THE

APPROACH TO PHILOSOPHY

THE
APPROACH TO PHILOSOPHY

THE APPROACH TO PHILOSOPHY

BY

RALPH BARTON PERRY, Ph.D.

ASSISTANT PROFESSOR OF PHILOSOPHY IN HARVARD UNIVERSITY

CHARLES SCRIBNER'S SONS

NEW YORK   CHICAGO   BOSTON

C

THIS VOLUME IS DEDICATED TO

MY FATHER

AS A TOKEN OF MY LOVE AND ESTEEM

PREFACE

IN an essay on "The Problem of Philosophy at the Present Time," Professor Edward Caird says that "philosophy is not a first venture into a new field of thought, but the rethinking of a secular and religious consciousness which has been developed, in the main, independently of philosophy." * If there be any inspiration and originality in this book, they are due to my great desire that philosophy should appear in its vital relations to more familiar experiences. If philosophy is, as is commonly assumed, appropriate to a phase in the development of every individual, it should *grow out* of interests to which he is already alive. And if the great philosophers are indeed never dead, this fact should manifest itself in their classic or historical representation of a perennial outlook upon the world. I am not seeking to attach to philosophy a fictitious liveliness, wherewith to insinuate it into the good graces of the student. I hope

* Edw. Caird: *Literature and Philosophy*, Vol. I, p. 207.

vii

rather to be true to the meaning of philosophy. For there is that in its stand-point and its problem which makes it universally significant entirely apart from dialectic and erudition. These are derived interests, indispensable to the scholar, but quite separable from that modicum of philosophy which helps to make the man. The present book is written for the sake of elucidating the inevitable philosophy. It seeks to make the reader more solicitously aware of the philosophy that is in him, or to provoke him to philosophy in his own interests. To this end I have sacrificed all else to the task of mediating between the tradition and technicalities of the academic discipline and the more common terms of life.

The purpose of the book will in part account for those shortcomings that immediately reveal themselves to the eye of the scholar. In Part I various great human interests have been selected as points of departure. I have sought to introduce the general stand-point and problem of philosophy through its implication in practical life, poetry, religion, and science. But in so doing it has been necessary for me to deal shortly with topics of great independent importance, and so risk the disfavor of those better skilled in these several matters. This is evidently true of the chapter which deals with natural science. But the problem which I there faced differed radically from those of the foregoing chapters, and the method of treatment is correspondingly different. In the case of natural science one has to deal with a body of knowledge which is frequently regarded as the only knowledge. To write a chapter about science from a philosophical stand-point is, in the present state of opinion, to undertake a polemic against exclusive naturalism, an attitude which is itself philosophical, and as such is well known in the history of philosophy as *positivism* or *agnosticism*. I have avoided the polemical spirit and method so far as possible, but have, nevertheless, here taken sides against a definite philosophical position. This chapter, together with the Conclusion, is therefore an exception to the purely introductory and expository representation which I have, on the whole, sought to give. The relatively great space accorded to the discussion of religion is, in my own belief, fair to the general interest in this topic, and to the intrinsic significance of its relation to philosophy.

I have in Part II undertaken to furnish the reader with a map of the country to which he has been led. To this end I have attempted a brief survey of the entire programme of philosophy. An accurate and full account of philosophical terms can be found in such books as Külpe's "Introduction to Philosophy" and Baldwin's "Dictionary of Philosophy," and an attempt to emulate their thoroughness would be superfluous, even if it were conformable to the general spirit of this book. The scope of Part II is due in part to a desire for brevity, but chiefly to the hope of furnishing an epitome that shall follow the course of the *natural and historical differentiation* of the general philosophical problem.

Finally, I have in Part III sought to present the tradition of philosophy in the form of general types. My purpose in undertaking so difficult a task is to acquaint the reader with philosophy in the concrete; to show how certain underlying principles may determine the whole circle of philosophical ideas, and give them unity and distinctive flavor. Part II offers a general classification of philosophical problems and conceptions independently of any special point of view. But I have in Part III sought to emphasize the point of view, or the internal consistency that makes a *system of philosophy* out of certain answers to the special problems of philosophy. In such a division into types, lines are of necessity drawn too sharply. There will be many historical philosophies that refuse to fit, and many possibilities unprovided for. I must leave it to the individual reader to overcome this abstractness through his own reflection upon the intermediate and variant standpoints.

Although the order is on the whole that of progressive complexity, I have sought to treat each chapter with independence enough to make it possible for it to be read separately; and I have provided a carefully selected bibliography in the hope that this book may serve as a stimulus and guide to the reading of other books.

The earlier chapters have already appeared as articles: Chapter I in the *International Journal of Ethics*, Vol. XIII, No. 4; Chapter II in the *Philosophical Review*, Vol. XI, No. 6; Chapter III in the *Monist*, Vol. XIV, No. 5; Chapter IV in the *International Journal of Ethics*, Vol. XV, No. 1; and some paragraphs of Chapter V in the *Journal of Philosophy, Psychology, and Scientific Methods*, Vol. I, No. 7. I am indebted to the editors of these periodicals for permission to reprint with minor changes.

In the writing of this, my first book, I have been often reminded that a higher critic, skilled in the study of internal evidence, could probably trace all of its ideas to suggestions that have come to me from my teachers and colleagues of the Department of Philosophy in Harvard University. I have unscrupulously forgotten what of their definite ideas I have adapted to my own use, but not that I received from them the major portion of my original philosophical capital. I am especially indebted to Professor William James for the inspiration and resources which I have received from his instruction and personal friendship.

RALPH BARTON PERRY.

CAMBRIDGE, March, 1905.

TABLE OF CONTENTS

PART I

APPROACH TO THE PROBLEM OF PHILOSOPHY

PART II

THE SPECIAL PROBLEMS OF PHILOSOPHY

PART III

SYSTEMS OF PHILOSOPHY

§ 124. Naturalism as Antagonistic to Religion...... 263
§ 125. Naturalism as the Basis for a Religion of Service, Wonder, and Renunciation.......... 265

CHAPTER IX. SUBJECTIVISM 267
§ 126. Subjectivism Originally Associated with Relativism and Scepticism 267
§ 127. Phenomenalism and Spiritualism........... 271
§ 128. Phenomenalism as Maintained by Berkeley. The Problem Inherited from Descartes and Locke 272
§ 129. The Refutation of Material Substance....... 275
§ 130. The Application of the Epistemological Principle 277
§ 131. The Refutation of a Conceived Corporeal World............................... 278
§ 132. The Transition to Spiritualism............. 280
§ 133. Further Attempts to Maintain Phenomenalism 281
§ 134. Berkeley's Spiritualism. Immediate Knowledge of the Perceiver.................... 284
§ 135. Schopenhauer's Spiritualism, or Voluntarism. Immediate Knowledge of the Will........ 285
§ 136. Panpsychism............................ 287
§ 137. The Inherent Difficulty in Spiritualism. No Provision for Objective Knowledge 288
§ 138. Schopenhauer's Attempt to Universalize Subjectivism. Mysticism 290
§ 139. Objective Spiritualism.................... 292
§ 140. Berkeley's Conception of God as Cause, Goodness, and Order........................ 293
§ 141. The General Tendency of Subjectivism to Transcend Itself 297
§ 142. Ethical Theories. Relativism 298
§ 143. Pessimism and Self-denial 299

TABLE OF CONTENTS

PART I

APPROACH TO THE PROBLEM OF PHILOSOPHY

CHAPTER I

THE PRACTICAL MAN AND THE PHILOSOPHER

§ 1. PHILOSOPHY suffers the distinction of being regarded as essentially an academic pursuit.   The

Is Philosophy a Merely Academic Interest?
term *philosophy*, to be sure, is used in common speech to denote a stoical manner of accepting the vicissitudes of life; but this conception sheds little or no light upon the meaning of philosophy as a branch of scholarship. The men who write the books on " Epistemology " or " Ontology," are regarded by the average man of affairs, even though he may have enjoyed a " higher education," with little sympathy and less intelligence.   Not even philology seems less concerned with the real business of life.   The pursuit of philosophy appears to be a phenomenon of extreme and somewhat effete culture, with its own peculiar traditions, problems, and aims, and with little or nothing to contribute to the real enterprises of society.   It is easy to prove to the satisfaction of the philosopher that such a view is radically

3

mistaken. But it is another and more serious matter to bridge over the very real gap that separates
philosophy and common-sense. Such an aim is
realized only when philosophy is seen to issue from
some special interest that is humanly important;
or when, after starting in thought at a point where
one deals with ideas and interests common to all,
one is led by the inevitableness of consistent thinking into the sphere of philosophy.

§ 2. There is but one starting-point for reflection when all men are invited to share in it.
Life as a Start- Though there be a great many special
ing-point for
Thought.   platforms where special groups of men
may take their stand together, there is only one
platform broad enough for all. This universal
stand-point, or common platform, is *life*. It is
our more definite thesis, then, that philosophy,
even to its most abstruse technicality, is rooted in
life; and that it is inseparably bound up with the
satisfaction of practical needs, and the solution of
practical problems.

Every man knows what it is to live, and his
immediate experience will verify those features of
the adventure that stand out conspicuously. To
begin with, life is our birthright. We did not ask
for it, but when we grew old enough to be self-

conscious we found ourselves in possession of it.
Nor is it a gift to be neglected, even if we had the
will.   As is true of no other gift of nature, we
must use it, or cease to be.   There is a unique
urgency about life.   But we have already implied
more, in so far as we have said that it must be
used, and have thereby referred to some form of
movement or activity as its inseparable attribute.
To live is to find one's self compelled to do something.   To do *something*—there is another implication of life: some outer expression, some medium
in which to register the degree and form of its
activity.   Such we recognize as the environment
of life, the real objects among which it is placed;
which it may change, or from which it may suffer
change.   Not only do we find our lives as unso-
licited active powers, but find, as well, an arena
prescribed for their exercise.   That we shall act,
and in a certain time and place, and with reference
to certain other realities, this is the general condition of things that is encountered when each one
of us discovers life.   In short, to live means to be
compelled to do something under certain circumstances.

There is another very common aspect of life
that would not at first glance seem worthy of men-

tion. Not only does life, as we have just described it, mean opportunity, but it means self-conscious opportunity. The facts are such as we have found them to be, and as each one of us has previously found them for himself. But when we discover life for ourselves, we who make the discovery, and we who live, are identical. From that moment we both live, and know that we live. Moreover, such is the essential unity of our natures that our living must now express our knowing, and our knowing guide and illuminate our living. Consider the allegory of the centipede. From the beginning of time he had manipulated his countless legs with exquisite precision. Men had regarded him with wonder and amazement. But he was innocent of his own art, being a contrivance of nature, perfectly constructed to do her bidding. One day the centipede discovered life. He discovered himself as one who walks, and the newly awakened intelligence, first observing, then foreseeing, at length began to direct the process. And from that moment the centipede, because he could not remember the proper order of his going, lost all his former skill, and became the poor clumsy victim of his own self-consciousness. This same self-consciousness is the inconvenience and the great glory of human life. We must stumble along as best we can, guided by the feeble light of our own little intelligence. If nature starts us on our way, she soon hands over the torch, and bids us find the trail for ourselves. Most men are brave enough to regard this as the best thing of all; some despair on account of it. In either case it is admittedly the true story of human life. We must live as separate selves, observing, foreseeing, and planning. There are two things that we can do about it. We can repudiate our natures, decline the responsibility, and degenerate to the level of those animals that never had our chance; or we can leap joyously to the helm, and with all the strength and wisdom in us guide our lives to their destination. But if we do the former, we shall be unable to forget what might have been, and shall be haunted by a sense of ignominy; and if we do the second, we shall experience the unique happiness of fulfilment and self-realization.

Life, then, is a situation that appeals to intelligent activity. Humanly speaking, there is no such thing as a situation that is not at the same time a theory. As we live we are all theorists. Whoever has any misgivings as to the practical

value of theory, let him remember that, speaking
generally of human life, it is true to say that there
is no practice that does not issue at length from
reflection. That which is the commonest experience of mankind is the conjunction of these two,
the thought and the deed. And as surely as we
are all practical theorists, so surely is philosophy
the outcome of the broadening and deepening
of practical theory. But to understand how the
practical man becomes the philosopher, we must
inquire somewhat more carefully into the manner
of his thought about life.

§ 3. Let anyone inspect the last moment in his
life, and in all probability he will find that his
The Practical mind was employed to discover the
Knowledge of
Means.   means to some end. He was already
bent upon some definite achievement, and was
thoughtful for the sake of selecting the economical
and effectual way. His theory made his practice
skilful. So through life his knowledge shows him
how to work his will. Example, experience, and
books have taught him the uses of nature and
society, and in his thoughtful living he is enabled
to reach the goal he has set for the next hour, day,
or year of his activity. The long periods of
human life are spent in elaborating the means to

some unquestioned end. Here one meets the
curious truth that we wake up in the middle of
life, already making headway, and under the guidance of some invisible steersman. When first we
take the business of life seriously, there is a considerable stock in trade in the shape of habits,
and inclinations to all sorts of things that we never
consciously elected to pursue. Since we do not
begin at the beginning, our first problem is to
accommodate ourselves to ourselves, and our first
deliberate acts are in fulfilment of plans outlined
by some predecessor that has already spoken for
us. The same thing is true of the race of men.
At a certain stage in their development men found
themselves engaged in all manner of ritual and
custom, and burdened with concerns that were not
of their own choosing. They were burning in-
cense, keeping festivals, and naming names, all
of which they must now proceed to justify with
myth and legend, in order to render intelligible
to themselves the deliberate and self-conscious
repetition of them. Even so much justification
was left to the few, and the great majority continued to seek that good which social usage coun-
tenanced and individual predisposition confirmed.
So every man of us acts from day to day for

love's sake, or wealth's sake, or power's sake, or
for the sake of some near and tangible object;
reflecting only for the greater efficiency of his
endeavor.

§ 4. But if this be the common manner of thinking about life, it does not represent the whole of
The Practical such thought.   Nor does it follow that
Knowledge of because it occupies us so much, it is
the End or
Purpose.   therefore correspondingly fundamental.
Like the myth makers of old, we all want more
or less to know the *reason of our ends*.   Here,
then, we meet with a somewhat different type of
reflection upon life, the reflection that underlies
the adoption of a life purpose.   It is obvious that
most ends are selected for the sake of other ends,
and so are virtually means.   Thus one may struggle for years to secure a college education.   This
definite end has been adopted for the sake of a
somewhat more indefinite end of self-advance-
ment, and from it there issues a whole series of
minor ends, which form a hierarchy of steps ascending to the highest goal of aspiration.   Now
upon the face of things we live very unsystematic
lives, and yet were we to examine ourselves in this
fashion, we should all find our lives to be marvels
of organization.   Their growth, as we have seen,

began before we were conscious of it; and we are commonly so absorbed in some particular flower or fruit that we forget the roots, and the design of the whole. But a little reflection reveals a remarkable unitary adjustment of parts. The unity is due to the dominance of a group of central purposes. Judged from the stand-point of experience, it seems bitter irony to say that everyone gets from life just what he wishes. But a candid searching of our own hearts will incline us to admit that, after all, the way we go and the length we go is determined pretty much by the kind and the intensity of our secret longing. That for which in the time of choice we are willing to sacrifice all else, is the formula that defines the law of each individual life. All this is not intended to mean that we have each named a clear and definite ideal which is our chosen goal. On the contrary, such a conception may be almost meaningless to some of us. In general the higher the ideal the vaguer and less vivid is its presentation to our consciousness. But, named or unnamed, sharp or blurred, vivid or half-forgotten, there may be found in the heart of every man that which of all things he wants to be, that which of all deeds he wants to do. If he has had the normal youth of dreaming, he has seen it, and warmed to the picture of his imagination; if he has been somewhat more thoughtful than the ordinary, his reason has defined it, and adopted it for his vocation; if neither, it has been present as an undertone throughout the rendering of his more inevitable life. He will recognize it when it is named as the desire to do the will of God, or to have as good a time as possible, or to make other people as happy as possible, or to be equal to his responsibilities, or to fulfil the expectation of his mother, or to be distinguished, wealthy, or influential. This list of ideals is miscellaneous, and ethically reducible to more fundamental concepts, but these are the terms in which men are ordinarily conscious of their most intimate purposes. We must now inquire respecting the nature of the thought that determines the selection of such a purpose, or justifies it when it has been unconsciously accepted.

§ 5. What is most worth while? So far as human action is concerned this obviously depends The Philosophy of the Devotee, the Man of Affairs, and the Voluptuary. upon what is possible, upon what is expected of us by our own natures, and upon what interests and concerns are conserved by the trend of events in our environment. What I had best do, presupposes what I have the strength and the skill to do, what I feel called upon to do, and what are the great causes that are entitled to promotion at my hands. It seems that practically we cannot separate the ideal from the real. We may feel that the highest ideal is an immediate utterance of conscience, as mysterious in origin as it is authoritative in expression. We may be willing to defy the universe, and expatriate ourselves from our natural and social environment, for the sake of the holy law of duty. Such men as Count Tolstoi have little to say of the possible, or the expedient, or the actual, and are satisfied to stand almost alone against the brutal facts of usage and economy. We all have a secret sense of chivalry, that prompts, however ineffectually, to a like devotion. But that which in such moral purposes appears to indicate a severance of the ideal and the real, is, if we will but stop to consider, only a severance of the ideal and the apparent. The martyr is more sure of reality than the adventurer. He is convinced that though his contemporaries and his environment be against him; the fundamental or eventual order of things is for him. He believes in a spiritual world more abiding, albeit less obvious, than the material world. Though every temporal event contradict him, he lives in the certainty that eternity is his. Such an one may have found his ideal in the voice of God and His prophets, or he may have been led to God as the justification of his irresistible ideal; but in either case the selection of his ideal is reasonable to him in so far as it is harmonious with the ultimate nature of things, or stands for the promise of reality. In this wise, thought about life expands into some conception of the deeper forces of the world, and life itself, in respect of its fundamental attachment to an ideal, implies some belief concerning the fundamental nature of its environment.

But lest in this account life be credited with too much gravity and import, or it seem to be assumed that life is all knight-errantry, let us turn to our less quixotic, and perhaps more effectual, man of affairs. He works for his daily bread, and for success in his vocation. He has selected his vocation for its promise of return in the form of wealth, comfort, fame, or influence. He likewise performs such additional service to his family and his community as is demanded of him by public opinion and his own sense of responsibility.

He may have a certain contempt for the man who sees visions. This may be his manner of testifying to his own preference for the ideal of usefulness and immediate efficiency. But even so he would never for an instant admit that he was pursuing a merely conventional good. He may be largely imitative in his standards of value, recognizing such aims as are common to some time or race; nevertheless none would be more sure than he of the truth of his ideal. Question him, and he will maintain that his is the reasonable life under the conditions of human existence. He may maintain that if there be a God, he can best serve Him by promoting the tangible welfare of himself and those dependent upon him. He may maintain that, since there is no God, he must win such rewards as the world can give. If he have something of the heroic in him, he may tell you that, since there is no God, he will labor to the uttermost for his fellow-men. Where he has not solved the problem of life for himself, he may believe himself to be obeying the insight of some one wiser than himself, or of society as expressed in its customs and institutions. But no man ever admitted that his life was purely a matter of expediency, or that in his dominant ideal he was the victim of chance. In the background of the busiest and most preoccupied life of affairs, there dwells the conviction that such living is appropriate to the universe; that it is called for by the circumstances of its origin, opportunities, and destiny.

Finally, the man who makes light of life has of all men the most transparent inner consciousness. In him may be clearly observed the relation between the ideal and the reflection that is assumed to justify it.

> " A Moment's Halt—a momentary taste
> Of Being from the Well amid the Waste—
> And Lo!—the phantom Caravan has reach'd
> The Nothing it set out from— . . . "

> " We are no other than a moving row
> Of Magic Shadow-shapes that come and go
> Round with the Sun-illumin'd Lantern held
> In Midnight by the Master of the Show."

Where the setting of life is construed in these terms, there is but one natural and appropriate manner of life. Once believing in the isolation and insignificance of life, one is sceptical of all worth save such as may be tasted in the moment of its purchase. If one's ideas and experiences are no concern of the world's, but incidents of a purely local and transient interest, they will real-

ize most when they realize an immediate gratification. Where one does not believe that he is a
member of the universe, and a contributor to its
ends, he does well to minimize the friction that
arises from its accidental propinquity, and to
kindle some little fire of enjoyment in his own
lonely heart. This is the life of abandonment to
pleasure, accompanied by the conviction that the
conditions of life warrant no more strenuous or
heroic plan.

§ 6. In such wise do we adopt the life purpose,
or justify it when unconsciously adopted. The
The Adoption pursuit of an ideal implies a belief in
of Purposes
and the its effectuality. Such a belief will in-
Philosophy
of Life. variably appear when the groundwork
of the daily living is laid bare by a little reflection.
And if our analysis has not been in error, there
is something more definite to be obtained from it.
We all believe in the practical wisdom of our fundamental ideals; but we believe, besides, that such
wisdom involves the sanction of the universe as
a whole. The momentousness of an individual's
life will be satisfied with nothing less final than
an absolutely wise disposition of it. For every individual, his life is all his power and riches, and
is not to be spent save for the *greatest good that*

he can reasonably pursue. But the solution of such a problem is not to be obtained short of a searching of entire reality. Every life will represent more or less of such wisdom and enlightenment; and in the end the best selection of ideal will denote the greatest wealth of experience. It is not always true that he who has seen more will live more wisely, for in an individual case instinct or authority may be better sources of aspiration than experience. But we trust instinct and authority because we believe them to represent a comprehensive experience on the part of the race as a whole, or on the part of God. He whose knowledge is broadest and truest would know best what is finally worth living for. On this account, most men can see no more reasonable plan of life than obedience to God's will, for God in the abundance of his wisdom, and since all eternity is plain before him, must see with certainty that which is supremely worthy.

We mean, then, that the selection of our ideals shall be determined by the largest possible knowledge of the facts pertaining to life. We mean to select as one would select who knew all about the antecedents and surroundings and remote consequences of life. In our own weakness and fini-

tude we may go but a little way in the direction
of such an insight, and may prefer to accept the
judgment of tradition or authority, but we recognize a distinct type of knowledge as alone worthy
to justify an individual's adoption of an ideal.
That type of knowledge is the knowledge that comprehends the universe in its totality.   Such knowledge does not involve completeness of information
respecting all parts of reality.   This, humanly
speaking, is both unattainable and inconceivable.
It involves rather a conception of the *kind* of reality that is fundamental.   For a wise purpose it
is unnecessary that we should know many matters
of fact, or even specific laws, provided we are convinced of the inner and essential character of the
universe.   Some of the alternatives are matters of
every-day thought and speech.   One cannot tell
the simplest story of human life without disclos-
ing them.   To live the human life means to pursue ideals, that is, to have a thing in mind, and
then to try to accomplish it.   Here is one kind of
reality and power.   The planetary system, on the
other hand, does not pursue ideals, but moves unconscious of itself, with a mechanical precision
that can be expressed in a mathematical formula;
and is representative of another kind of reality

and power. Hence a very common and a very
practical question: Is there an underlying law,
like the law of gravitation, fundamentally and permanently governing life, in spite of its apparent
direction by ideal and aspiration? Or is there
an underlying power, like purpose, fundamentally
and permanently governing the planetary system
and all celestial worlds, in spite of the apparent
control of blind and irresistible forces? This is
a practical question because nothing could be more
pertinent to our choice of ideals. Nothing could
make more difference to life than a belief in the
life or lifelessness of its environment. The faiths
that generate or confirm our ideals always refer to
this great issue. And this is but one, albeit the
most profound, of the many issues that arise from
the desire to obtain some conviction of the inner
and essential character of life. Though so intimately connected with practical concerns, these
issues are primarily the business of thought. In
grappling with them, thought is called upon for
its greatest comprehensiveness, penetration, and
self-consistency. By the necessity of concentration, thought is sometimes led to forget its origin
and the source of its problems. But in naming
itself philosophy, thought has only recognized the

definiteness and earnestness of its largest task. Philosophy is still thought about life, representing but the deepening and broadening of the common practical thoughtfulness.

We who began together at the starting-point of *life*, have now entered together the haven of *philosophy*. It is not a final haven, but only the point of departure for the field of philosophy proper. Nevertheless that field is now in the plain view of the man who occupies the practical stand-point. He must recognize in philosophy a kind of reflection that differs only in extent and persistence from the reflection that guides and justifies his life. He may not consciously identify himself with any one of the three general groups which have been characterized. But if he is neither an idealist, nor a philistine, nor a pleasure lover, surely he is compounded of such elements, and does not escape their implications. He desires something most of all, even though his highest ideal be only an inference from the gradation of his immediate purposes. This highest ideal represents what he conceives to be the greatest worth or value attainable in the universe, and its adoption is based upon the largest generalization that he can make or borrow. The complete justi-

fication of his ideal would involve a true knowledge of the essential character of the universe.
For such knowledge he substitutes either authority
or his own imperfect insight. But in either case
his life is naturally and organically correlated
with a *thought about the universe in its totality,
or in its deepest and essential character.* Such
thought, the activity and its results, is philosophy. Hence he who lives is, *ipso facto,* a philosopher. He is not only a potential philosopher, but
a partial philosopher. He has already begun to
be a philosopher. Between the fitful or prudential
thinking of some little man of affairs, and the sus-
tained thought of the devoted lover of truth, there
is indeed a long journey, but it is a straight journey along the same road. Philosophy is neither
accidental nor supernatural, but inevitable and
normal. Philosophy is not properly a vocation,
but the ground and inspiration of all vocations.
In the hands of its devotees it grows technical and
complex, as do all efforts of thought, and to pursue philosophy bravely and faithfully is to encounter obstacles and labyrinths innumerable. The
general problem of philosophy is mother of a
whole brood of problems, little and great. But

whether we be numbered among its devotees, or their beneficiaries, an equal significance attaches to the truth that philosophy is continuous with life.

CHAPTER II

POETRY AND PHILOSOPHY

§ 7. As the ultimate criticism of all human interests, philosophy may be approached by avenues **Who is the** as various as these interests. Only **Philosopher-Poet?** when philosophy is discovered as the implication of well-recognized special interests, is the significance of its function fully appreciated. For the sake of such a further understanding of philosophy, those who find either inspiration or entertainment in poetry are invited in the present chapter to consider certain of the relations between poetry and philosophy.

We must at the very outset decline to accept unqualifiedly the poet's opinion in the matter, for he would not think it presumptuous to incorporate philosophy in poetry. "No man," said Coleridge, "was ever yet a great poet without being at the same time a great philosopher." This would seem to mean that a great poet is a great philosopher, and more too. We shall do better to begin with the prosaic and matter of fact minimum of

24

truth: some poetry is philosophical. This will enable us to search for the portion of philosophy that is in some poetry, without finally defining their respective boundaries. It may be that all true poetry is philosophical, as it may be that all true philosophy is poetical; but it is much more certain that much actual poetry is far from philosophical, and that most actual philosophy was not conceived or written by a poet. The mere poet and the mere philosopher must be tolerated, if it be only for the purpose of shedding light upon the philosopher-poet and the poet-philosopher. And it is to the philosopher-poet that we turn, in the hope that under the genial spell of poetry we may be brought with understanding to the more forbidding land of philosophy.

§ 8. Poetry is well characterized, though not defined, as an interpretation of life. The term **Poetry as Appreciation.** "life" here signifies the human purposive consciousness, and active pursuit of ends. An interpretation of life is, then, a selection and account of such values in human experience as are actually sought or are worth the seeking. For the poet all things are good or bad, and never only matters of fact. He is neither an annalist nor a statistician, and is even an observer

only for the sake of a higher design. He is one
who appreciates, and expresses his appreciation so
fittingly that it becomes a kind of truth, and a permanently communicable object. That " unbodied
joy," the skylark's song and flight, is through the
genius of Shelley so faithfully embodied, that it
may enter as a definite joy into the lives of countless human beings. The sensuous or suggestive
values of nature are caught by the poet's quick
feeling for beauty, and fixed by his creative activity. Or with his ready sympathy he may perceive
the value of some human ideal or mastering passion, and make it a reality for our common feeling.
Where the poet has to do with the base and hate-
ful, his attitude is still appreciative. The evil is
apprehended as part of a dramatic whole having
positive moral or æsthetic value. Moral ideas
may appear in both poetry and life as the inspiration and justification of struggle. Where there is
no conception of its moral significance, the repul-
sive possesses for the poet's consciousness the
æsthetic value of diversity and contrast. Even
where the evil and ugly is isolated, as in certain
of Browning's dramatic monologues, it forms, both
for the poet and the reader, but a part of some
larger perception of life or character, which is sub-

lime or beautiful or good.   Poetry involves, then,
the discovery and presentation of human experiences that are satisfying and appealing.   It is a
language for human pleasures and ideals.   Poetry
is without doubt a great deal more than this, and
only after a careful analysis of its peculiar language could one distinguish it from kindred arts;
but it will suffice for our purposes to characterize
and not differentiate.   Starting from this most
general truth respecting poetry, we may now look
for that aspect of it whereby it may be a witness
of philosophical truth.

§ 9. For the answer to our question, we must
turn to an examination of the intellectual elements
Sincerity in   of poetry.   In the first place, the com-
Poetry.
Whitman.   mon demand that the poet shall be accurate in his representations is suggestive of an
indispensable intellectual factor in his genius.
As we have seen, he is not to reproduce nature,
but the human appreciative experience of nature.
Nevertheless, he must even here be true to his
object.   His art involves his ability to express
genuinely and sincerely what he himself experiences in the presence of nature, or what he can
catch of the inner lives of others by virtue of his
intelligent sympathy.   No amount of emotion or

even of imagination will profit a poet, unless he can render a true account of them. To be sure, he need not define, or even explain; for it is his function to transfer the immediate qualities of experience: but he must be able to speak the truth, and, in order to speak it, he must have known it. In all this, however, we have made no demand that the poet should see more than one thing at a time. Sincerity of expression does not require what is distinctly another mode of intelligence, *comprehensiveness of view*. It is easier, and accordingly more usual, to render an account of the moments and casual units of experience, than of its totality. There are poets, little and great, who possess the intellectual virtue of sincerity, without the intellectual power of synthesis and reconciliation. This distinction will enable us to separate the intelligence exhibited in all poetry, from that distinct form of intelligence exhibited in such poetry as is properly to be called philosophical.

The "barbarian" in poetry has recently been defined as "the man who regards his passions as their own excuse for being; who does not domesticate them either by understanding their cause or by conceiving their ideal goal." [1]   One will read-

---

[1] George Santayana, in his *Poetry and Religion*, p. 176.

ily appreciate the application of this definition to
Walt Whitman.   What little unity there is in this
poet's world, is the composition of a purely sensuous experience,

> " The earth expending right hand and left hand,
>   The picture alive, every part in its best light,
>   The music falling in where it is wanted, and stopping
>   where it is not wanted."

In many passages Whitman manifests a marvellous ability to discover and communicate a fresh
gladness about the commonest experiences.   We
cannot but rejoice with him in all sights and
sounds.   But though we cannot deny him truth,
his truth is honesty and not understanding.   The
experiences in which he discovers so much worth,
are random and capricious, and do not constitute
a universe.   To the solution of ultimate questions
he contributes a sense of mystery, and the conviction

> " That you are here—that life exists and identity,
>   That the powerful play goes on, and you may contribute
>   a verse."

His world is justly described by the writer just
quoted as " a phantasmagoria of continuous visions, vivid, impressive, but monotonous and hard
to distinguish in memory, like the waves of the sea

or the decorations of some barbarous temple, sublime only by the infinite aggregation of parts." [2]

As is Walt Whitman, so are many poets greater
and less.   Some who have seen the world-view, ex-
hibit the same particularism in their lyric moods;
although, generally speaking, a poet who once
has comprehended the world, will see the parts of
it in the light of that wisdom.   But Walt Whitman is peculiarly representative of the poetry that
can be true, without being wise in the manner that
we shall come shortly to understand as the manner
of philosophy.   He is as desultory in his poet raptures as is the common man when he lives in his
immediate experiences.   The truth won by each is
the clear vision of one thing, or of a limited collection of things, and not the broad inclusive vision
of all things.

§ 10. The transition from Whitman to Shakespeare may seem somewhat abrupt, but the very
Constructive
Knowledge in
Poetry.
Shakespeare. differences between these poets serve
to mark out an interesting affinity.
Neither has put any unitary construction upon human life and its environment.
Neither, as poet, is the witness of any world-view;
which will mean for us that neither is a philos-

[2] Santayana : *op. cit.*, p. 180.

opher-poet. As respects Shakespeare, this is a
hard saying. We are accustomed to the critical
judgment that finds in the Shakespearian dramas
an apprehension of the universal in human life.
But though this judgment is true, it is by no means
conclusive as respects Shakespeare's relation to the
philosophical type of thought. For there can be
universality without philosophy. Thus, to know
the groups and the marks of the vertebrates is to
know a truth which possesses generality, in contradistinction to the particularism of Whitman's
poetic consciousness. Even so to know well the
groups and marks of human character, vertebrate
and invertebrate, is to know that of which the average man, in his hand to hand struggle with life,
is ignorant. Such a wisdom Shakespeare possessed to a unique degree, and it enabled him to
reconstruct human life. He did not merely perceive human states and motives, but he understood
human nature so well that he could create consistent men and women. Moreover, Shakespeare's
knowledge was not only thus universal in being
a knowledge of general groups and laws, but also
in respect of its extensity. His understanding
was as rich as it was acute. It is true, then, that
Shakespeare read human life as an open book,

knowing certainly the manner of human thinking
and feeling, and the power and interplay of human
motives.   But it is equally true, on the other hand,
that he possessed no unitary conception of the
meaning and larger relations of human life. Such
a conception might have been expressed either by
means of the outlook of some dominating and persistent type of personality, or by a pervading suggestion of some constant world-setting for the
variable enterprise of mankind.   It could appear
only provided the poet's appreciation of life in detail were determined by an interpretation of the
meaning of life as a whole.   Shakespeare apparently possessed no such interpretation.   Even
when Hamlet is groping after some larger truth
that may bear upon the definite problems of life,
he represents but one, and that a strange and un-
usual, type of human nature.   And Hamlet's reflections, it should be noted, have no outcome.
There is no Shakespearian answer to the riddles
that Hamlet propounds.   The poet's genius is not
less amazing for this fact; indeed, his peculiar distinction can only be comprehended upon this basis.
Shakespeare put no construction upon life, and by
virtue of this very reserve accomplished an art of
surpassing fidelity and vividness.   The absence of

philosophy in Shakespeare, and the presence of the most characteristic quality of his genius, may both be imputed by the one affirmation, that *there is no Shakespearian point of view.*

This truth signifies both gain and loss. The philosophical criticism of life may vary from the ideal objectivity of absolute truth, to the subjectivity of a personal religion. Philosophy aims to correct the partiality of particular points of view by means of a point of view that shall comprehend their relations, and effect such reconciliations or transformations as shall enable them to constitute a universe. Philosophy always assumes the hypothetical view of omniscience. The necessity of such a final criticism is implicit in every scientific item of knowledge, and in every judgment that is passed upon life. Philosophy makes a distinct and peculiar contribution to human knowledge by its heroic effort to measure all knowledges and all ideals by the standard of totality. Nevertheless it is significant that no human individual can possibly possess the range of omniscience. The most adequate knowledge of which any generation of men is capable, will always be that which is conceived by the most synthetic and vigorously metaphysical minds; but every individual philosophy will nevertheless be a premature synthesis. The effort to complete knowledge is the indispensable test of the adequacy of prevailing conceptions, but the completed knowledge of any individual mind will shortly become an historical monument. It will belong primarily to the personal life of its creator, as the articulation of his personal covenant with the universe. There is a sound justification for such a conclusion of things in the case of the individual, for the conditions of human life make it inevitable; but it will always possess a felt unity, and many distinct features, that are private and subjective. Now such a projection of personality, with its coloring and its selection, Shakespeare has avoided; and very largely as a consequence, his dramas are a storehouse of genuine human nature. Ambition, mercy, hate, madness, guilelessness, conventionality, mirth, bravery, deceit, purity—these, and all human states and attributes save piety, are upon his pages as real, and as mysterious withal, as they are in the great historical society. For an ordinary reader, these states and attributes are more real in Hamlet or Lear than in his own direct experience, because in Hamlet and Lear he can see them with the eye and intelligence of genius. But Shakespeare is the world all over again, and there is loss as well as gain in such realism. Here is human life, no doubt, and a brilliant pageantry it is; but human life as varied and as problematic as it is in the living. Shakespeare's fundamental intellectual resource is the historical and psychological knowledge of such principles as govern the construction of human natures. The goods for which men undertake, and live or die, are any goods, justified only by the actual human striving for them. The virtues are the old winning virtues of the secular life, and the heroisms of the common conscience. Beyond its empirical generality, his knowledge is universal only in the sense that space and time are universal. His consciousness *contains* its representative creations, and expresses them unspoiled by any transforming thought. His poetic consciousness is like the very stage to which he likens all the world: men and women meet there, and things happen there. The stage itself creates no unity save the occasion and the place. Shakespeare's consciousness is universal because it is a fair field with no favors. But even so it is particular, because, though each may enter and depart in peace, when all enter together there is anarchy and a babel of voices. All Shakespeare is like all the world seen through the eyes of each of its inhabitants. Human experience in Shakespeare is human experience as everyone feels it, as comprehensive as the aggregate of innumerable lives. But human experience in philosophy is the experience of all as thought by a synthetic mind. Hence the wealth of life depicted by Shakespeare serves only to point out the philosopher's problem, and to challenge his powers. Here he will find material, and not results; much to philosophize about, but no philosophy.

§ 11. The discussion up to this point has attributed to poetry very definite intellectual factors

Philosophy in Poetry. The World-View. Omar Khayyam.

that nevertheless do not constitute philosophy. Walt Whitman speaks his feeling with truth, but in general manifests no comprehensive insight. Shakespeare has not only sincerity of expression but an understanding mind. He has a knowledge not only of particular experiences, but of human nature; and a consciousness full and varied like society itself. But there is a kind of knowledge possessed by neither, the knowledge sought by coördinating all aspects of human experience, both particular and general. Not even Shakespeare is wise as one who, having seen the whole, can fundamentally interpret a part. But though the philosopher-poet may not yet be found, we cannot longer be ignorant of his nature. He will be, like all poets, one who appreciates experiences or finds things good, and he will faithfully reproduce the values which he discovers. But he must *justify himself in view of the fundamental nature of the universe.* The values which he apprehends must be harmonious, and so far above the plurality of goods as to transcend and unify them. The philosopher-poet will find reality as a whole to be something that accredits the order of values in his inner life. He will not only find certain things to be most worthy objects of action or contemplation, but he will see why they are worthy, because he will have construed the judgment of the universe in their favor.

In this general sense, Omar Khayyam is a philosopher-poet. To be sure his universe is quite the opposite of that which most poets conceive, and is perhaps profoundly antagonistic to the very spirit of poetry; but it is none the less true that the joys to which Omar invites us are such as his universe prescribes for human life.

> "Some for the Glories of This World; and some
> Sigh for the Prophet's Paradise to come;
> Ah, take the Cash, and let the Credit go,
> Nor heed the rumble of a distant Drum."

Herein is both poetry and philosophy, albeit but a poor brand of each. We are invited to occupy ourselves only with spiritual cash, because the universe is spiritually insolvent. The immediately gratifying feelings are the only feelings that the world can guarantee. Omar Khayyam is a philosopher-poet, because his immediate delight in " youth's sweet-scented manuscript " is part of a consciousness that vaguely sees, though it cannot grasp, " this sorry scheme of things entire."

" Drink for you know not whence you come, nor why;
Drink for you know not why you go, nor where."

§ 12. But the poet in his world-view ordinarily sees other than darkness. The same innate spir-
Wordsworth. itual enterprise that sustains religious faith leads the poet more often to find the universe positively congenial to his ideals, and to ideals in general. He interprets human experience in the light of the spirituality of all the world. It is to Wordsworth that we of the present age are chiefly indebted for such imagery, and it will profit us to consider somewhat carefully the philosophical quality of his poetry.

Walter Pater, in introducing his appreciation of Wordsworth, writes that " an intimate consciousness of the expression of natural things, which weighs, listens, penetrates, where the earlier mind passed roughly by, is a large element in the complexion of modern poetry." We recognize at once the truth of this characterization as applied to Wordsworth. But there is something more distinguished about this poet's sensibility even than its extreme fineness and delicacy; a quality that is suggested, though not made explicit, by Shelley's allusion to Wordsworth's experience as " a sort of thought in sense." Nature possessed for him not merely enjoyable and describable characters of great variety and minuteness, but an immediately apprehended unity and meaning. It would be a great mistake to construe this meaning in sense as analogous to the crude symbolism of the educator Froebel, to whom, as he said, " the world of crystals proclaimed, in distinct and univocal terms, the laws of human life." Wordsworth did not attach ideas to sense, but regarded sense itself as a communication of truth. We readily call to mind his unique capacity for apprehending the characteristic flavor of a certain place in a certain moment of time, the individuality of a situation. Now in such moments he felt that he was receiving intelligences, none the less direct and significant for their inarticulate form. Like the boy on Windermere, whom he himself describes,

> " while he hung
> Loitering, a gentle shock of mild surprise
> Has carried far into his heart the voice
> Of mountain torrents; or the visible scene
> Would enter unawares into his mind,
> With all its solemn imagery, its rocks,
> Its woods, and that uncertain heaven received
> Into the bosom of the steady lake."

For our purpose it is essential that we should recognize in this appreciation of nature, expressed in almost every poem that Wordsworth wrote, a consciousness respecting the fundamental nature of the world. Conversation, as we know, denotes an interchange of commensurable meanings. Whatever the code may be, whether words or the most subtle form of suggestion, communication is impossible without community of nature. Hence, in believing himself to be holding converse with the so-called physical world, Wordsworth conceives that world as fundamentally like himself. He finds the most profound thing in all the world to be the universal spiritual life. In nature this life manifests itself most directly, clothed in its own proper dignity and peace. But it may be discovered in the humanity that is most close to nature, in the avocations of plain and simple people, and the unsophisticated delights of children; and, with the perspective of contemplation, even " among the multitudes of that huge city."

So Wordsworth is rendering a true account of his own experience of reality when, as in " The Prelude," he says unequivocally:

> " A gracious spirit o'er this earth presides,
> And in the heart of man; invisibly
> It comes to works of unreproved delight,
> And tendency benign; directing those
> Who care not, know not, think not, what they do."

Wordsworth is not a philosopher-poet because by searching his pages we can find an explicit philosophical creed such as this, but because all the joys of which his poet-soul compels him to sing have their peculiar note, and compose their peculiar harmony, by virtue of such an indwelling consciousness. Here is one who is a philosopher in and through his poetry. He is a philosopher in so far as the detail of his appreciation finds fundamental justification in a world-view. From the immanence of " the universal heart " there follows, not through any mediate reasoning, but by the immediate experience of its propriety, a conception of that which is of supreme worth in life. The highest and best of which life is capable is contemplation, or the consciousness of the universal indwelling of God.

Of those who fail to live thus fittingly in the midst of the divine life, Walter Pater speaks for Wordsworth as follows:

"To higher or lower ends they move too often with something of a sad countenance, with hurried and ignoble gait, becoming, unconsciously, something like thorns, in their anxiety to bear grapes; it being possible for people, in the pursuit of even great ends, to become themselves thin and impoverished in spirit and temper, thus diminishing the sum of perfection in the world at its very sources."[3]

The quiet and worshipful spirit, won by the cultivation of the emotions appropriate to the presence of nature and society, is the mark of the completest life and the most acceptable service. Thus for Wordsworth the meaning of life is inseparable from the meaning of the universe. In apprehending that which is good and beautiful in human experience, he was attended by a vision of the totality of things. Herein he has had to do, if not with the form, at any rate with the very substance of philosophy.

§ 13. Unquestionably the supreme philosopher-poet is Dante. He is not only philosophical in the temper of his mind, but his greatest poem is the incarnation of a definite system of

Dante.

---

[3] *Appreciations*, p. 59.

philosophy, the most definite that the world has seen. That conception of the world which in the thirteenth century found argumentative and orderly expression in the "Summa Theologiæ" of Thomas of Aquino, and constituted the faith of the church, is visualized by Dante, and made the basis of an interpretation of life.

The "Divina Commedia" deals with all the heavens to the Empyrean itself, and with all spiritual life to the very presence of God. It derives its imagery from the cosmology of the day, its dramatic motive from the Christian and Greek conceptions of God and his dealings with the world. Sin is punished because of the justice of God; knowledge, virtue, and faith lead, through God's grace and mercy manifested in Christ, to a perpetual union with Him. Hell, purgatory, and paradise give place and setting to the events of the drama. But the deeper meaning of the poem is allegorical. In a letter quoted by Lowell, Dante writes:

"The literal subject of the whole work is the state of the soul after death, simply considered. But if the work be taken allegorically the subject is man, as by merit or demerit, through freedom of the will, he renders himself liable to the reward or punishment of justice." [4]

[4] Letter to Can Grande. See Lowell's *Essay on Dante*, p. 34.

In other words, the inner and essential meaning
of the poem has to do not with external retribution,
but with character, and the laws which determine
its own proper ruin or perfection. The punish-
ments described in the " Inferno " are accounts of
the state of guilt itself, implications of the will
that has chosen the part of brutishness. Sin itself
is damnable and deadening, but the knowledge
that the soul that sinneth shall die is the first way
of emancipation from sin. The guidance of Virgil
through hell and purgatory signifies the knowledge
of good and evil, or moral insight, as the guide
of man through this life of struggle and progress.
The earthly paradise, at the close of the " Purgatorio," represents the highest state to which human
character can attain when choice is determined by
ordinary experience, intelligence, and understanding. Here man stands alone, endowed with an
enlightened conscience. Here are uttered the last
words of Virgil to Dante, the explorer of the spiritual country :

"Expect no more or word or sign from me. Free, up-
right, and sane is thine own free will, and it would be
wrong not to act according to its pleasure; wherefore thee
over thyself I crown and mitre." [5]

[5] *Purgatorio*, Canto XXVII.   Translation by Norton.

But moral self-reliance is not the last word. As Beatrice, the image of tenderness and holiness, comes to Dante in the earthly paradise, and leads him from the summit of purgatory into the heaven of heavens, and even to the eternal light; so there is added to the mere human, intellectual, and moral resources of the soul, the sustaining power of the divine grace, the illuminating power of divine truth, and the transforming power of divine love. Through the aid of this higher wisdom, the journey of life becomes the way to God. Thus the allegorical truth of the " Divina Commedia " is not merely an analysis of the moral nature of man, but the revelation of a universal spiritual order, manifesting itself in the moral evolution of the individual, and above all in his ultimate community with the eternal goodness.

"Thou shouldst not, if I deem aright, wonder more at thy ascent, than at a stream if from a high mountain it descends to the base. A marvel it would be in thee, if, deprived of hindrance, thou hadst sat below, even as quiet by living fire in earth would be."[6]

Such, in brief, is Dante's world-view, so suggestive of the freer idealistic conceptions of later thought as to justify a recent characterization of him as one who, " accepting without a shadow of a doubt

[6] *Paradiso*, Canto I.

or hesitation all the constitutive ideas of mediæval thought and life, grasped them so firmly and gave them such luminous expression that the spirit in them broke away from the form." [7]

But it must be added, as in the case of Words-worth, that Dante is a philosopher-poet not be-cause St. Thomas Aquinas appears and speaks with authority in the Thirteenth Canto of the " Para-diso," nor even because a philosophical doctrine can be consistently formulated from his writings, but because his consciousness of life is informed with a sense of its universal bearings.   There is a famous passage in the Twenty-second Canto of the " Paradiso," in which Dante describes himself as looking down upon the earth from the starry heaven.

" 'Thou art so near the ultimate salvation,' began Bea-trice, 'that thou oughtest to have thine eyes clear and sharp.   And therefore ere thou further enterest it, look back downward, and see how great a world I have already set beneath thy feet, in order that thy heart, so far as it is able, may present itself joyous to the triumphant crowd which comes glad through this round ether.'   With my sight I returned through each and all the seven spheres, and saw this globe such that I smiled at its mean sem-blance; and that counsel I approve as the best which holds it of least account; and he who thinks of other things may be called truly worthy."

[7] Edward Caird, in his *Literature and Philosophy*, Vol. I, p. 24.

Dante's scale of values is that which appears from
the starry heaven. His austere piety, his invin-
cible courage, and his uncompromising hatred of
wrong, are neither accidents of temperament nor
blind reactions, but compose the proper character
of one who has both seen the world from God,
and returned to see God from the world. He was,
as Lowell has said, " a man of genius who could
hold heartbreak at bay for twenty years, and would
not let himself die till he had done his task ";
and his power was not obstinacy, but a vision of
the ways of God. He knew a truth that justified
him in his sacrifices, and made a great glory of
his defeat and exile. Even so his poetry or appreciation of life is the expression of an inward
contemplation of the world in its unity or essence.
It is but an elaboration of the piety which he
attributes to the lesser saints of paradise, when he
has them say:

"Nay, it is essential to this blessed existence to hold ourselves within the divine will, whereby our very wills are
made one.   So that as we are from stage to stage throughout this realm, to all the realm is pleasing, as to the King
who inwills us with His will.   And His will is our peace;
it is that sea whereunto is moving all that which It creates
and which nature makes." [8]

[8] *Paradiso*, Canto III.

§ 14. There now remains the brief task of distinguishing the philosopher-poet from the philosopher himself. The philosopher-poet is one who, having made the philosophical point of view his own, expresses himself in the form of poetry. The philosophical point of view is that from which the universe is comprehended in its totality. The wisdom of the philosopher is the knowledge of each through the knowledge of all. Wherein, then, does the poet, when possessed of such wisdom, differ from the philosopher proper ? To this question one can give readily enough the general answer, that the difference lies in the mode of utterance. Furthermore, we have already given some account of the peculiar manner of the poet. He invites us to experience with him the beautiful and moving in nature and life. That which the poet has to express, and that which he aims to arouse in others, is an appreciative experience. He requires what Wordsworth calls " an atmosphere of sensation in which to move his wings." Therefore if he is to be philosophical in intelligence, and yet essentially a poet, he must find his universal truth in immediate experience. He must be one who, in seeing the many, sees the one. The philosopher-poet is he

The Difference between Poetry and Philosophy.

who visualizes a fundamental interpretation of the world. "A poem," says one poet, "is the very image of life expressed in its eternal truth."

The philosopher proper, on the other hand, has the sterner and less inviting task of <u>rendering such an interpretation articulate to thought.</u> That which the poet sees, the philosopher must define. That which the poet divines, the philosopher must calculate. The philosopher must dig for that which the poet sees shining through. As the poet transcends thought for the sake of experience, the philosopher must transcend experience for the sake of thought. As the poet sees all, and all in each, so the philosopher, knowing each, must think all consistently together, and then know each again. It is the part of philosophy to collect and criticise evidence, to formulate and coördinate conceptions, and finally to define in exact terms. The reanimation of the structure of thought is accomplished primarily in religion, which is a general conception of the world made the basis of daily living.

For religion there is no subjective correlative less than life itself. Poetry is another and more circumscribed means of restoring thought to life. By the poet's imagination, and through the art of his expression, thought may be sensuously perceived. "If the time should ever come," says Wordsworth, "when what is now called Science, thus familiarized to men, shall be ready to put on, as it were, a form of flesh and blood, the Poet will lend his divine spirit to aid the transfiguration, and will welcome the Being thus produced, as a dear and genuine inmate of the household of man." [9] As respects truth, philosophy has an indubitable priority. The very sternness of the philosopher's task is due to his supreme dedication to truth. But if validity be the merit of philosophy, it can well be supplemented by immediacy, which is the merit of poetry. Presuppose in the poet conviction of a sound philosophy, and we may say with Shelley, of his handiwork, that "it is the perfect and consummate surface and bloom of all things; it is as the odor and the color of the rose to the texture of the elements which compose it, as the form and splendor of unfaded beauty to the secrets of anatomy and corruption." "Indeed," as he adds, "what were our consolations on this side of the grave—and our aspirations beyond it— if poetry did not ascend to bring light and fire

[9] Observations prefixed to the second edition of *Lyrical Ballads*.

from those eternal regions where the owl-winged faculty of calculation dare not ever soar ? " [10]

The unity in outlook, attended by differences of method and form, which may exist between poet and philosopher, is signally illustrated by the relation between Goethe and Spinoza. What Goethe saw and felt, Spinoza proved and defined. The universal and eternal substance was to Spinoza, as philosopher, a theorem, and to Goethe, as poet, a perception and an emotion. Goethe writes to Jacobi that when philosophy " lays itself out for division," he cannot get on with it, but when it " confirms our original feeling as though we were one with nature," it is welcome to him. In the same letter Goethe expresses his appreciation of Spinoza as the complement of his own nature:

"His all-reconciling peace contrasted with my all-agitating endeavor; his intellectual method was the opposite counterpart of my poetic way of feeling and expressing myself; and even the inflexible regularity of his logical procedure, which might be considered ill-adapted to moral subjects, made me his most passionate scholar and his devoted adherent. Mind and heart, understanding and sense, were drawn together with an inevitable elective affinity, and this at the same time produced an intimate union between individuals of the most different types." [11]

[10] *A Defence of Poetry.*
[11] Quoted by Caird in his *Literature and Philosophy*, Vol. I, p. 60

It appears, then, that some poets share with all philosophers that point of view from which the horizon line is the boundary of all the world. Poetry is not always or essentially philosophical, but may be so; and when the poetic imagination restores philosophy to immediacy, human experience reaches its most exalted state, excepting only religion itself, wherein God is both seen and also served.   Nor is the part of philosophy in poetry and religion either ignoble or presumptuous, for, humanly speaking, " the owl-winged faculty of calculation " is the only safe and sure means of access to that place on high,

> " Where the nightingale doth sing
> Not a senseless, trancèd thing,
> But a divine melodious truth;
> Philosophic numbers smooth;
> Tales and golden histories
> Of heaven and its mysteries."

CHAPTER III

§ 15. THE least religious experience is so mysterious and so complex that a moderate degree of **The Possibility of Defining Religion.** reflection upon it tends to a sense of intellectual impotence. " If I speak," says Emerson, " I define and confine, and am less." One would gladly set down religion among the unspeakable things and avoid the imputation of degrading it. It is certain that the enterprise of defining religion is at present in disrepute. It has been undertaken so often and so unsuccessfully that contemporary students for the most part prefer to supply a list of historical definitions of religion, and let their variety demonstrate their futility. Metaphysicians and psychologists agree that in view of the differences of creed, ritual, organization, conduct, and temperament that have been true of different religions in different times and places, one may as well abandon the idea that there is a constant element.

But on the other hand we have the testimony afforded by the name religion; and the ordinary judgments of men to the effect that it signifies something to be religious, and to be more or less religious. There is an elementary logical principle to the effect that a group name implies certain common group characters. Impatience with abstract or euphemistic definitions should not blind us to the truth. Even the psychologist tends in his description of religious phenomena to single out and emphasize what he calls a *typical* religious experience. And the same applies to the idealist's treatment of the matter.[1] Religion, he reasons, is essentially a development of which the true meaning can be seen only in the higher stages. The primitive religion is therefore only implicit religion. But lower stages cannot be regarded as belonging to a single development with higher stages, if there be not some actual promise of the later in the earlier, or some element which endures throughout. It is unavoidable, then, to assume that in dealing with religion we are dealing with a specific and definable experience.

§ 16. The profitableness of undertaking such a definition is another matter. It may well be that

[1] Cf. Caird: *The Evolution of Religion*, Lectures II, III.

in so human and practical an affair as religion,
definition is peculiarly inappropriate.   But is there
not a human and practical value in the
very defining of religion?   Is there not
a demand for it in the peculiar relation that exists between religion and the progress
of enlightenment?   Religion associates itself with
the habits of society.   The progress of enlightenment means that more or less all the time, and very
profoundly at certain critical times, society must
change its habits.   The consequence is that religion
is likely to be abandoned with the old habits.   The
need of a new religion is therefore a chronic one.
The reformer in religion, or the man who wishes
to be both enlightened and religious, is chiefly occupied with the problem of disentangling religion
pure and undefiled from definite discredited practices and opinions.   And the solution of the problem turns upon some apprehension of the essence
of religion.   There is a large amount of necessary
and unnecessary tragedy due to the extrinsic connection between ideas and certain modes of their
expression.   There can be no more serious and
urgent duty than that of expressing as directly,
and so as truly as possible, the great permanent
human concerns.   The men to whom educational

The Profit-
ableness of
Defining
Religion.

reform has been largely due have been the men
who have remembered for their fellows what this
whole business of education is after all for.   Co-
menius and Pestalozzi served society by stripping
educational activity of its historical and institutional accessories, and laying bare the genuine
human need that these are designed to satisfy.
There is a similar virtue in the insistent attempt
to distinguish between the essential and the acces-
sory in religion.

§ 17. Although declining to be discouraged by
the conspicuousness of past failures in this connec-

The True
Method of
Defining
Religion.
tion, one may well profit by them.   The
amazing complexity of religious phenomena must somehow be seen to be consistent with their common nature.   The religious
experience must not only be found, but must also
be reconciled with " the varieties of religious experience."   The inadequacy of the well-known
definitions of religion may be attributed to several
causes.   The commonest fallacy is to define religion in terms of *a* religion.   My definition of religion must include my brother's religion, even
though he live on the other side of the globe, and
my ancestor's religion, in spite of his prehistoric
remoteness.   Error may easily arise through the

attempt to define religion in terms of my own religion, or what I conceive to be the true religion. Whatever the relation between ideal religion and actual religion, the field of religion contains by common consent cults that must on their own grounds condemn one another; religions that are bad religions, and yet religions.

A more enlightened fallacy, and a more dangerous one, is due to the supposition that religion can be defined exclusively in terms of some department of human nature. There have been descriptions of religion in terms of feeling, intellect, and conduct respectively. But it is always easy to overthrow such a description, by raising the question of its application to evidently religious experiences that belong to some other aspect of life. Religion is not feeling, because there are many phlegmatic, God-fearing men whose religion consists in good works. Religion is not conduct, for there are many mystics whose very religion is withdrawal from the field of action. Religion is not intellection, for no one has ever been able to formulate a creed that is common to all religions. Yet without a doubt one must look for the essence of religion in human nature. The present psychological interest in religion has emphasized this truth.

How, then, may we describe it in terms of certain constant conditions of human life, and yet escape the abstractness of the facultative method? Modern psychology suggests an answer in demonstrating the interdependence of knowledge, feeling, and volition.[2] The perfect case of this unity is *belief*. The believing experience is cognitive in intent, but practical and emotional as well in content. I believe what I take for granted; and the object of my belief is not merely known, but also felt and acted upon. *What I believe expresses itself in my total experience.*

There is some hope, then, of an adequate definition of the religious experience, if it be regarded as belonging to the psychological type of belief.[3] Belief, however, is a broader category than religion. There must be some *religious type* of believing. An account of religion in terms of believing, and the particular type of it here in question, would, then, constitute the central stem of a psychology of religion, and affords the proper conceptions for a description of the religious experience. Even here the reservation must be made that belief is always more than the believing *state*, in that it

[2] Cf. Leuba: *Introduction to a Psychological Study of Religion, Monist*, Vol. XI, p. 195.
[3] Cf. Leuba: *Ibid.*

means to be *true*.[4] Hence to complete an account of religion one should consider its object, or its cognitive implications. But this direct treatment of the relation between religion and philosophy must be deferred until in the present chapter we shall have come to appreciate the inwardness of the religious consciousness. To this end we must permit ourselves to be enlightened by the experience of religious people as viewed from within. It is not our opinion of a man's religion that is here in question, but the content and meaning which it has for him.

"I would have you," says Fielding, in his " Hearts of Men," "go and kneel beside the Mahommedan as he prays at the sunset hour, and put your heart to his and wait for the echo that will surely come. . . . I would have you go to the hillman smearing the stone with butter that his god may be pleased, to the woman crying to the forest god for her sick child, to the boy before his monks learning to be good. No matter where you go, no matter what the faith is called, if you have the hearing ear, if your heart is in unison with the heart of the world, you will hear always the same song."[5]

§ 18. The general identification of religion with belief is made without serious difficulty. The essential factor in belief, is, as we have seen, the reaction of the whole person-

Religion as Belief.

[4] Cf. § 29.   [5] P. 322.

ality to a fixed object or accepted situation. A
similar principle underlies common judgments
about a man's religion. He is accounted most religious whose religion penetrates his life most intimately. In the man whose religion consists in the
outer exercise of attendance upon church, we recognize the sham. He *appears* to be religious.
He does one of the things which a religious man
would do; but an object of religious faith is not
the constant environment of his life. He may or
may not feel sure of God from his pew, but God
is not among the things that count in his daily
life. God does not enter into his calculations or
determine his scale of values. Again, discursive
thinking is regarded as an interruption of religion.
When I am at pains to justify my religion, I am
already doubting; and for common opinion doubt
is identical with irreligion. In so far as I am
religious, my religion stands in no need of justification, even though I regard it as justifiable. In
my religious experience I am taking something for
granted; in other words I act about it and feel
about it in a manner that is going to be determined
by the special conditions of my mood and temperament. The mechanical and prosaic man acknowledges God in his mechanical and prosaic

way. He believes in divine retribution as he
believes in commercial or social retribution.   He
is as careful to prepare for the next world as he
is to be respectable in this.   The poet, on the other
hand, believes in God after the manner of his
genius.   Though he worship God in spirit he may
conduct his life in an irregular manner peculiar
to himself.   Difference of mood in the same individual may be judged by the same measure.
When God is most real to him, brought home to
him most vividly, or consciously obeyed, in these
moments he is most religious.   When, on the other
hand, God is merely a name to him, and church
a routine, or when both are forgotten in the daily
occupations, he is least religious.   His life on the
whole is said to be religious in so far as periods
of the second type are subordinated to periods of
the first type.   Further well-known elements of
belief, corollaries of the above, are evidently present in religion.   A certain *imagery remains constant* throughout an individual's experience.   He
comes back to it as to a physical object in space.
And although religion is sporadically an exclusive
and isolated affair, it tends strongly to be social.
The religious object, or God, is a social object,
common to me and to my neighbor, and presup-

posed in our collective undertakings. This reduction of religion to the type of the believing state
should thus provide us with an answer to that old
and fundamental question concerning the relative
priority of faith and works. The test of the faith
is in the works, and the works are religious in so
far as they are the expression of the faith. Religion is not the doing of anything nor the feeling of anything nor the thinking of anything,
but the reacting as a whole, in terms of all possible activities of human life, to some accepted
situation.

§ 19. We may now face the more interesting
but difficult question of the special character of

Religion as religious belief. In spite of the fact
Belief in a that in these days the personality of God
Disposition or
Attitude. is often regarded as a transient feature
of religion, that type of belief which throws most
light upon the religious experience is the *belief in
persons.* Our belief in persons consists in the
practical recognition of a more or less persistent
disposition toward ourselves. The outward behavior of our fellow-men is construed in terms of
the practical bearing of the attitude which it implies. The extraordinary feature of such belief
is the disproportion between its vividness and the

direct evidence for it. Of this we are most aware in connection with those personalities which we regard as distinctly friendly or hostile to ourselves. We are always more or less clearly in the presence of our friends and enemies. Their well-wishing or their ill-wishing haunts the scene of our living. There is no more important constituent of what the psychologists call our "general feeling tone." There are times when we are entirely possessed by a state that is either exuberance in the presence of those who love us, or awkwardness and stupidity in the presence of those whom we believe to suspect and dislike us. The latter state may easily become chronic. Many men live permanently in the presence of an accusing audience. The inner life which expresses itself in the words, "Everybody hates me!" is perhaps the most common form of morbid self-consciousness. On the other hand, buoyancy of spirits springs largely from a constant faith in the good-will of one's fellows. In this case one is filled with a sense of security, and is conscious of a sympathetic reinforcement that adds to private joys and compensates for private sorrows. And this sense of attitude is wonderfully discriminating. We can feel the presence of a "great man," a "formidable person," a superior

or inferior, one who is interested or indifferent to
our talk, and all the subtlest degrees of approval
and disapproval.

A similar sensibility may quicken us even in
situations where no direct individual attitude to
ourselves is implied. We regard places and communities as congenial when we are in sympathy
with the prevailing purposes or standards of value.
We may feel ill at ease or thoroughly at home
in cities where we know no single human soul.
Indeed, in a misanthrope like Rousseau (and who
has not his Rousseau moods!) the mere absence of
social repression arouses a most intoxicating sense
of tunefulness and security. Nature plays the
part of an indulgent parent who permits all sorts
of personal liberties.

"The view of a fine country, a succession of agreeable prospects, a free air, a good appetite, and the health
I gain by walking; the freedom of inns, and the distance
from everything that can make me recollect the dependence of my situation, conspire to free my soul, and
give boldness to my thoughts, throwing me, in a manner,
into the immensity of things, where I combine, choose,
and appropriate them to my fancy, without restraint or
fear. I dispose of all nature as I please."[6]

§ 20. In such confidence or distrust, inspired

[6] Rousseau: *Confessions*, Book IV, p. 125.

originally by the social environment, and similarly suggested by other surroundings of life, we have the key to the religious consciousness. But it is now time to add that in the case of religion these attitudes are concerned with the universal or supernatural rather than with present and normal human relationships. Religious reactions are "total reactions."

Religion as Belief in the Disposition of the Residual Environment, or Universe.

"To get at them," says William James, "you must go behind the foreground of existence and reach down to that curious *sense of the whole residual cosmos as an everlasting presence*, intimate or alien, terrible or amusing, lovable or odious, which in some degree everyone possesses. This *sense of the world's presence*, appealing as it does to our peculiar individual temperament, makes us either strenuous or careless, devout or blasphemous, gloomy or exultant about life at large; and our reaction, involuntary and inarticulate and often half unconscious as it is, is the completest of all our answers to the question, 'What is the character of this universe in which we dwell?' " [7]

This *residual environment*, or profounder realm of tradition and nature, may have any degree of unity from chaos to cosmos. For religion its sig-

[7] William James: *The Varieties of Religious Experience*, p. 35. The italics are mine. I am in the present chapter under constant obligation to this wonderfully sympathetic and stimulating book.

nificance lies in the idea of original and far-reaching power rather than in the idea of totality. But that which is at first only " beyond," is *practically* the same object as that which comes in the development of thought to be conceived as the " world " or the " universe." We may therefore use these latter terms to indicate the object of religion, until the treatment of special instances shall define it more precisely. Religion is, then, man's *sense of the disposition of the universe to himself*. We shall expect to find, as in the social phenomena with which we have just dealt, that the manifestation of this sense consists in a general reaction appropriate to the disposition so attributed. He will be fundamentally ill at ease, profoundly confident, or will habitually take precautions to be safe. The ultimate nature of the world is here no speculative problem. The savage who could feel some joy at living in the universe would be more religious than the sublimest dialectician. It is in the vividness of the sense of this presence that the acuteness of religion consists. I am religious in so far as the whole tone and temper of my living reflects a belief as to what the universe thinks of such as me.

§ 21. The examples that follow are selected

because their differences in personal flavor serve

Examples of Religious Belief. to throw into relief their common religious character. Theodore Parker, in describing his own boyhood, writes as follows:

" I can hardly think without a shudder of the terrible effect the doctrine of eternal damnation had on me. How many, many hours have I wept with terror as I lay on my bed, till, between praying and weeping, sleep gave me repose. But before I was nine years old this fear went away, and I saw clearer light in the goodness of God. But for years, say from seven till ten, I said my prayers with much devotion, I think, and then continued to repeat, 'Lord, forgive my sins,' till sleep came on me." [8]

Compare with this Stevenson's Christmas letter to his mother, in which he says:

" The whole necessary morality is kindness; and it should spring, of itself, from the one fundamental doctrine, Faith. If you are sure that God, in the long run, means kindness by you, you should be happy; and if happy, surely you should be kind." [9]

Here is destiny frowning and destiny smiling, but in each case so real, so present, as to be immediately responded to with helpless terror and with grateful warm-heartedness.

The author of the " Imitatio Christi " speaks thus of the daily living of the Christian:

[8] Chadwick: *Theodore Parker*, p. 18.
[9] Stevenson: *Letters*, Vol. I, p. 229.

" The life of a Christian who has dedicated himself to the service of God should abound with eminent virtues of all kinds, that he may be really the same person which he is by outward appearance and profession. Indeed, he ought not only to be the same, but much more, in his inward disposition of soul; because he professes to serve a God who sees the inward parts, a searcher of the heart and reins, a God and Father of spirits: and therefore, since we are always in His sight, we should be exceedingly careful to avoid all impurity, all that may give offence to Him whose eyes cannot behold iniquity. We should, in a word, so far as mortal and frail nature can, imitate the blessed angels in all manner of holiness, since we, as well as they, are always in His presence. . . . And good men have always this notion of the thing. For they depend upon God for the success of all they do, even of their best and wisest undertakings." [10]

Such is to be the practical acknowledgment of God in the routine of life.   The more direct response to this presence appears abundantly in St. Augustine's conversation and reminiscence with God.

" How evil have not my deeds been; or if not my deeds my words; or if not my words my will? But Thou, O Lord, art good and merciful, and Thy right hand had respect unto the profoundness of my death, and removed from the bottom of my heart that abyss of corruption. And this was the result, that I willed not to do what I willed, and willed to do what thou willedst. . . . How sweet did it suddenly become to me to be without the delights of trifles! And what at one time I

[10] Thomas à Kempis: *Imitation of Christ*, Chap. XIX. Translation by Stanhope, p. 44.

feared to lose, it was now a joy to me to put away.   For
Thou didst cast them away from me, Thou true and
highest sweetness.   Thou didst cast them away, and
instead of them didst enter in Thyself—sweeter than
all pleasure, though not to flesh and blood; brighter
than all light, but more veiled than all mysteries; more
exalted than all honor, but not to the exalted in their
own conceits.   Now was my soul free from the gnawing
cares of seeking and getting. . . . And I babbled
unto Thee my brightness, my riches, and my health,
the Lord my God."[11]

In these two passages we meet with religious conduct and with the supreme religious experience,
the direct worship of God.   In each case the heart
of the matter is an individual's indubitable conviction of the world's favorable concern for him.
The deeper order of things constitutes the real and
the profoundly congenial community in which he
lives.

§ 22.   Let us now apply this general account of
the religious experience to certain typical religious
Typical Religious Phenomena: Conversion. phenomena: *conversion; piety;* and religious *instruments, symbolisms, and
modes of conveyance.*   Although recent
study of the phenomenon of *conversion* has
brought to light a considerable amount of interest-

[11] St. Augustine: *Confessions*, Book I, Chap. I.   Translation in Schaff: *Nicene and Post-Nicene Fathers*, Vol. I, p. 129.

ing material, there is some danger of misconceiving its importance. The pyschology of conversion is primarily the psychology of crisis or radical alteration, rather than the psychology of religion. For the majority of religious men and women conversion is an insignificant event, and in very many cases it never occurs at all. Religion is more purely present where it is normal and monotonous. But this phenomenon is nevertheless highly significant in that religion and irreligion are placed in close juxtaposition, and the contribution of religion at its inception thereby emphasized. In general it is found that conversion takes place during the period of adolescence. But this is the time of the most sudden expansion of the environment of life; a time when there is the awakening consciousness of many a new presence. This is sometimes expressed by saying that it is a period of acute self-consciousness. Life is conscious of itself as over against its inheritance; the whole setting of life sweeps into view. Some solution of the life problem, some coming to terms with the universe, is the normal issue of it. Religious conversion signifies, then, that in this fundamental adjustment a man defines and accepts for his life a certain attitude on the part of the universe. The examples cited by the psychologists, as well as the generalizations which they derive, bear out this interpretation.

"General Booth, the founder of the Salvation Army, considers that the first vital step in saving outcasts consists in making them feel that some decent human being cares enough for them to take an interest in the question whether they are to rise or sink." [12]

The new state is here one of courage and hope stimulated by the glow of friendly interest. The convert is no longer "out in the cold." He is told that the world wishes him well, and this is brought home to him through representations of the tenderness of Christ, and through the direct ministerings of those who mediate it. But somehow the convert must be persuaded to realize all this. He must *believe* it before it can mean anything to him. He is therefore urged to pray—a proceeding that is at first ridiculous to him, since it involves taking for granted what he disbelieves. But therein lies the critical point. It is peculiar to the object in this case that it can exist only for one who already believes in it. The psychologists call this the element of "self-surrender." To be converted a man must somehow suffer his

[12] James: *Varieties of Religious Experience*, p. 203.

surroundings to put into him a new heart, which
may thereupon confirm its object. Such belief is
tremendously tenacious because it so largely creates its own evidence. Once believe that " God,
in the long run, means kindness by you," and you
are likely to stand by it to the end—the more so
in this case because the external evidence either way
is to the average man so insufficient. Such a belief
as this is inspired in the convert, not by reasoning,
but by all the powers of suggestion that personality
and social contagion can afford.

§ 23. The psychologists describe *piety* as a sense
of unity. One feels after reading their accounts

Piety.   that they are too abstract. For there
are many kinds of unity, characteristic of widely
varying moods and states. Any state of rapt attention is a state of unity, and this occurs in the
most secular and humdrum moments of life. Nor
does it help matters to say that in the case of religion this unity must have been preceded by a state
of division; for we cannot properly characterize
any state of mind in terms of another state unless
the latter be retained in the former. And that
which is characteristic of the religious sense of
unity would seem to be just such an overcoming of
difference. There is a recognition of two distinct

attitudes, which may be more or less in sympathy with one another, but which are both present even in their fullest harmony. Were I to be taken out of myself so completely as to forget myself, I should inevitably lose that sense of sympathy from which arises the peculiar exultation of religious faith, a heightened experience of the same type with the freedom and spontaneity that I experience in the presence of those with whom I feel most in accord. The further graces and powers of religion readily submit to a similar description. My sense of positive sympathy expresses itself in an attitude of well-wishing; living in an atmosphere of kindness I instinctively endeavor to propagate it. My buoyancy is distinctly of that quality which to a lesser degree is due to any sense of social security; my power is that of one who works in an environment that reënforces him. I experience the objective or even cosmical character of my enterprises. They have a momentum which makes me their instrument rather than their perpetrator. A paradoxical relation between religion and morality has always interested observers of custom and history. Religion is apparently as capable of the most fiendish malevolence as of the most saintly gentleness. Fielding writes that,

" When religion is brought out or into daily life and used as a guide or a weapon in the world it has no effect either for good or evil. Its effect is simply in strengthening the heart, in blinding the eyes, in deafening the ears. It is an intensive force, an intoxicant. It doubles or trebles a man's powers. It is an impulsive force sending him headlong down the path of emotion, whether that path lead to glory or to infamy. It is a tremendous stimulant, that is all." [13]

Religion does not originate life purposes or define their meaning, but stimulates them by the same means that works in all corporate and social activity.   To work with the universe is the most tremendous incentive that can appeal to the individual will.   Hence in highly ethical religions the power for good exceeds that of any other social and spiritual agency.   Such religion makes present, actual, and real, that good on the whole which the individual otherwise tends to distinguish from that which is good for *him*.   In daily life the morally valid and the practically urgent are commonly arrayed against one another; but the ethical religion makes the valid urgent.

§ 24. The *instruments* of religion are legion, and it is in order here only to mention certain

Religious Instruments, Symbolism, and Modes of Conveyance.

prominent cases in which their selection would seem to have direct reference to the provocation and perpetuation of

[13] Fielding: *op. cit.*, p. 152.

such a sense of attitude as we have been describing. This is true in a general way of all *symbolism*. There is no essential difference between the religious symbol and such symbols as serve to remind us of human relationships. In both cases the perceptual absence of will is compensated for by the presence of some object associated with that will. The function of this object is due to its power to revive and perpetuate a certain special social atmosphere. But the most important vehicle of religion has always been personality. It is, after all, to priests, prophets, and believers that religious cults have owed their long life. The traits that mark the prophet are both curious and sublime. He is most remarkable for the confidence with which he speaks for the universe. Whether it be due to lack of a sense of humor or to a profound conviction of truth, is indifferent to our purpose. The power of such men is undoubtedly in their suggestion of a force greater than they, whose designs they bring directly and socially to the attention of men. The prophet in his prophesying is indeed not altogether distinguished from God, and it is through the mediation of a directly perceptible human attitude that a divine attitude gets itself fixed in the imagination of the believer.

What is true of the prophet is equally true of the preacher whose function it is not to represent God in his own person, but to depict him with his tongue. It is generally recognized that the preacher is neither a moralizer nor a theologian. But it is less perfectly understood that it is his function to suggest the presence of God. His proper language is that of the imagination, and the picture which he portrays is that of a reciprocal social relationship between man and the Supreme Master of the situation of life. He will not define God or prove God, but introduce Him and talk about Him. And at the same time the association of prayer and worship with his sermon, and the atmosphere created by the meeting together of a body of disciples, will act as the confirmation of his suggestions of such a living presence.

The *conveyance* of any single religious cult from generation to generation affords a signal illustration of the importance in religion of the recognition of attitude. Religions manage somehow to survive any amount of transformation of creed and ritual. It is not what is done, or what is thought, that identifies the faith of the first Christians with that of the last, but a certain reckoning with the disposition of God. The successive generations of Christians are introduced into the spiritual world of their fathers, with its furnishing of hopes and fears remaining substantially the same; and their Christianity consists in their continuing to live in it with only a slight and gradual renovation. To any given individual God is more or less completely represented by his elders in the faith in their exhortations and ministerings; and through them he fixes as the centre of his system an image of God his accuser or redeemer.

§ 25. The complete verification of this interpretation of the religious experience would require the application of it to the different historical cults. In general the examination of such instances is entirely beyond the scope of this chapter; but a brief consideration may be given to those which seem to afford reasonable grounds for objection.

Historical Types of Religion. Primitive Religions.

First, it may be said that in *primitive religions,* notably in fetichism, tabooism, and totemism, there is no recognition of a cosmical unity. It is quite evident that there is no conception of a universe. But it is equally evident that the natural and historical environment in its generality has a very specific practical significance for the primitive believer. It is often said with truth that these

earliest religions are more profoundly pantheistic
than polytheistic.   Man recognizes an all-pervad-
ing interest that is capable of being directed to
himself.   The selection of a deity is not due to
any special qualification for deification possessed
by the individual object itself, but to the tacit presumption that, as Thales said, " all things are full
of gods." The disposition of residual reality manifests to the believer no consistency or unity, but it
is nevertheless the most constant object of his will.
He lives in the midst of a capriciousness which he
must appease if he is to establish himself at all.

§ 26. Secondly, in the case of *Buddhism* we are
Buddhism.   said to meet with a religion that is essentially atheistic.

"Whether Buddhas arise, O priests, or whether
Buddhas do not arise, it remains a fact and the fixed
and necessary constitution of being, that all its constituents are transitory." [14]

The secret of life lies in the application of this
truth:

> " O builder! I've discovered thee!
> This fabric thou shalt ne'er rebuild!
> Thy rafters all are broken now,
> And pointed roof demolished lies!
> This mind has demolition reached,
> And seen the last of all desire! " [14]

[14] Warren: *Buddhism in Translations*, p. 14.
[15] *Ibid.*, p. 83.

The case of Buddha himself and of the exponents of his purely esoteric doctrine, belong to the reflective type which will presently be given special consideration. But with the ordinary believer, even where an extraneous but almost inevitable polytheism is least in evidence, the religious experience consists in substantially the same elements that appear in theistic religions. The individual is here living appropriately to the ultimate nature of things, with the ceaseless periods of time in full view. That which is brought home to him is the illusoriness and hollowness of things when taken in the spirit of active endeavor. The only profound and abiding good is nothingness. While nature and society conspire to mock him, Nirvana invites him to its peace. The religious course of his life consists in the use of such means as can win him this end. From the stand-point of the universe he has the sympathy only of that wisdom whose essence is self-destruction. And this truth is mediated by the imagination of divine sympathy, for the Blessed One remains as the perpetual incarnation of his own blessedness.

§ 27. Finally there remains the consideration of the bearing of this interpretation upon the more

refined and disciplined religions. The religion
of the critically enlightened man is less naive

Critical Religion. and credulous in its imagery. God
tends to vanish into an ideal or a uni-
versal, into some object of theoretical definition. Here we are on that borderland where an
assignment of individual cases can never be
made with any certainty of correctness. We
can generalize only by describing the conditions
that such cases must fulfil if they are properly to be denominated religious. And there can
be no question of the justice of deriving such
a description from the reports of historical and institutional religions. An idealistic philosophy
will, then, be a religion just in so far as it is rendered practically vivid by the imagination. Such
imagination must create and sustain a social relationship. The question of the legitimacy of this
imagination is another matter. It raises the issue
concerning the judgment of truth implied in religion, and this is the topic of the next chapter.
At any rate the religious experience *may be* realized by virtue of the metaphorical or poetical representation of a situation as one of intercommuni-
cation between persons, where reflective definition
at the same time denies it. The human worshipper

may supply the personality of God from himself, viewing himself as from the divine stand-point. But whatever faculty supplies this indispensable social quality of religion, he who defines God as the ultimate goodness or the ultimate truth, has certainly not yet worshipped Him. He begins to be religious only when such an ideal determines the atmosphere of his daily living; when he regards the immanence of such an ideal in nature and history as the object of his will; and when he responds to its presence in the spirit of his conduct and his contemplation.

CHAPTER IV

THE PHILOSOPHICAL IMPLICATIONS OF RELIGION

§ 28. It has been maintained that religion is closely analogous to one's belief in the disposition

Résumé of Psychology of Religion. toward one's self of men or communities. In the case of religion this disposition is attributed to the more or less vaguely conceived residual environment that is recognized as lying outside of the more familiar natural and social relations. After the rise of science this residual environment tends to be conceived as a unity which is ultimate or fundamental, but for the religious consciousness it is more commonly regarded as a general source of influence practically worthy of consideration. Such a belief, like all belief, is vitally manifested, with such emphasis upon action, feeling, or intellection as temperament and mood may determine.

§ 29. But if the psychology of belief is the proper starting-point for a description of the re-

Religion Means to be True. ligious experience, it is none the less suggestive of the fact that religion, just

82

because it *is* belief, is not wholly a matter for psychology. For religion *means to be true,* and thus submits itself to valuation as a case of knowledge. The psychological study of religion is misleading when accepted as a substitute for philosophical criticism. The religious man takes his religion not as a narcotic, but as an enlightenment. Its subjective worth is due at any rate in part to the supposition of its objective worth. As in any case of insight, that which warms the heart must have satisfied the mind. The religious experience purports to be the part of wisdom, and to afford only such happiness as increasing wisdom would confirm. And the charm of truth cannot survive its truthfulness. Hence, though religion may be described, it cannot be justified, from the stand-point of therapeutics. Were such the case it would be the real problem of religious leaders to find a drug capable of giving a constantly pleasant tone to their patient's experience.[1] There would be no difference between priests and physicians who make a specialty of nervous diseases, except that the former would aim at a more fundamental and perpetual

[1] As Plato interprets the scepticism of Protagoras to mean that one state of mind cannot be more *true* than another, but only *better* or worse. Cf. *Theœtetus,* 167.

suggestion of serenity. Now no man wants to be
even a blessed fool. He does not want to dwell
constantly in a fictitious world, even if it be after
his own heart. He may from the cynical point of
view actually do so, but if he be religious he thinks
it is reality, and is satisfied only in so far as he
thinks so. He regards the man who has said in
his heart that there is no God as the fool, and not
because he may have to suffer for it, but because
he is cognitively blind to the real nature of things.
Piety, on the other hand, he regards as the standard
experience, the most veracious life. Hence, it is
not an accident that religion has had its creeds and
its controversies, its wars with science and its appeals to philosophy. The history of these affairs
shows that religion commonly fails to understand
the scope of its own demand for truth; but they
have issued from the deep conviction that one's
religion is, implicitly, at least, in the field of truth;
that there are theoretical judgments whose truth
would justify or contradict it.

This general fact being admitted, there remains
the task to which the present discussion addresses
itself, that of defining the kind of *theoretical judgment* implied in religion, and the relation to this
central cognitive stem of its efflorescences of myth,

theology, and ritual. It is impossible to separate
the stem and the efflorescence, or to determine the
precise spot at which destruction of the tissue
would prove fatal to the plant, but it is possible to
obtain some idea of the relative vitality of the
parts.

§ 30. The difficulty of reaching a definite state-
ment in this matter is due to the fact that the truth
Religion   in which any religious experience cen-
Means to be
Practically   tres is a practical and not a scientific
True.
God is a Dis-   truth.   A practical truth does not composition from   mit itself to any single scientific state-
which Conse-
quences May   ment, and can often survive the over-
Rationally
be Expected.   throw of that scientific statement in
which at any given time it has found expression.
In other words, an indefinite number of scientific
truths are compatible with a single practical truth.
An instance of this is the consistency with my expectation of the alternation of day and night, of
either the Ptolemaic or Copernican formulation of
the solar system.   Now expectation that the sun
will rise to-morrow is an excellent analogue of my
religious belief.   Celestial mechanics is as relevant
to the one as metaphysics to the other.   Neither is
overthrown until a central practical judgment is
discredited, and either could remain true through

a very considerable alteration of logical definition ;
but neither is on this account exempt from theoretical responsibility.   In so far as religion deliberately enters the field of science, and defines its
formularies with the historical or metaphysical
method, this difficulty does not, of course, exist.
Grant that the years of Methuselah's life, or the precise place and manner of the temptation of Jesus,
or the definition of Christ in the terms of the
Athanasian Creed, are constitutive of Christianity,
and the survival of that religion will be determined
by the solution of ordinary problems of historical
or metaphysical research.   But the Christian will
very properly claim that his religion is only externally and accidentally related to such propositions,
since they are never or very rarely intended in his
experience.   As religious he is occupied with
Christ as his saviour or with God as his protector
and judge.   The history of Jesus or the metaphysics of God essentially concern him only in so
far as they may or may not invalidate this relationship.   He cares only for the power and disposition
of the divine, and these are affected by history and
metaphysics only in so far as he has definitely put
them to such proof.

For my religion is my sense of a practical situation, and only when that has been proved to be folly has my religion become untrue. My God is my practical faith, my plan of salvation. My religion is overthrown if I am convinced that I have misconceived the situation and mistaken what I should do to be saved. The conception of God is very simple practically, and very complex theoretically, a fact that confirms its practical genesis. My conception of God contains *an idea of my own interests, an idea of the disposition of the universe toward my interests,* and *some working plan for the reconciliation of these two terms.* These three elements form a practical unity, but each is capable of emphasis, and a religion may be transformed through the modification of any one of them. It appears, then, as has always been somewhat vaguely recognized, that the truth of religion is ethical as well as metaphysical or scientific. My religion will be altered by a change in my conception of what constitutes my real interest, a change in my conception of the fundamental causes of reality, or a change in my conception of the manner in which my will may or may not affect these causes. God is neither an entity nor an ideal, but always a relation of entity to ideal: *reality regarded from the stand-point of its favorableness or unfavorable-*

ness to human life, and prescribing for the latter
the propriety of a certain attitude.

§ 31. The range of historical examples is limit-

Historical
Examples of
Religious
Truth and
Error.
The Religion
of Baal. less, but certain of these are especially
calculated to emphasize the application
of a criterion to religion.   Such is the
case with Elijah's encounter with the
prophets of Baal, as narrated in the Old Testament.

"And Elijah came near unto all the people, and said,
How long halt ye between two opinions? If Yahweh
be God, follow him: but if Baal, then follow him. . . .
And call ye on the name of your god, and I will call on
the name of Yahweh: and the God that answereth by
fire, let him be God. . . . And Elijah said unto the
prophets of Baal, Choose you one bullock for yourselves,
and dress it first; for ye are many; and call on the name
of your god, but put no fire under. And they took the
bullock which was given them, and they dressed it, and
called on the name of Baal from morning even until
noon, saying, O Baal, hear us. But there was no voice,
nor any that answered. . . . And it came to pass
at noon, that Elijah mocked them, and said, Cry aloud:
for he is a god; either he is musing, or he is gone aside,
or he is in a journey, or peradventure he sleepeth, and
must be awaked. And they cried aloud, and cut themselves after their manner with knives and lances, till the
blood gushed out upon them. . . . But there was
neither voice, nor any to answer, nor any that regarded."[2]

[2] Quoted with some omissions from *I Kings*, 18: 21-29.
The Hebrew term *Yahweh*, the name of the national deity,
has been substituted for the English translation, "the Lord."

The religion of the followers of Baal here consists in a belief in the practical virtue of a mode
of address and form of ritual associated with the
traditions and customs of a certain social group.
The prophets of this cult agree to regard the experiment proposed by Elijah as a crucial test, and
that which is disproved from its failure is a plan
of action. These prophets relied upon the presence of a certain motivity, from which a definite response could be evoked by an appeal which
they were peculiarly able to make; but though
" they prophesied until the time of the offering
of the evening oblation," there was none that
regarded.

§ 32. An equally familiar and more instructive
example is the refutation of the Greek national
Greek   religion by Lucretius. The conception
Religion.   of life which Lucretius finds unwar-
ranted is best depicted in Homer. There we hear
of a society composed of gods and men. Though
the gods, on the one hand, have their own history,
their affairs are never sharply sundered from those
of men, who, on the other hand, must constantly
reckon with them, gauge their attitude, and seek
their favor by paying tribute to their individual
humors and preferences. In the Ninth Book of

the "Iliad," Phœnix addresses himself to the re-
calcitrant Achilles as follows:

> "It fits not one that moves
> The hearts of all, to live unmov'd, and succor hates for
>   loves.
> The Gods themselves are flexible; whose virtues, honors,
>   pow'rs,
> Are more than thine, yet they will bend their breasts as
>   we bend ours.
> Perfumes, benign devotions, savors of offerings burn'd,
> And holy rites, the engines are with which their hearts
>   are turn'd,
> By men that pray to them." [3]

Here is a general recognition of that which
makes sacrifice rational.   It is because he conceives
this presupposition to be mistaken, that Lucretius
declares the practices and fears which are founded
upon it to be folly.   It is the same with all that is
practically based upon the expectation of a life
beyond the grave.   The correction of the popular
religion is due in his opinion to that true view of
the world taught by Epicurus, whose memory
Lucretius thus invokes at the opening of the Third
Book of the "De Rerum Natura":

"Thee, who first wast able amid such thick darkness
to raise on high so bright a beacon and shed a light on
the true interests of life, thee I follow, glory of the Greek
race, and plant now my footsteps firmly fixed in thy
imprinted marks. . . .   For soon as thy philosophy

[3] *Iliad*, Book IX, lines 467 *sq.*   Translation by Chapman.

issuing from a godlike intellect has begun with loud
voice to proclaim the nature of things, the terrors of the
mind are dispelled, the walls of the world part asunder,
I see things in operation throughout the whole void: the
divinity of the gods is revealed and their tranquil abodes
which neither winds do shake nor clouds drench with
rains nor snow congealed by sharp frost harms with
hoary fall: an ever cloudless ether o'ercanopies them,
and they laugh with light shed largely round. Nature
too supplies all their wants and nothing ever impairs
their peace of mind. But on the other hand the Acheru-
sian quarters [4] are nowhere to be seen, though earth is
no bar to all things being descried, which are in operation underneath our feet throughout the void." [5]

In another passage, after describing the Phry-
gian worship of Cybele, he comments as follows:

"All which, well and beautifully as it is set forth and
told, is yet widely removed from true reason. For the
nature of gods must ever in itself of necessity enjoy
immortality together with supreme repose, far removed
and withdrawn from our concerns; since exempt from
every pain, exempt from all dangers, strong in its own
resources, not wanting aught of us, it is neither gained
by favors nor moved by anger. . . . The earth
however is at all time without feeling, and because it
receives into it the first-beginnings of many things, it
brings them forth in many ways into the light of the
sun." [6]

If the teaching of Epicurus be true it is evident

[4] The supposed abode of departed spirits.
[5] Lucretius: *De Rerum Natura*, Book III, lines 1 *sq.* Translated by Munro.
[6] *Ibid.*, Book II, lines 644 *sq.*

that those who offered hecatombs with the idea that they were thereby mitigating anger, or securing special dispensation, were playing the fool. They were appealing to a fictitious motivity, one not grounded in " the nature of things." To one for whom the walls of the world had parted asunder, such a procedure was no longer possible; though he might choose to " call the sea Neptune " and reverence the earth as " mother of the gods." [7]

§ 33. The history of religion contains no more impressive and dramatic chapter than that which records the development of the religion of the Jews. Passing over its obscure beginnings in the primitive Semitic cult, we find this religion first clearly defined as tribal self-interest sanctioned by Yahweh.[8]   God's interest

Judaism and Christianity.

[7] It would be interesting to compare the equally famous criticism of Greek religion in Plato's *Republic*, Book II, 377 *sq.*

[8] Cf. W. Robertson Smith's admirable account of the Semitic religions:

"What is requisite to religion is a practical acquaintance with the rules on which the deity acts and on which he expects his worshippers to frame their conduct—what in II Kings, 17:26 is called the 'manner,' or rather the 'customary law' (*mishpat*), of the god of the land. This is true even of the religion of Israel. When the prophets speak of the knowledge of God, they always mean a practical knowledge of the laws and principles of His government in Israel, and a summary expression for religion as a whole is 'the knowledge and fear of Jehovah,' *i. e.*, the knowledge

in his chosen people determines the prosperity of him who practises the social virtues.

"The name of Yahweh is a strong tower: the righteous runneth into it, and is safe."

"He that is steadfast in righteousness shall attain unto life."

"To do justice and judgment is more acceptable to Yahweh than sacrifice." [9]

But in time it is evident to the believer that his experience does not bear out this expectation. Neither as a Jew nor as a righteous man does he prosper more than his neighbor.   He comes, therefore, to distrust the virtue of his wisdom.

"Then I saw that wisdom excelleth folly, as far as light excelleth darkness. The wise man's eyes are in his head, and the fool walketh in darkness: and yet I perceived that one event happeneth to them all. Then said I in my heart, As it happeneth to the fool, so will it happen even to me; and why was I then more wise? Then I said in my heart, that this also was vanity. For of the wise man, even as of the fool, there is no remembrance forever; seeing that in the days to come all will have been already forgotten. And how doth the wise man die even as the fool! So I hated life; because the work that is wrought under the sun was grievous unto me: for all is vanity and a striving after wind." [10]

It is evident that he who expects the favor of for-

of what Jehovah prescribes, combined with a reverent obedience." *The Religion of the Semites*, p. 23.

[9] *Proverbs*, 18:10; 11:19; 21:3.

[10] *Ecclesiastes*, 2:13 *sq.*

tune in return for his observance of precept is mistaken. The "work that is wrought under the sun" makes no special provision for him during his lifetime. Unless the cry of vanity is to be the last word there must be a reinterpretation of the promise of God. This appears in the new ideal of patient submission, and the chastened faith that expects only the love of God. And those whom God loves He will not forsake. They will come to their own, if not here, then beyond, according to His inscrutable but unswerving plan.

"The sacrifices of God are a broken spirit: a broken and a contrite heart, O God, thou wilt not despise."
"For thus saith the high and lofty One that inhabiteth eternity, whose name is Holy: I dwell in the high and holy place, with him also that is of a contrite and humble spirit, to revive the spirit of the humble, and to revive the heart of the contrite ones."[11]

In this faith Judaism merges into Christianity.[12] In the whole course of this evolution God is regarded as the friend of his people, but his people learn to find a new significance in his friendship. That which is altered is the conduct which that friendship requires and the expecta-

[11] *Psalms*, 51:17; *Isaiah*, 57:15.
[12] In this discussion of Judaism I am much indebted to Matthew Arnold's *Literature and Dogma*, especially Chapters I and II.

tion which it determines. The practical ideal which the relationship sanctions, changes gradually from that of prudence to that of goodness for its own sake. God, once an instrument relevant to human temporal welfare, has come to be an object of disinterested service.

No such transformation as this was absolutely realized during the period covered by the writings of the Old Testament, nor has it even yet been realized in the development of Christianity. But the evolution of both Judaism and Christianity has taken this direction. The criterion of this evolution is manifestly both ethical and metaphysical. A Christian avows that he rates purity of character above worldly prosperity, so that the former cannot properly be prized for the sake of the latter. Furthermore, he shares more or less unconsciously such philosophical and scientific opinions as deny truth to the conception of special interferences and dispensations from a supernatural agency. Therefore he looks for no fire from heaven to consume his sacrifice. But his religion is nevertheless a practical expectation. He believes that God is good, and that God loves him and sustains him. He believes that there obtains between himself, in so far as good, and the

universe *sub specie eternitatis,* a real sympathy and
reciprocal reenforcement.   He believes that he
secures through the profoundly potent forces of
the universe that which he regards as of most worth ;
and that somewhat is added to these forces by virtue of his consecration.   The God of the Christians
cannot be defined short of some such account as
this, inclusive of an ideal, an attitude, and an expectation.   In other words the God of the Christians is to be known only in terms of the Christ-
like outlook upon life, in which the disciple is
taught to emulate the master.   When moral and
intellectual development shall have discredited
either its scale of values, or its conviction that
cosmical events are in the end determined in accordance with that scale of values, then Christianity must either be transformed, or be untenable for
the wise man.   If we have conceived the essence
of Christianity too broadly or vaguely, it does not
much matter for our present purposes.   Its essence is, at any rate, some such inwardness of life
resolving ideality and reality into one, and drawing upon objective truth only to the extent required
for the confirming of that relation.

§ 34. We conclude, then, our attempt to emphasize the cognitive factor in religion, with the thesis

The Cognitive Factor in Religion. that every religion centres in a practical secret of the universe. *To be religious is to believe that a certain correlation of forces, moral and factual, is in reality operative, and that it determines the propriety and effectiveness of a certain type of living. Whatever demonstrates the futility, vanity, or self-deception of this living, discredits the religion. And, per contra, except as they define or refute such practical truth, religion is not essentially concerned with theoretical judgments.*

§ 35. But neither religion nor any other human interest consists in essentials. Such a practical

The Place of Imagination in Religion. conviction as that which has been defined inevitably flowers into a marvelous complexity, and taps for its nourishment every spontaneity of human nature. If it be said that only the practical conviction is essential, this is not the same as to say that all else is superfluous. There may be no single utterance that my religion could not have spared, and yet were I to be altogether dumb my religion would, indeed, be as nothing. For if I believe, I accept a presence in my world, which as I live will figure in my dreams, or in my thoughts, or in my habits.

And each of these expressions of myself will have a truth if it do but bear out my practical acceptance of that presence. The language of religion, like that of daily life, is not the language of science except it take it upon itself to be so. There is scarcely a sentence which I utter in my daily intercourse with men which is not guilty of transgressions against the canons of accurate and definite thinking. Yet if I deceive neither myself nor another, I am held to be truthful, even though my language deal with chance and accident, material purposes and spiritual causes, and though I vow that the sun smiles or the moon lets down her hair into the sea. Science is a special interest in the discovery of unequivocal and fixed conceptions, and employs its terms with an unalterable connotation. But no such algebra of thought is indispensable to life or conversation, and its lack is no proof of error. Such is the case also with that eminently living affair, religion. I may if I choose, and I will if my reasoning powers be at all awakened, be a theologian. But theology, like science, is a special intellectual spontaneity. St. Thomas, the master theologian, did not glide unwittingly from prayer into the *quæstiones* of the " Summa Theologiæ," but turned to them as to a fresh adventure.

Theology is inevitable, because humanly speaking adventure is inevitable. For man, with his intellectual spontaneity, every object is a problem; and did he not seek sooner or later to define salvation, there would be good reason to believe that he did not practically reckon with any. But this is *similarly* and *independently* true of the imagination, the most familiar means with which man clothes and vivifies his convictions, the exuberance with which he plays about them and delights to confess them. The imagination of religion, contributing what Matthew Arnold called its " poetry and eloquence," does not submit itself to such canons as are binding upon theology or science, but exists and flourishes in its own right.

The indispensableness to religion of the imagination is due to that faculty's power of realizing what is not perceptually present. Religion is not interested in the apparent, but in the secret essence or the transcendent universal. And yet this interest is a practical one. Imagination may introduce one into the vivid presence of the secret or the transcendent. It is evident that the religious imagination here coincides with poetry. For it is at least one of the interests of poetry to cultivate and satisfy a sense for the universal; to obtain an

immediate experience or appreciation that shall
have the vividness without the particularism of
ordinary perception.   And where a poet elects so
to view the world, we allow him as a poet the
privilege, and judge him by the standards to which
he submits himself.   That upon which we pass
judgment is the *fitness of his expression*.   This
expression is not, except in the case of the theoretical mystic, regarded as constituting the most
valid form of the idea, but is appreciated expressly
for its fulfilment of the condition of immediacy.
The same sort of critical attitude is in order with
the fruits of the religious imagination.   These
may or may not fulfil enough of the requirements of that art to be properly denominated
poetry; but like poetry they are the translation of
ideas into a specific language.   They must not,
therefore, be judged as though they claimed to
excel in point of validity, but only in point of consistency with the context of that language.   And
*the language of religion is the language of the
practical life*.   Such translation is as essential to
an idea that is to enter into the religious experience, as translation into terms of immediacy is
essential to an idea that is to enter into the appreciative consciousness of the poet.   No object can

find a place in my religion until it is conjoined with my purposes and hopes; until it is taken for granted and acted upon, like the love of my friends, or the courses of the stars, or the stretches of the sea.

§ 36. The religious imagination, then, is to be understood and justified as that which brings the *The Special* objects of religion within the range of *Functions of* *the Religious* living. The central religious object, as *Imagination.* has been seen, is an *attitude* of the residuum or totality of things. To be religious one must have a sense for the *presence of an attitude,* like his sense for the presence of his human fellows, with all the added appreciation that is proper in the case of an object that is unique in its mystery or in its majesty. It follows that the religious imagination fulfils its function in so far as it provides the object of religion with properties similar to those which lend vividness and reality to the normal social relations.

The presence of one's fellows is in part the perceptual experience of their bodies. To this there corresponds in religion some extraordinary or subtle appearance. The gods may in visions or dreams be met with in their own proper embodiments; or, as is more common, they may be re-

garded as present for practical purposes: in some
inanimate object, as in the case of the fetish; in
some animal species, as in the case of the totem;
in some place, as in the case of the shrine; or even
in some human being, as in the case of the inspired
prophet and miracle worker.   In more refined and
highly developed religions the medium of God's
presence is less specific.   He is perceived with

> " —a sense sublime
> Of something far more deeply interfused,
> Whose dwelling is the light of setting suns,
> And the round ocean and the living air,
> And the blue sky, and in the mind of man."

God is here found in an interpretation of the common and the natural, rather than in any individual
and peculiar embodiment.   And here the poet's
appreciation, if not his art, is peculiarly indispensable.

But, furthermore, his fellows are inmates of
" the household of man " in that he knows their
history.   They belong to the temporal context of
actions and events.   Similarly, the gods must be
historical.   The sacred traditions or books of religion are largely occupied with this history.   The
more individual and anthropomorphic the gods,
the more local and episodic will be the account of
their affairs.   In the higher religions the acts of

God are few and momentous, such as creation or special providence; or they are identical with the events of nature and human history when these are *construed* as divine. To find God in this latter way requires an interpretation of the course of events in terms of some moral consistency, a faith that sees some purpose in their evident destination.

There is still another and a more significant way in which men recognize one another: the way of address and conversation. And men have invariably held a similar intercourse with their gods. To this category belong communion and prayer, with all their varieties of expression. I have no god until I address him. This will be the most direct evidence of what is at least from my point of view a social relation. There can be no general definition of the form which this address will take. There may be as many special languages, as many attitudes, and as much playfulness and subtlety of symbolism as in human intercourse. But, on the other hand, there are certain utterances that are peculiarly appropriate to religion. In so far as he regards his object as endowed with both power and goodness the worshipper will use the language of adoration; and the sense of his depend-

ence will speak in terms of consecration and
thanksgiving.

> "O God, thou art my God; early will I seek thee:
> My soul thirsteth for thee, my flesh longeth for thee,
> In a dry and weary land, where no water is.
> So have I looked upon thee in the sanctuary,
> To see thy power and thy glory.
> For thy loving-kindness is better than life;
> My lips shall praise thee."

These are expressions of a hopeful faith; but,
on the other hand, God may be addressed in terms
of hatred and distrust.

> "Who is most wretched in this dolorous place?
> I think myself; yet I would rather be
> My miserable self than He, than He
> Who formed such creatures to his own disgrace.

> "The vilest thing must be less vile than Thou
> From whom it had its being, God and Lord!
> Creator of all woe and sin! abhorred,
> Malignant and implacable." [13]

In either case there may be an indefinite degree
of hyperbole. The language of love and hate, of
confidence and despair, is not the language of description. In this train of the religious consciousness there is occasion for whatever eloquence man
can feel, and whatever rhetorical luxuriance he
can utter.

[13] James Thomson: *The City of Dreadful Night.* Quoted
by James, in *The Will to Believe, etc.,* p. 45,

§ 37. Such considerations as these serve to account for the exercise and certain of the fruits of

The Relation between Imagination and Truth in Religion. the religious imagination, and to designate the general criterion governing its propriety. But *how is one to determine the boundary between the imaginative and the cognitive?* It is commonly agreed that what religion says and does is not all intended literally. But when is expression of religion only poetry and eloquence, and when is it matter of conviction? If we revert again to the cognitive aspect of religion, it is evident that there is but one test to apply: *whatever either fortifies or misleads the will is literal conviction.* This test cannot be applied absolutely, because it can properly be applied only to the intention of an individual experience. However I may express my religion, that which I express, is, we have seen, an expectation. The degree to which I literally mean what I say is then the degree to which it determines my expectations. Whatever adds no item to these expectations, but only recognizes and vitalizes them, is pure imagination. But it follows that it is entirely impossible from direct inspection to define any given *expression* of religious experience as myth, or to define the degree to which it is myth,

It submits to such distinctions only when viewed from the stand-point of the concrete religious experience which it expresses. Any such given expression could easily be all imagination to one, and all conviction to another. Consider the passage which follows:

" And I saw the heaven opened; and behold, a white horse, and he that sat thereon, called Faithful and True; and in righteousness he doth judge and make war. And his eyes are a flame of fire, and upon his head are many diadems; and he hath a name written, which no one knoweth but he himself. And he is arrayed in a garment sprinkled with blood : and his name is called The Word of God."[14]

Is this all rhapsody, or is it in part true report? There is evidently no answer to the question so conceived. But if it were to express my own religious feeling it would have some specific proportion of literal and metaphorical significance, according to the degree to which its detail contributes different practical values to me. It might then be my guide-book to the heavens, or only my testimony to the dignity and mystery of the function of Christ.

The development of religion bears in a very important way upon this last problem. The factor

[14] *Revelation*, 19 : 11–13.

of imagination has undoubtedly come to have a more clearly recognized role in religion. There can be no doubt that what we now call myths were once beliefs, and that what we now call poetry was once history. If we go back sufficiently far we come to a time when the literal and the metaphorical were scarcely distinguishable, and this because science had not emerged from the early animistic extension of social relations. Men *meant* to address their gods as they addressed their fellows, and expected them to hear and respond, as they looked for such reactions within the narrower circle of ordinary intercourse. The advance of science has brought into vogue a description of nature that inhibits such expectations. The result has been that men, continuing to use the same terms, essentially expressive as they are of a practical relationship, have come to regard them as only a general expression of their attitude. The differences of content that are in excess of factors of expectation remain as poetry and myth. On the other hand, it is equally possible, if not equally common, for that which was once imagined to come to be believed. Such a transformation is, perhaps, normally the case when the inspired utterance passes from its author to the cult. The prophets and sweet singers are likely to possess an exuberance of imagination not appreciated by their followers; and for this reason almost certainly misunderstood. For these reasons it is manifestly absurd to fasten the name of myth or the name of creed upon any religious utterance whatsoever, unless it be so regarded from the stand-point of the personal religion which it originally expressed, or unless one means by so doing to define it as an expression of his own religion. He who defines " the myth of creation," or " the poetical story of Samson," as parts of the pre-Christian Judaic religion, exhibits a total loss of historical sense. The distinction between cognition and fancy does not exist among objects, but only in the *intending* experience; hence, for me to attach my own distinction to any individual case of belief, viewed apart from the believer, is an utterly confusing projection of my own personality into the field of my study.

§ 38. Only after such considerations as these are we qualified to attack that much-vexed question as to whether religion deals invariably with a personal god. It is often assumed in discussion of this question that " personal god," as well as " god," is a dis-

The Philosophy Implied in Religion and in Religions.

tinct and familiar kind of entity, like a dragon or centaur; its existence alone being problematical. This is doubly false to the religious employment of such an object. If it be true that in religion we mean by God a practical interpretation of the world, *whatsoever be its nature*, then the personality of God must be a derivative of the attitude, and not of the nature of the world. Given the practical outlook upon life, there is no definable world that cannot be construed under the form of God. My god is my world practically recognized in respect of its fundamental or ultimate attitude to my ideals. In the sense, then, conveyed by this term *attitude* my god will invariably possess the characters of personality. But the degree to which these characters will coincide with the characters which I assign to human persons, or the terms of any logical conception of personality, cannot be absolutely defined. Anthropomorphisms may be imagination or they may be literal conviction. This will depend, as above maintained, upon the degree to which they determine my expectations. Suppose the world to be theoretically conceived as governed by laws that are indifferent to all human interests. The practical expression of this conception appears in the naturalism of Lucretius, or

Diogenes, or Omar Khayyam. Living in the vivid presence of an indifferent world, I may picture my gods as leading their own lives in some remote realm which is inaccessible to my petitions, or as regarding me with sinister and contemptuous cruelty. In the latter case I may shrink and cower, or return them contempt for contempt. I mean this literally only if I look for consequences following directly from the emotional coloring which I have bestowed upon them. It may well be that I mean merely to regard myself *sub specie eternitatis*, in which case I am *personifying* in the sense of free imagination. In the religion of enlightenment the divine attitude tends to belong to the poetry and eloquence of religion rather than to its cognitive intent. This is true even of optimistic and idealistic religion. The love and providence of God are less commonly supposed to warrant an expectation of special and arbitrary favors, and have come more and more to mean the play of my own feeling about the general central conviction of the favorableness of the cosmos to my deeper or moral concerns. But the factor of personality cannot possibly be entirely eliminated, for the religious consciousness *creates* a social relationship between man and the universe. Such an interpretation of

life is not a case of the pathetic fallacy, unless it
incorrectly *reckons with* the inner feeling which it
attributes to the universe.   It is an obvious practical truth that the total or residual environment
is significant for life.   Grant this and you make
rational a recognition of that significance, or a
more or less constant sense of coincidence or conflict with cosmical forces.   Permit this consciousness to stand, and you make some expression of it
inevitable.   Such an expression may, furthermore,
with perfect propriety and in fulfilment of human
nature, set forth and transfigure this central belief
until it may enter into the context of immediacy.

Thus any conception of the universe whatsoever may afford a basis for religion.   But there is
no religion that does not virtually make a more
definite claim upon the nature of things, and this
entirely independently of its theology, or explicit
attempt to define itself.   Every religion, even in
the very living of it, is naturalistic, or dualistic,
or pluralistic, or optimistic, or idealistic, or pessi-
mistic.   And there is in the realm of truth that
which justifies or refutes these definite practical
ways of construing the universe.   But no historical
religion is ever so vague even as this in its philosophical implications.   Indeed, we shall always

be brought eventually to the inner meaning of some individual religious experience, where no general criticism can be certainly valid.

There is, then, a place in religion for that which is not directly answerable to philosophical or scientific standards. But there is always, on the other hand, an element of hope which conceives the nature of the world, and means to be grounded in reality. In respect of that element, philosophy is indispensable to religion. The meaning of religion is, in fact, the central problem of philosophy. There is a virtue in religion like that which Emerson ascribes to poetry. " The poet is in the right attitude; he is believing; the philosopher, after some struggle, having only reasons for believing." But whatever may be said to the disparagement of its dialectic, philosophy is the justification of religion, and the criticism of religions. To it must be assigned the task of so refining positive religion as to contribute to the perpetual establishment of true religion. And to philosophy, with religion, belongs the task of holding fast to the idea of the universe. There is no religion except before you begin, or after you have rested from, your philosophical speculation. But in the universe these interests have a common object. As philosophy is the articulation and vindication of religion, so is religion the realization of philosophy. In philosophy thought is brought up to the elevation of life, and in religion philosophy, as the sum of wisdom, enters into life.

CHAPTER V

NATURAL SCIENCE AND PHILOSOPHY

§ 39. In the case of natural science we meet not only with a special human interest, but with a

The True Relations of Philosophy and Science. Misconceptions and Antagonisms. theoretical discipline. We are confronted, therefore, with a new question: that of the relation within the body of human knowledge of two of its constituent members. Owing to the militant temper of the representatives of both science and philosophy, this has long since ceased to be an academic question, and has frequently been met in the spirit of rivalry and partisanship. But the true order of knowledge is only temporarily distorted by the brilliant success of a special type of investigation; and the conquests of science are now so old a story that critical thought shows a disposition to judge of the issue with sobriety and logical highmindedness.

In the seventeenth century a newly emancipated and too sanguine reason proposed to know the whole of nature at once in terms of mathematics

and mechanics.   Thus the system of the English-
man Hobbes was science swelled to world-propor-
tions, simple, compact, conclusive, and all-comprehensive.   Philosophy proposed to do the work of
science, but in its own grand manner.   The last
twenty years of Hobbes's life, spent in repeated
discomfiture at the hands of Seth Ward, Wallis,
Boyle, and other scientific experts of the new
Royal Society, certified conclusively to the failure
of this enterprise, and the experimental specialist
thereupon took exclusive possession of the field of
natural law.   But the idealist, on the other hand,
reconstructed nature to meet the demands of philosophical knowledge and religious faith.   There
issued, together with little mutual understanding
and less sympathy, on the one hand *positivism,* or
exclusive experimentalism, and on the other hand
a rabid and unsympathetic transcendentalism.
Hume, who consigned to the flames all thought
save " abstract reasoning concerning quantity or
number," and " experimental reasoning concerning matter of fact and existence "; Comte, who
assigned metaphysics to an immature stage in the
development of human intelligence; and Tyndall,
who reduced the religious consciousness to an emotional experience of mystery, are typical of the one

attitude. The other is well exhibited in Schelling's reference to " the blind and thoughtless mode of investigating nature which has become generally established since the corruption of philosophy by Bacon, and of physics by Boyle." Dogmatic experimentalism and dogmatic idealism signify more or less consistently the abstract isolation of the scientific and philosophical motives.

There is already a touch of quaintness in both of these attitudes. We of the present are in the habit of acknowledging the autonomy of science, and the unimpeachable validity of the results of experimental research in so far as they are sanctioned by the consensus of experts. But at the same time we recognize the definiteness of the task of science, and the validity of such reservations as may be made from a higher critical point of view. Science is to be transcended in so far as it is understood as a whole. Philosophy is critically empirical; empirical, because it regards all *bona fide* descriptions of experience as knowledge; critical, because attentive to the conditions of both general and special knowledge. And in terms of a critical empiricism so defined, it is one of the problems of philosophy *to define and appraise the generating problem of science,* and so to determine the value assignable to natural laws in the whole system of knowledge.

§ 40. If this be the true function of philosophy with reference to science, several current notions The Spheres of of the relations of the spheres of these Philosophy and Science. disciplines may be disproved. In the first place, philosophy will not be all the sciences regarded as one science. Science tends to unify without any higher criticism. The various sciences already regard the one nature as their common object, and the one system of interdependent laws as their common achievement. The philosopher who tries to be all science at once fails ignominiously because he tries to replace the work of a specialist with the work of a dilettante; and if philosophy be identical with that body of truth accumulated and organized by the coöperative activity of scientific men, then philosophy is a name and there is no occasion for the existence of the philosopher as such. Secondly, philosophy will not be the assembling of the sciences; for such would be a merely clerical work, and the philosopher would much better be regarded as non-existent than as a book-keeper. Nor, thirdly, is philosophy an auxiliary discipline that may be called upon in emergencies for the solution of some baffling problem of science. A problem defined by science must be solved in the scientific manner. Science will accept no aid from the gods when engaged in her own campaign, but will fight it out according to her own principles of warfare. And as long as science moves in her own plane, she can acknowledge no permanent barriers.   There is then no need of any superscientific research that shall replace, or piece together, or extend the work of science. But the savant is not on this account in possession of the entire field of knowledge. It is true that he is not infrequently moved to such a conviction when he takes us about to view his estates. Together we ascend up into heaven, or make our beds in sheol, or take the wings of the morning and dwell in the uttermost parts of the sea—and look in vain for anything that is not work done, or work projected, by natural science. Persuade him, however, to *define* his estates, and he has circumscribed them. In his definition he must employ conceptions more fundamental than the working conceptions that he employs within his field of study. Indeed, in viewing his task as definite and specific he has undertaken the solution of the problem of philosophy. The logical self-consciousness has been awakened, and there is no honorable way of putting it to sleep again. This is precisely what takes place in any account of the generating problem of science. To define science is to define at least one realm that is other than science, the realm of active intellectual endeavor with its own proper categories. One cannot reflect upon science and assign it an end, and a method proper to that end, without bringing into the field of knowledge a broader field of experience than the field proper to science, broader at any rate by the presence in it of the scientific activity itself.

Here, then, is the field proper to philosophy. The scientist *qua* scientist is intent upon his own determinate enterprise. The philosopher comes into being as one who is interested in observing what it is that the scientist is so intently doing. In taking this interest he has accepted as a field for investigation that which he would designate as the totality of interests or the inclusive experience. He can carry out his intention of defining the scientific attitude only by standing outside it, and determining it by means of nothing less than an exhaustive searching out of all attitudes. Philosophy is, to be sure, itself a definite activity and an attitude, but an attitude required by definition to be conscious of itself, and, if you please, conscious of its own consciousness, until its attitude shall have embraced in its object the very principle of attitudes. Philosophy defines itself and all other human tasks and interests. None have furnished a clearer justification of philosophy than those men of scientific predilections who have claimed the title of agnostics. A good instance is furnished by a contemporary physicist, who has chosen to call his reflections " antimetaphysical."

"Physical science does not pretend to be a *complete* view of the world; it simply claims that it is working toward such a complete view in the future. The highest philosophy of the scientific investigator is precisely this *toleration* of an incomplete conception of the world and the preference for it, rather than an apparently perfect, but inadequate conception."[1]

It is apparent that if one were to challenge such a statement, the issue raised would at once be philosophical and not scientific. The problem here stated and answered, requires for its solution the widest inclusiveness of view, and a peculiar interest in critical reflection and logical coördination.

§ 41. One may be prepared for a knowledge of

[1] Ernst Mach: *Science of Mechanics.* Translation by McCormack, p. 464. No one has made more important contributions than Professor Mach to a certain definite modern philosophical movement. Cf. § 207.

the economic and social significance of the railway
even if one does not know a throttle from a piston-rod, provided one has broad and well-balanced knowledge of the inter-play of human social interests. One's proficiency here requires one to stand off from society, and to obtain a perspective that shall be as little distorted as possible. The reflection of the philosopher of science requires a similar quality of perspective. All knowledges, together with the knowing of them, must be his object yonder, standing apart in its wholeness and symmetry. Philosophy is the least dogmatic, the most empirical, of all disciplines, since it is the only investigation that can permit itself to be forgetful of nothing.

The Procedure of a Philosophy of Science.

But the most comprehensive view may be the most distorted and false. The true order of knowl-edge is the difficult task of logical analysis, requir-ing as its chief essential some determination of the scope of the working conceptions of the differ-ent independent branches of knowledge. In the case of natural science this would mean an exam-ination of the method and results characteristic of this field, for the sake of defining the kind of truth which attaches to the laws which are being gradually formulated. But one must immediately reach either the one or the other of two very general conclusions. If the laws of natural science cover all possible knowledge of reality, then there is left to philosophy only the logical function of justifying this statement. Logic and natural science will then constitute the sum of knowledge. If, on the other hand, it be found that the aim of natural science is such as to exclude certain aspects of reality, then philosophy will not be restricted to logical criticism, but will have a cognitive field of its own. The great majority of philosophers have assumed the latter of these alternatives to be true, while most aggressive scientists have intended the former in their somewhat blind attacks upon "metaphysics." Although the selection of either of these alternatives involves us in the defence of a specific answer to a philosophical question, the issue is inevitable in any introduction to philosophy because of its bearing upon the extent of the field of that study. Furthermore there can be no better exposition of the meaning of philosophy of science than an illustration of its exercise. The following, then, is to be regarded as on the one hand a tentative refutation of *positivism,* or the *claim of natural science to be coextensive with knowable reality;* and on the other hand a programme for the procedure of philosophy with reference to natural science.

§ 42. Science issues through imperceptible stages from organic habits and instincts which

The Origin of the Scientific Interest. signify the possession by living creatures of a power to meet the environment on its own terms. Every organism possesses such a working knowledge of nature, and among men the first science consists in those habitual adjustments common to men and infra-human organisms. Man is already practising science before he recognizes it. As *skill* it distinguishes itself early in his history from lore, or untested tradition. Skill is familiarity with general kinds of events, together with ability to identify an individual with reference to a kind, and so be prepared for the outcome. Thus man is inwardly prepared for the alternation of day and night, and the periods of the seasons. He practically anticipates the procession of natural events in the countless emergencies of his daily life. But science in the stricter sense begins when skill becomes *free* and *social*.

§ 43. Skill may be said to be *free* when the essential terms of the action have been abstracted from the circumstances attending them in individ-

ual experiences, and are retained as ideal plans ap-
Skill as Free. plicable to any practical occasion. The
monkey who swings with a trapeze from his perch
on the side of the cage, counts upon swinging back
again without any further effort on his own part.
His act and its successful issue signify his practical familiarity with the natural motions of bodies.
We can conceive such a performance to be accompanied by an almost entire failure to grasp its essentials. It would then be necessary for nearly
the whole situation to be repeated in order to induce
in the monkey the same action and expectation.
He would require a similar form, color, and distance. But he might, on the other hand, regard
as practically identical all suspended and freely
swinging bodies capable of affording him support,
and quite independently of their shape, size, time,
or place. In this latter case his skill would be
applicable to the widest possible number of cases
that could present themselves. Having a discern-
ing eye for essentials, he would lose no chance of
a swing through looking for more than the bare
necessities. When the physicist describes the pendulum in terms of a formula such as $t = 2\pi\sqrt{l/g}$
he exhibits a similar discernment. He has found
that the time occupied by an oscillation of any pen-

dulum may be calculated exclusively in terms of its length and the acceleration due to gravity. The monkey's higher proficiency and the formula alike represent a knowledge that is free in the sense that it is contained in terms that require no single fixed context in immediacy. The knowledge is valid wherever these essential terms are present; and calculations may be based upon these essential terms, while attendant circumstances vary *ad infinitum*. Such knowledge is said to be *general* or *universal*.

There is another element of freedom, however, which so far has not been attributed to the monkey's knowledge, but which is evidently present in that of the physicist. The former has a practical ability to deal with a pendulum when he sees it. The latter, on the other hand, knows about a pendulum whether one be present or not. His knowledge is so retained as always to be available, even though it be not always applicable. His knowledge is not merely skill in treating a situation, but the possession of resources which he may employ at whatever time, and in whatever manner, may suit his interests. Knowing what he does about the pendulum, he may act from the idea of such a contrivance, and with the aid of it construct some more complex mechanism. His formulas are his instruments, which he may use on any occasion. Suppose that a situation with factors *a, b,* and *c* requires factor *d* in order to become *M,* as desired. Such a situation might easily be hopeless for an organism reacting directly to the stimulus *abc,* and yet be easily met by a free knowledge of *d.* One who knows that *l, m,* and *n* will produce *d,* may by these means provide the missing factor, complete the sum of required conditions, *abcd,* and so obtain the end *M.* Such indirection might be used to obtain any required factor of the end, or of any near or remote means to the end. There is, in fact, no limit to the complexity of action made possible upon this basis; for since it is available in idea, the whole range of such knowledge may be brought to bear upon any individual problem.

§ 44. But knowledge of this free type becomes at the same time *social* or *institutional.* It con-
Skill as Social. sists no longer in a skilful adaptation of the individual organism, but in a system of terms common to all intelligence, and preserved in those books and other monuments which serve as the articulate memory of the race. A knowledge that is social must be composed of unequivocal conceptions and fixed symbols. The mathe-

matical laws of the exact sciences represent the
most successful attainment of this end so far as
form is concerned.   Furthermore, the amount of
knowledge may now be increased from generation
to generation through the service of those who make
a vocation of its pursuit.   Natural science is thus
a cumulative racial proficiency, which any individual may bring to bear upon any emergency of
his life.

§ 45.   Such proficiency as science affords is in
every case the anticipation of experience.   This

Science for
Accommoda-
tion and Con-
struction.
has a twofold value for mankind, that
of *accommodation,* and that of construc-
tion.   Primitively, where mere survival
is the function of the organism as a whole, the
value of accommodation is relatively fundamental.
The knowledge of what may be expected enables
the organism to save itself by means of its own
counter-arrangement of natural processes.   Construction is here for the sake of accommodation.
But with the growth of civilization construction
becomes a positive interest, and man tends to save
himself for definite ends.   Accommodation comes
to take place for the sake of construction.   Science
then supplies the individual with the ways and
means wherewith to execute life purposes which

themselves tend to assume an absolute value that
cannot be justified merely on the ground of science.

§ 46. If natural science be animated by any
special cognitive interest, this motive should ap-

*Method and
Fundamental
Conceptions
of Natural
Science.
The De-
scriptive
Method.*
pear in the development of its method
and fundamental conceptions. If that
interest has been truly defined, it should
now enable us to understand the progressive and permanent in scientific investigation as directly related to it. For the aim
of any discipline exercises a gradual selection from
among possible methods, and gives to its laws their
determinate and final form.

The descriptive method is at the present day
fully established. A leading moral of the history
of science is the superior usefulness of an exact
account of the workings of nature to an explanation in terms of some qualitative potency. Explanation has been postponed by enlightened science
until after a more careful observation of actual
processes shall have been made; and at length it
has been admitted that there is no need of any
explanation but perfect description. Now the
practical use of science defined above, requires no
knowledge beyond the actual order of events. For
such a purpose sufficient reason signifies only suffi-

cient conditions. All other considerations are irrelevant, and it is proper to ignore them. Such
has actually been the fate of the so-called metaphysical solution of special problems of nature.
The case of Kepler is the classic instance. This
great scientist supplemented his laws of planetary
motion with the following speculation concerning
the agencies at work:

" We must suppose one of two things: either that the
moving spirits, in proportion as they are more removed
from the sun, are more feeble; or that there is one moving
spirit in the centre of all the orbits, namely, in the sun,
which urges each body the more vehemently in proportion as it is nearer; but in more distant spaces languishes in
consequence of the remoteness and attenuation of its
virtue." [2]

The following passage from Hegel affords an
interesting analogy:

" The moon is the waterless crystal which seeks to
complete itself by means of our sea, to quench the thirst
of its arid rigidity, and therefore produces ebb and
flow." [3]

No scientist has ever sought to refute either of
these theories. They have merely been neglected.

[2] Whewell: *History of the Inductive Sciences*, Vol. I, p. 289.
Quoted from Kepler: *Mysterium Cosmographicum*.
[3] Quoted by Sidgwick in his *Philosophy, its Scope and
Relations*, p. 89.

They were advanced in obedience to a demand for the ultimate explanation of the phenomena in question, and were obtained by applying such general conceptions as were most satisfying to the reasons of their respective authors. But they contributed nothing whatsoever to a practical familiarity with the natural course of events, in this case the times and places of the planets and the tides. Hence they have not been used in the building of science. In our own day investigators have become conscious of their motive, and do not wait for historical selection to exclude powers and reasons from their province. They deliberately seek to formulate exact descriptions. To this end they employ symbols that shall serve to identify the terms of nature, and formulas that shall define their systematic relationship. These systems must be exact, or deductions cannot be made from them. Hence they tend ultimately to assume a mathematical form of expression.

§ 47. But science tends to employ for these systems only such conceptions as relate to *prediction;*

Space, Time, and Prediction. and of these the most fundamental are *space* and *time*. The first science to establish its method was the science of astronomy, where measurement and computation in terms of

space and time were the most obvious means of
description; and the general application of the
method of astronomy by Galileo and Newton, or
the development of mechanics, is the most important factor in the establishment of modern science upon a permanent working basis. The persistence of the term *cause*, testifies to the fact that
science is primarily concerned with the determination of *events*. Its definitions of objects are
means of identification, while its laws are dynamical, *i. e.*, have reference to the conditions under
which these objects arise. Thus the chemist may
know less about the properties of water than
the poet; but he is preëminently skilled in its pro-
duction from elements, and understands similarly
the compounds into which it may enter. Now the
general conditions of all anticipation, whereby it
becomes exact and verifiable, are spacial and temporal. A predictable event must be assigned to
what is here now, or there now; or what is here
then, or there then. An experimentally verifiable
system must contain space-time variables, for which
can be substituted the here and now of the experi-
menter's immediate experience. Hence science
deals primarily with calculable places and moments. The mechanical theory of nature owes its

success to a union of space and time through its
conceptions of *matter* and *motion*.[4] And the projected theory of energetics must satisfy the same
conditions.

§ 48. But, furthermore, science has, as we have
seen, an interest in freeing its descriptions from
the peculiar angle and relativity of an
individual's experience, for the sake of
affording him knowledge of that with which he
must meet. Science enlightens the will by ac-
quainting it with that which takes place in spite
of it, and for which it must hold itself in readiness. To this end the individual benefits himself
in so far as he eliminates himself from the objects
which he investigates. His knowledge is useful
in so far as it is valid for his own indefinitely
varying stand-points, and those of other wills recognized by him in his practical relations. But in

The Quantita-
tive Method.

---

[4] The reader is referred to Mr. Bertrand Russell's chapters
on *matter* and *motion* in his *Principles of Mathematics*,
Vol. I. Material particles he defines as "many-one relations of all times to some places, or of all terms of a continuous one-dimensional series t to some terms of a continuous three-dimensional series s." Similarly, " when
different times, throughout any period however short, are
correlated with different places, there is motion; when
different times, throughout some period however short,
are all correlated with the same place, there is rest." *Op.
cit.*, p. 473.

attempting to describe objects in terms other than
those of a specific experience, science is compelled
to describe them in terms of one another.   For this
purpose *the quantitative method* is peculiarly ser-
viceable.   With its aid objects permit themselves
to be described as multiples of one another, and as
occupying positions in relation to one another.
When all objects are described strictly in terms of
one another, they are expressed in terms of arbitrary units, and located in terms of arbitrary
spacial or temporal axes of reference.   Thus
there arises the universe of the scientific imagination, a vast complexity of material displacements
and transformations, without color, music, pleasure, or any of all that rich variety of qualities
that the least of human experiences contains.   It
does not completely rationalize or even completely
describe such experiences, but formulates their succession.   To this end they are reduced to terms
that correspond to no specific experience, and for
this very reason may be translated again into all
definable hypothetical experiences.   The solar system for astronomy is not a bird's-eye view of
elliptical orbits, with the planets and satellites in
definite phases.   Nor is it this group of objects
from any such point of view, or from any number

of such points of view; but a formulation of their
motions that will serve as the key to an infinite
number of their appearances. Or, consider the
picture of the ichthysauria romping in the meso-
zoic sea, that commonly accompanies a text-book
of geology. Any such picture, and all such pict-
ures, with their coloring and their temporal and
spacial perspective, are imaginary. No such special and exclusive manifolds can be defined as having been then and there realized. But we have a
geological knowledge of this period, that fulfils the
formal demands of natural science, in so far as we
can construct this and countless other specific experiences with reference to it.

§ 49. Science, then, is to be understood as
springing from the practical necessity of anticipating the environment. This anticipation appears first as congenital or
acquired reactions on the part of the organism.
Such reactions imply a fixed coördination or system in the environment whereby a given circumstance determines other circumstances; and science
proper arises as the formulation of such systems.
The requirement that they shall apply to the
phenomena that *confront* the will, determines their
spacial, temporal, and quantitative form. The

The General
Development
of Science.

progress of science is marked by the growth of
these conceptions in the direction of comprehen
siveness on the one hand, and of refinement and
delicacy on the other.   Man lives in an environment that is growing at the same time richer and
more extended, but with a compensatory simplifi-
cation in the ever closer systematization of scientific conceptions under the form of the order of
nature.

§ 50. At the opening of this chapter it was
maintained that it is a function of philosophy to
The Determi- criticise science through its generating
nation of the
Limits of Nat- problem, or its self-imposed task viewed
ural Science. as determining its province and selecting
its categories.   The above account of the origin
and method of science must suffice as a definition
of its generating problem, and afford the basis of
our answer to the question of its limits.   Enough
has been said to make it clear that philosophy is
not in the field of science, and is therefore not
entitled to contest its result in detail or even to
take sides within the province of its special problems.   Furthermore, philosophy should not aim to
restrain science by the imposition of external barriers.   Whatever may be said of the sufficiency of
its categories in any region of the world, that body

of truth of which mathematics, mechanics, and physics are the foundations, must be regarded as a whole that tends to be all-comprehensive in its own terms. There remains for philosophy, then, the critical examination of these terms, and the appraisal as a whole of the truth that they may express.

§ 51. The impossibility of embracing the whole of knowledge within natural science is due to the

Natural Science is Abstract.

fact that the latter is *abstract*. This follows from the fact that natural science is governed by a selective interest. The formulation of definitions and laws in exclusively mechanical terms is not due to the exhaustive or even preëminent reality of these properties, but to their peculiar serviceableness in a verifiable description of events. Natural science does not affirm that reality is essentially constituted of matter, or essentially characterized by motion; but is *interested* in the mechanical aspect of reality, and describes it quite regardless of other evident aspects and without meaning to prejudice them. It is unfortunately true that the scientist has rarely been clear in his own mind on this point. It is only recently that he has partially freed himself from the habit of construing his terms as final and exhaustive.[5] This he was able to do even to his own satisfaction, only by allowing loose rein to the imagination. Consider the example of the atomic theory. In order to describe such occurrences as chemical combination, or changes in volume and density, the scientist has employed as a unit the least particle, physically indivisible and qualitatively homogeneous. Look for the atom in the body of science, and you will find it in physical laws governing expansion and contraction, and in chemical formulas. There the real responsibility of science ends. But whether through the need of popular exposition, or the undisciplined imagination of the investigator himself, atoms have figured in the history of thought as round corpuscles of a grayish hue scurrying hither and thither, and armed with special appliances wherewith to lock in molecular embrace. Although this is nonsense, we need not on that account conclude that there

[5] That the scientist still permits himself to teach the people a loose exoteric theory of reality, is proven by Professor Ward's citation of instances in his *Naturalism and Agnosticism*. So eminent a physicist as Lord Kelvin is quoted as follows : "You can imagine particles of something, the thing whose motion constitutes light. This thing we call the luminiferous ether. That is the only substance we are confident of in dynamics. One thing we are sure of, and that is the reality and substantiality of the luminiferous ether." Vol. I, p. 113.

are no atoms. There are atoms in precisely the sense intended by scientific law, in that the formulas computed with the aid of this concept are true of certain natural processes. The conception of ether furnishes a similar case. Science is not responsible for the notion of a quivering gelatinous substance pervading space, but only for certain laws that, *e. g.*, describe the velocity of light in terms of the vibration. It is true that there is such a thing as ether, not as gratuitously rounded out by the imagination, with various attributes of immediate experience, but just in so far as this concept is employed in verified descriptions of radiation, magnetism, or electricity. Strictly speaking science asserts nothing about the existence of ether, but only about the behavior, *e. g.*, of light. If true descriptions of this and other phenomena are reached by employing units of wave propagation in an elastic medium, then ether is proved to exist in precisely the same sense that linear feet are proved to exist, if it be admitted that there are 90,000,000 x 5,280 of them between the earth and the sun. And to imagine in the one case a jelly with all the qualities of texture, color, and the like, that an individual object of sense would possess, is much the same as in the other to imagine the heavens filled with foot-rules and tape-measures. There is but one safe procedure in dealing with scientific concepts: to regard them as true so far as they describe, and no whit further. To supplement the strict meaning which has been verified and is contained in the formularies of science, with such vague predicates as will suffice to make entities of them, is mere ineptness and confusion of thought. And it is only such a supplementation that obscures their abstractness. For a mechanical description of things, true as it doubtless is, is even more indubitably incomplete.

§ 52. But though the abstractness involved in scientific description is open and deliberate, we **The Meaning of Abstractness in Truth.** must come to a more precise understanding of it, if we are to draw any conclusion as to what it involves. In his "Principles of Human Knowledge," the English philosopher Bishop Berkeley raises the question as to the universal validity of mathematical demonstrations. If we prove from the image or figure of an isosceles right triangle that the sum of its angles is equal to two right angles, how can we know that this proposition holds of all triangles?

"To which I answer, that, though the idea I have in view whilst I make the demonstration be, for instance,

that of an isosceles rectangular triangle whose sides are
of a determinate length, I may nevertheless be certain
it extends to all other rectilinear triangles, of what sort
or bigness soever. And that because neither the right
angle, nor the equality, nor determinate length of the
sides are at all concerned in the demonstration. It is
true the diagram I have in view includes all these particulars; but then there is not the least mention made of
them in the proof of the proposition."[*]

Of the total conditions present in the concrete
picture of a triangle, one may in one's calculations
neglect as many as one sees fit, and work with the
remainder. Then, if one has clearly distinguished
the conditions used, one may confidently assert
that whatever has been found true of them holds
regardless of the neglected conditions. These may
be missing or replaced by others, provided the
selected or (for any given investigation) essential
conditions are not affected. That which is true
once is true always, provided time is not one of
its conditions; that which is true in one place is
true everywhere, provided location is not one of its
conditions. But, given any concrete situation, the
more numerous the conditions one ignores in one's
calculations, the less adequate are one's calculations to that situation. The number of its inhabi-

[*] Berkeley: *Principles of Human Knowledge*, Introduction. Edition of Fraser, p. 248.

tants, and any mathematical operation made with that number, is true, but only very abstractly true of a nation. A similar though less radical abstractness appertains to natural science. Simple qualities of sound or color, and distinctions of beauty or moral worth, together with many other ingredients of actual experience attributed therein to the objects of nature, are ignored in the mechanical scheme. There is a substitution of certain mechanical arrangements in the case of the first group of properties, the simple qualities of sense, so that they may be assimilated to the general scheme of events, and their occurrence predicted. But their intrinsic qualitative character is not reckoned with, even in psychology, where the physiological method finally replaces them with brain states. Over and above these neglected properties of things there remain the purposive activities of thought. It is equally preposterous to deny them and to describe them in mechanical terms. It is plain, then, that natural science calculates upon the basis of only a fraction of the conditions that present themselves in actual experience. Its conclusions, therefore, though true so far as they go, and they may be abstractly true of everything, are completely true of nothing.

§ 53. Such, in brief, is the general charge of inadequacy which may be urged against natural

But Scientific
Truth is Valid
for Reality.

science, not in the spirit of detraction, but for the sake of a more sound belief concerning reality. The philosopher falls into error no less radical than that of the dogmatic scientist, when he charges the scientist with untruth, and attaches to his concepts the predicate of unreality. The fact that the concepts of science are selected, and only inadequately true of reality, should not be taken to mean that they are sportive or arbitrary. They are not " devices " or abbreviations, in any sense that does not attach to such symbolism as all thought involves. Nor are they merely " hypothetical," though like all thought they are subject to correction.[7] The scientist does not merely assert that the equation for energy is true if nature's capacity for work be measurable, but *that such is actually the case.* The statistician does not arrive at results contingent upon the supposition that men are numerable, but declares his sums and averages to be categorically true. Similarly scientific laws are true; only, to be sure, so

[7] The reader who cares to pursue this topic further is referred to the writer's discussion of *"Professor Ward's Philosophy of Science"* in the *Journal of Philosophy Psychology and Scientific Methods,* Vol. I, No. 13.

far as they go, but with no condition save the condition that attaches to all knowledge, viz., that it shall not need correction.   The philosophy of science, therefore, is not the adversary of science, but supervenes upon science in the interests of the ideal of final truth.   No philosophy of science is sound which does not primarily seek by an analysis of scientific concepts to understand science on its own grounds.   Philosophy may understand science better than science understands itself, but only by holding fast to the conviction of its truth, and including it within whatever account of reality it may be able to formulate.

§ 54. Though philosophy be the most ancient and most exalted of human disciplines, it is not **Relative Practical Value of Science and Philosophy.** infrequently charged with being the most unprofitable.   Science has amassed a fortune of information, which has facilitated life and advanced civilization.   Is not philosophy, on the other hand, all programme and idle questioning?   In the first place, no questioning is idle that is logically possible.   It is true that philosophy shows her skill rather in the asking than in the answering of questions.   But the formal pertinence of a question is of the greatest significance.   No valid though unanswered question can have a purely negative value, and especially as respects the consistency or completeness of truth. But, in the second place, philosophy with all its limitations serves mankind as indispensably as science. If science supplies the individual with means of self-preservation, and the instruments of achievement, philosophy supplies the ideals, or the objects of deliberate construction. Such reflection as justifies the adoption of a fundamental life purpose is always philosophical. For every judgment respecting final worth is a judgment *sub specie eternitatis*. And the urgency of life requires the individual to pass such judgments. It is true that however persistently reflective he may be in the matter, his conclusion will be premature in consideration of the amount of evidence logically demanded for such a judgment. But he must be as wise as he can, or he will be as foolish as conventionality and blind impulse may impel him to be. Philosophy determines for society what every individual must practically determine upon for himself, the most reasonable plan of reality as a whole which the data and reflection of an epoch can afford. It is philosophy's service to mankind to compensate for the enthusiasm and concentration of the specialist, a service needed in every " present day." Apart from the philosopher, public opinion is the victim of sensationalism, and individual opinion is further warped by accidental propinquity. It is the function of philosophy to interpret knowledge for the sake of a sober and wise belief. The philosopher is the true prophet, appearing before men in behalf of that which is finally the truth. He is the spokesman of the most considerate and comprehensive reflection possible at any stage in the development of human thought. Owing to a radical misconception of function, the man of science has in these later days begun to regard himself as the wise man, and to teach the people. Popular materialism is the logical outcome of this determination of belief by natural science. It may be that this is due as much to the indifference of the philosopher as to the forwardness of the scientist, but in any case the result is worse than conservative loyalty to religious tradition. For religion is corrected surely though slowly by the whole order of advancing truth. Its very inflexibility makes it proof against an over-emphasis upon new truth. It has generally turned out in time that the obstinate man of religion was more nearly right than the adaptable intellectual man of fashion. But philosophy, as a critique of science for the sake of faith, should provide the individual religious believer with intellectual enlightenment and gentleness. The quality, orderliness, and inclusiveness of knowledge, finally determine its value; and the philosopher, premature as his synthesis may some day prove to be, is the wisest man of his own generation. From him the man of faith should obtain such discipline of judgment as shall enable him to be fearless of advancing knowledge, because acquainted with its scope, and so intellectually candid with all his visions and his inspirations.

PART II

THE SPECIAL PROBLEMS OF PHILOSOPHY

CHAPTER VI

METAPHYSICS AND EPISTEMOLOGY

§ 55. THE stand-point and purpose of the philosopher define his task, but they do not necessarily

**The Impossi-
bility of an
Absolute
Division of the
Problem of
Philosophy.**
prearrange the division of it. That the
task is a complex one, embracing many
subordinate problems which must be
treated *seriatim*, is attested both by the
breadth of its scope and the variety of the interests from which it may be approached. But this
complexity is qualified by the peculiar importance
which here attaches to unity. That which lends
philosophical quality to any reflection is a steadfast adherence to the ideals of inclusiveness and
consistency. Hence, though the philosopher must
of necessity occupy himself with subordinate problems, these cannot be completely isolated from one
another, and solved successively. Perspective is
his most indispensable requisite, and he has solved
no problem finally until he has provided for the
solution of all. His own peculiar conceptions are

those which *order* experience, and reconcile such
aspects of it as other interests have distinguished.
Hence the compatibility of any idea with all other
ideas is the prime test of its philosophical sufficiency. On these grounds it may confidently be
asserted that the work of philosophy cannot be
assigned by the piece to different specialists, and
then assembled. There are no special philosophical problems which can be finally solved upon
their own merits. Indeed, such problems could
never even be named, for in their discreteness they
would cease to be philosophical.

The case of *metaphysics* and *epistemology*
affords an excellent illustration. The former of
these is commonly defined as the theory of reality or of first principles, the latter as the theory
of knowledge. But the most distinctive philosophical movement of the nineteenth century issues
from the idea that knowing and being are identical.[1] The prime reality is defined as a knowing
mind, and the terms of reality are interpreted as
terms of a cognitive process. Ideas and logical
principles *constitute* the world. It is evident that
in this Hegelian philosophy epistemology embraces

[1] The post-Kantian movement in Germany—especially
in so far as influenced by Hegel. See Chap. XII.

metaphysics. In defining the relations of knowledge to its object, one has already defined one's
fundamental philosophical conception, while *logic*,
as the science of the universal necessities of
thought, will embrace the first principles of reality. Now, were one to divide and arrange the problems of philosophy upon this basis, it is evident
that one would not have deduced the arrangement
from the general problem of philosophy, but from
a single attempted solution of that problem. It
might serve as an exposition of Hegel, but not as
a general philosophical programme.

Another case in point is provided by the present-
day interest in what is called " *pragmatism.*" [2]
This doctrine is historically connected with Kant's
principle of the " primacy of the practical reason," in which he maintained that the consciousness of duty is a profounder though less scientific
insight than the knowledge of objects. The current doctrine maintains that thought with its fruits
is an expression of interest, and that the will which
evinces and realizes such an interest is more original and significant than that which the thinking
defines. Such a view attaches a peculiar importance to the springs of conduct, and in its more

[2] Cf. § 203.

systematic development [3] has regarded *ethics* as
the true propædeutic and proof of philosophy. But
to make ethics the key-stone of the arch, is to define a special philosophical system; for it is the
very problem of philosophy to dispose the parts of
knowledge with a view to systematic construction.
The relation of the provinces of metaphysics, epistemology, logic, and ethics cannot, then, be defined
without entering these provinces and answering
the questions proper to them.

§ 56. Since the above terms exist, however,
there can be no doubt but that important divisions
The Depend-   within the general aim of philosophy
ence of the
Order of Phil- have actually been made. The inevi-
osophical
Problems   tableness of it appears in the variety of
upon the Ini-
tial Interest.   the sources from which that aim may
spring. The point of departure will always determine the emphasis and the application which
the philosophy receives. If philosophy be needed
to supplement more special interests, it will receive a particular character from whatever interest it so supplements. He who approaches it from
a definite stand-point will find in it primarily an
interpretation of that stand-point.

§ 57. There are two sources of the philosophical

---

[3] *E. g.*, the system of Fichte. Cf. § 177.

aim, which are perennial in their human significance. He, firstly, who begins with the demands
Philosophy as of life and its ideals, looks to philoso-
the Interpreta-
tion of Life. phy for a reconciliation of these with
the orderly procedure of nature. His philosophy
will receive its form from its illumination of life,
and it will be an ethical or religious philosophy.
Spinoza, the great seventeenth-century philosopher
who justified mysticism after the manner of mathematics,[4] displays this temper in his philosophy:

"After experience had taught me that all the usual
surroundings of social life are vain and futile; seeing
that none of the objects of my fears contained in themselves anything either good or bad, except in so far as
the mind is affected by them, I finally resolved to inquire whether there might be some real good having
power to communicate itself, which would affect the
mind singly, to the exclusion of all else: whether, in fact,
there might be anything of which the discovery and
attainment would enable me to enjoy continuous, supreme, and unending happiness."[5]

In pursuance of this aim, though he deals with
the problem of being in the rigorous logical fashion of his day, the final words of his great work
are, " Of Human Freedom ":

"Whereas the wise man, in so far as he is regarded as
such, is scarcely at all disturbed in spirit, but, being

    [4] See Chap. XI.
    [5] Spinoza: *On the Improvement of the Understanding.*
Translation by Elwes, p. 3.

conscious of himself, and of God, and of things, by a
certain eternal necessity, never ceases to be, but always
possesses true acquiescence of his spirit.   If the way which
I have pointed out as leading to this result seems exceedingly hard, it may nevertheless be discovered.   Needs
must it be hard, since it is so seldom found.   How would
it be possible if salvation were ready to our hand, and
could without great labor be found, that it should be by
almost all men neglected?   But all things excellent are
as difficult as they are rare." [6]

§ 58.   On the other hand, one who looks to philosophy for the extension and correction of scien-
Philosophy as   tific knowledge will be primarily inter-
the Extension
of Science.   ested in the philosophical definition of
ultimate conceptions, and in the method wherewith
such a definition is obtained.   Thus the philosophy
of the scientist will tend to be logical and metaphysical.   Şuch is the case with Descartes and
Leibniz, who are nevertheless intimately related to
Spinoza in the historical development of philosophy.

" Several years have now elapsed," says the former,
"since I first became aware that I had accepted, even
from my youth, many false opinions for true, and that
consequently what I afterward based on such principles
was highly doubtful; and from that time I was convinced of the necessity of undertaking once in my life to
rid myself of all the opinions I had adopted, and of com-

[6] Spinoza: *Ethics*, Part V, Proposition XLII.   Translation
by Elwes, p. 270.

mencing anew the work of building from the foundation, if I desired to establish a firm and abiding superstructure in the sciences."[7]

Leibniz's mind was more predominantly logical even than Descartes's. He sought in philosophy a supreme intellectual synthesis, a science of the universe.

"Although," he says retrospectively, "I am one of those who have worked much at mathematics, I have none the less meditated upon philosophy from my youth up; for it always seemed to me that there was a possibility of establishing something solid in philosophy by clear demonstrations. . . . I perceived, after much meditation, that it is impossible to find *the principles of a real unity* in matter alone, or in that which is only passive, since it is nothing but a collection or aggregation of parts *ad infinitum*."[8]

§ 59. Though these types are peculiarly representative, they are by no means exhaustive. There

The Historical Differentiation of the Philosophical Problem.

are as many possibilities of emphasis as there are incentives to philosophical reflection. It is not possible to exhaust the aspects of experience which may serve as bases from which such thought may issue, and to which, after its synthetic insight, it may return. But it is evident that such divisions of philosophy rep-

[7] Descartes: *Meditations*, I. Translation by Veitch, p. 97.

[8] Leibniz: *New System of the Nature of Substances*. Translation by Latta, pp. 299, 300.

resent in their order, and in the sharpness with
which they are sundered, the intellectual autobiog-
raphy of the individual philosopher.   There is but
one method by which that which is peculiar either
to the individual, or to the special position which
he adopts, may be eliminated.   Though it is impossible to tabulate the empty programme of philosophy, we may name certain special problems that
have appeared *in its history*.   Since this history
comprehends the activities of many individuals, a
general validity attaches to it.   There has been,
moreover, a certain periodicity in the emergence of
these problems, so that it may fairly be claimed for
them that they indicate inevitable phases in the
development of human reflection upon experience.
They represent a normal differentiation of interest
which the individual mind, in the course of its
own thinking, tends to follow.   It is true that it
can never be said with assurance that any age is
utterly blind to any aspect of experience.   This is
obviously the case with the practical and theoretical interests which have just been distinguished.
There is no age that does not have some practical
consciousness of the world as a whole, nor any
which does not seek more or less earnestly to universalize its science.   But though it compel us to

deal abstractly with historical epochs, there is abundant compensation in the possibility which this method affords of finding the divisions of philosophy in the manifestation of the living philosophical spirit.

§ 60. To Thales, one of the Seven Wise Men of Greece, is commonly awarded the honor of being

Metaphysics Seeks a Most Fundamental Conception. the founder of European philosophy. If he deserve this distinction, it is on account of the question which he raised, and not on account of the answer which he gave to it. Aristotle informs us that Thales held " water " to be " the material cause of all things." [9] This crude theory is evidently due to an interest in the totality of things, an interest which is therefore philosophical. But the interest of this first philosopher has a more definite character. It looks toward the definition in terms of some single conception, of *the constitution* of the world. As a child might conceivably think the moon to be made of green cheese, so philosophy in its childhood thinks here of all things as made of water. Water was a well-known substance, possessing well-known predicates. To define all nature in terms of it, was to maintain that in spite of superficial

[9] Burnet: *Early Greek Philosophy*, p. 42.

differences, all things have these predicates in common. They are the predicates which qualify for reality, and compose a community of nature from which all the individual objects and events of nature arise. The successors of Thales were evidently dissatisfied with his fundamental conception, because of its lack of generality. They seized upon vaguer substances like air and fire, for the very definiteness of the nature of water forbids the identification of other substances with it. But what is so obviously true of water is scarcely less true of air and fire; and it appeared at length that only a substance possessing the most general characters of body, such as shape, size, and mobility, could be thought as truly primeval and universal. In this wise a conception like our modern physical conception of matter came at length into vogue. Now the problem of which these were all tentative solutions is, in general, the problem of *metaphysics;* although this term belongs to a later era, arising only from the accidental place of the discussion of first principles *after physics* in the system of Aristotle. *The attempt to secure a most fundamental conception which attaches some definite meaning to the reality including and informing every particular thing, is metaphysics.*

§ 61. It must not be supposed that metaphysics is dogmatically committed to the reduction of all
Monism and Pluralism. reality to a unity of nature. It is quite consistent with its purpose that the parts of reality should be found to compose a group, or an indefinite multitude of irreducibly different entities. But it is clear that even such an account of things deals with what is true of all reality, and even in acknowledging the variety of its constituents, attributes to them some kind of relationship. The degree to which such a relationship is regarded as intimate and essential, determines the degree to which any metaphysical system is *monistic,*[10] rather than *pluralistic.* But the significance of this difference will be better appreciated after a further differentiation of the metaphysical problem has been noted.

§ 62. It has already been suggested that the test of Thales's conception lay in the possibility of
Ontology and Cosmology Concern Being and Process. deriving nature from it. A world principle must be fruitful. Now an abstract distinction has prevailed more or less persistently in metaphysics, between *the general definition of being,* called *ontology,* and the

---

[10] No little ambiguity attaches to the term "monism" in current usage, because of its appropriation by those who

study of the processes wherewith being is divided into things and events.   This latter study has to do primarily with the details of experience enumerated and systematized by the natural sciences. *To reconcile* these*, or the course of nature, with the fundamental definition of being,* is the problem of *cosmology*.   Cosmology is the construing of the *prima facie* reality in terms of the essential reality.   It is the proof and the explanation of ontology.   Since the most familiar part of the *prima facie* reality, the part almost exclusively noticed by the naive mind, is embraced within the field of the physical sciences, the term cosmology has come more definitely to signify the *philosophy of nature*.   It embraces such an examination of space, time, matter, causality, etc., as seeks to answer the most general questions about them, and provide for them in the world thought of as most profoundly real.   Such a study receives its philosophical character from its affiliation with ontology, as the latter would find its application in cosmology.

§ 63. But in addition to the consideration of

maintain that the universe is unitary and homogeneous in *physical terms* (cf. § 108).   It should properly be used to emphasize the unity of the world in any terms.

the various parts of nature, cosmology has commonly dealt with a radical and far-
reaching alternative that appeared at
the very dawn of metaphysics. Differences may arise within a world constituted of
a single substance or a small group of ultimate
substances, by changes in the relative position and
grouping of the parts. Hence the virtue of the
conception of motion. The theory which explains
all differences by motions of the parts of a qualitatively simple world, is called *mechanism*. Another source of change familiar to naive experience is *will*, or the action of living creatures.
According to the mechanical theory, *changes occur
on account of the natural motions of the parts
of matter;* according to the latter or *teleological*
conception, *changes are made by a formative
agency directed to some end.* Among the early
Greek philosophers, Leucippus was an exponent of
mechanism.

Mechanical and Teleological Cosmologies.

"He says that the worlds arise when many bodies
are collected together into the mighty void from the
surrounding space and rush together. They come into
collision, and those which are of similar shape and like
form become entangled, and from their entanglement
the heavenly bodies arise." [11]

[11] Burnet: *Op. cit.*, p. 358.

Anaxagoras, on the other hand, was famed for his doctrine of the Nous, or Intelligence, to whose direction he attributed the whole process of the world. The following is translated from extant fragments of his book, " περὶ φύσεως " :

" And Nous had power over the whole revolution, so that it began to revolve in the beginning. And it began to revolve first from a small beginning; but the revolution now extends over a larger space, and will extend over a larger still. And all the things that are mingled together and separated off and distinguished are all known by the Nous. And Nous set in order all things that were to be and that were, and all things that are not now and that are, and this revolution in which now revolve the stars and the sun and the moon, and the air and the ether that are separated off." [12]

§ 64. It is clear, furthermore, that the doctrine of Anaxagoras not only names a distinct kind of

Dualism.   cause, but also ascribes to it an independence and intrinsic importance that do not belong to motion. Whereas motion is a property of matter, intelligence is an originative power working out purposes of its own choosing. Hence we have here to do with a new ontology. If we construe ultimate being in terms of mind, we have a definite substitute for the physical theories outlined above. Such a theory is scarcely to be attributed to any Greek philosopher of the early

[12] Burnet: *Op. cit.*, p. 284.

period ; it belongs to a more sophisticated stage in the development of thought, after the rise of the problem of epistemology. But Anaxagoras's sharp distinction between the material of the world on the one hand, and the author of its order and evolution on the other, is in itself worthy of notice. It contains the germ of a recurrent philosophical *dualism*, which differs from pluralism in that it finds two and only two fundamental divisions of being, the physical, material, or potential on the one hand, and the mental, formal, or ideal on the other.

§ 65. Finally, the alternative possibilities which these cosmological considerations introduce, bear

The New Meaning of Monism and Pluralism.

directly upon the general question of the interdependence of the parts of the world, a question which has already appeared as pertinent in ontology. Monism and pluralism now obtain a new meaning. Where the world process is informed with some singleness of plan, as teleology proposes, the parts are reciprocally necessary, and inseparable from the unity. Where, on the other hand, the processes are random and reciprocally fortuitous, as Leucippus proposes, the world as a whole is an aggregate rather than a unity. In this way uniformity in kind of being may prevail in a world the relations of whose parts are due to chance, while diversity in kind of being may prevail in a world knit together by some thorough-going plan of organization. Thus monism and pluralism are conceptions as proper to cosmology as to ontology.

But enough has been said to demonstrate the interdependence of ontology and cosmology, of the theory of being and the theory of differentiation and process. Such problems can be only abstractly sundered, and the distinctive character of any metaphysical system will usually consist in some theory determining their relation. Philosophy returns to these metaphysical problems with its thought enriched and its method complicated, after becoming thoroughly alive to the problems of epistemology, logic, and ethics.

§ 66. *Epistemology* is *the theory of the possibility of knowledge,* and issues from criticism and

Epistemology Seeks to Understand the Possibility of Knowledge.
scepticism. If we revert again to the history of Greek philosophy, we find a first period of enterprising speculation giving place to a second period of hesitancy and doubt. This phase of thought occurs simultaneously with the brilliantly humanistic age of Pericles, and it is undoubtedly true that energy is

withdrawn from speculation largely for the sake of expending it in the more lively and engaging pursuits of politics and art. But there are patent reasons within the sphere of philosophy itself for entailment of activity and taking of stock. For three centuries men have taken their philosophical powers for granted, and used them without questioning them. Repeated attacks upon the problem of reality have resulted in no concensus of opinion, but only in a disagreement among the wise men themselves. A great variety of mere theories has been substituted for the old unanimity of religious tradition and practical life. It is natural under these circumstances to infer that in philosophy man has overreached himself. He would more profitably busy himself with affairs that belong to his own sphere, and find a basis for life in his immediate relations with his fellows. The sophists, learned in tradition, and skilled in disputation, but for the most part entirely lacking in originality, are the new prophets. As teachers of rhetoric and morals, they represent the practical and secular spirit of their age; while in their avoidance of speculation, and their critical justification of that course, they express its sceptical philosophy.

§ 67. In their self-justification certain of the sophists attached themselves to a definite doctrine

Scepticism, Dogmatism, and Agnosticism.

maintained by those of their predecessors and contemporaries who were atomists, or followers of that same Leucippus whom we have quoted. This doctrine was the result of an attempt to construe perception in terms of the motion of atoms. Outer objects were said to give off fine particles which, through the mediation of the sense organs, impinged upon the soul-atom. But it was evident even to the early exponents of this theory that according to such an account, each perceiver is relegated to a world peculiar to his own stand-point. His perception informs him concerning his own states as affected by things, rather than concerning the things themselves. Upon this ground the great sophist Protagoras is said to have based his dictum: Πάντων χρημάτων μέτρον ἄνθρωπος,—" Man is the measure of all things." This is the classic statement of the doctrine of relativity. But we have now entered into the province of epistemology, and various alternatives confront us. Reduce thought to perception, define perception as relative to each individual, and you arrive at *scepticism, or the denial of the possibility of valid knowledge.* Plato expounds this consequence in the well-known discussion of Protagoras that occurs in the " Theætetus."

"I am charmed with his doctrine, that what appears is to each one, but I wonder that he did not begin his book on Truth with a declaration that a pig or a dog-faced baboon, or some other yet stranger monster which has sensation, is the measure of all things; then he might have shown a magnificent contempt for our opinion of him by informing us at the outset that while we were reverencing him like a God for his wisdom, he was no better than a tadpole, not to speak of his fellow-men— would not this have produced an overpowering effect? For if truth is only sensation, and no man can discern another's feelings better than he, or has any superior right to determine whether his opinion is true or false, but each, as we have several times repeated, is to himself the sole judge, and everything that he judges is true and right, why, my friend, should Protagoras be preferred to the place of wisdom and instruction, and deserve to be well paid, and we poor ignoramuses have to go to him, if each one is the measure of his own wisdom? . . . The attempt to supervise or refute the notions or opinions of others would be a tedious and enormous piece of folly, if to each man his own are right; and this must be the case if Protagoras's Truth is the real truth, and the philosopher is not merely amusing himself by giving oracles out of the shrine of his book." [13]

This is the full swing of the pendulum from *dogmatism,* or the uncritical conviction of truth.   A modified form of scepticism has been developed in these later days under the influence of natural sci-

[13] Plato: *Theætetus,* 161.   Translation by Jowett.   References to Plato are to the marginal paging.

ence, and is called *agnosticism* or *positivism*. It
accepts the Protagorean doctrine only in the sense
of attributing to human knowledge as a whole an
incapacity for exceeding the range of perception.
Beyond this realm of natural science, where
theories can be sensibly verified, lies the unknowable realm, more real, but forever inaccessible.

§ 68. It is important to note that both scepticism and agnosticism agree in regarding *percep-*

The Source
and Criterion
of Knowledge
According to
Empiricism
and Rational-
ism.
Mysticism.

tion as the essential factor in knowledge.
So far at any rate as our knowledge is
concerned, the certification of being consists in perceivability. Knowledge is
coextensive with actual and possible
human experience. This account of the source
and criterion of knowledge is called *empiricism*,
in distinction from the counter-theory of *rationalism*.

The rationalistic motive was a quickening influence in Greek philosophy long before it became
deliberate and conspicuous in Socrates and Plato.
Parmenides, founder of the Eleatic School, has
left behind him a poem divided into two parts:
" The Way of Truth " and " The Way of Opinion." [14]   In the first of these he expounds his

---

[14] Burnet: *Early Greek Philosophy*, pp. 184, 187.

esoteric philosophy, which is a definition of being established by dialectical reasoning. He finds that being must be single, eternal, and changeless, because otherwise it cannot be thought and defined without contradiction. The method which Parmenides here employs presupposes that knowledge consists in understanding rather than perception. Indeed, he regards the fact that the world of the senses is manifold and mutable as of little consequence to the wise man. The world of sense is the province of vulgar opinion, while that of reason is the absolute truth revealed only to the philosopher. The truth has no concern with appearance, but is answerable only to the test of rationality. *That world is real which one is able by thinking to make intelligible.* The world is what a world must be in order to be possible at all, and the philosopher can deduce it directly from the very conditions of thought which it must satisfy. He who would know reality may disregard what seems to be, provided he can by reflective analysis discover certain general necessities to which being must conform. This is rationalism in its extreme form.

The rationalism of Socrates was more moderate, as it was more fruitful than that of Parmenides.

As is well known, Socrates composed no philosophical books, but sought to inculcate wisdom in
his teaching and conversation. His method of
inculcating wisdom was to evoke it in his inter-
locutor by making him considerate of the meaning
of his speech. Through his own questions he
sought to arouse the questioning spirit, which
should weigh the import of words, and be satisfied with nothing short of a definite and consistent
judgment.   In the Platonic dialogues the Socratic
method obtains a place in literature. In the
" Theætetus," which is, perhaps, the greatest of all
epistemological treatises, Socrates is represented as
likening his vocation to that of the midwife.

"Well, my art of midwifery is in most respects like
theirs, but differs in that I attend men, and not women,
and I look after their souls when they are in labor, and
not after their bodies: and the triumph of my art is in
thoroughly examining whether the thought which the
mind of the young man brings forth is a false idol or a
noble and true birth. And, like the midwives, I am
barren, and the reproach which is often made against
me, that I ask questions of others and have not the wit
to answer them myself, is very just; the reason is that
the god compels me to be a midwife, but does not allow
me to bring forth.   And therefore I am not myself at all
wise, nor have I anything to show which is the invention
or birth of my own soul, but those who converse with
me profit. . . . It is quite clear that they never

learned anything from me; the many fine discoveries to which they cling are of their own making." [15]

The principle underlying this method is the insistence that a proposition, to be true of reality, must at least bespeak a mind that is true to itself, internally luminous, and free from contradiction. That which is to me nothing that I can express in form that will convey precise meaning and bear analysis, is so far nothing at all. Being is not, as the empiricist would have it, ready at hand, ours for the looking, but is the fruit of critical reflection. Only reason, overcoming the relativity of perception, and the chaos of popular opinion, can lay hold on the universal truth.

A very interesting tendency to clothe the articulations of thought with the immediacy of perception is exhibited in *mysticism*, which attributes the highest cognitive power to an experience that transcends thought, an ineffable insight that is the occasional reward of thought and virtuous living. This theory would seem to owe its great vigor to the fact that it promises to unite the universality of the rational object with the vivid presence of the empirical object, though it sacrifices the definite content of both. The mystic, empiricist, and

[15] Plato: *Theœtetus*, 150 B.   Translation by Jowett.

rationalist are in these several ways led to revise
their metaphysics upon the basis of their epistemology, or to define reality in terms dictated by
the means of knowing it.

§ 69. But within the general field of epistemology there has arisen another issue of even

The Relation
of Knowledge
to its Object
According to
Realism, and
the Represent-
ative Theory.

greater significance in its bearing upon
metaphysics. The first issue, as we
have seen, has reference to the criterion
of knowledge, to the possibility of arriving at certainty about reality, and the choice of
means to that end. A second question arises, concerning *the relation between the knowledge and its
object or that which is known.* This problem
does not at first appear as an epistemological difficulty, but is due to the emphasis which the moral
and religious interests of men give to the conception of the self. My knowing is a part of me, a
function of that soul whose welfare and eternal
happiness I am seeking to secure. Indeed, my
knowing is, so the wise men have always taught,
the greatest of my prerogatives. Wisdom appertains to the philosopher, as folly to the fool. But
though my knowledge be a part of me, and in me,
the same cannot, lightly at any rate, be said of
what I know. It would seem that I must dis-

tinguish between the knowledge, which is my act or state, an event in my life, and the known, which is object, and belongs to the context of the outer world. *The object of knowledge* would then be quite *independent of the circumstance that I know it.* This theory has acquired the name of *realism*,[16] and is evidently as close to common sense as any epistemological doctrine can be said to be. If the knowledge consists in some sign or symbol which in my mind stands for the object, but is

[16] Much ambiguity attaches to the terms "realism" and "idealism" in current usage. The first had at one time in the history of philosophy a much narrower meaning than that which it now possesses. It was used to apply to those who, after Plato, believed in the independent reality of ideas, universals, or general natures. *Realists* in this sense were opposed to *nominalists* and *conceptualists*. Nominalism maintained the exclusive reality of individual substances, and reduced ideas to particular signs having, like the *name*, a purely symbolical or descriptive value. Conceptualism sought to unite realism and nominalism through the conception of mind, or an individual substance whose meanings may possess universal validity. Though this dispute was of fundamental importance throughout the mediæval period, the issues involved have now been restated. Realism in the old sense will, if held, come within the scope of the broader epistemological realism defined above. Nominalism is covered by empirical tendencies, and conceptualism by modern idealism.

The term *idealism* is sometimes applied to Plato on account of his designation of ideas as the ultimate realities. This would be a natural use of the term, but in our own day it has become inseparably associated with the doctrine

quite other than the object, realism is given the form known as the *representative theory*. This theory is due to a radical distinction between the inner world of consciousness and the outer world of things, whereby in knowledge the outer object requires a substitute that is qualified to belong to the inner world. Where, on the other hand, no specific and exclusive nature is attributed to the inner world, realism may flourish without the representative theory. In such a case the object would be regarded as itself capable of entering into any number of individual experiences or of remaining outside them all, and without on either account forfeiting its identity. This view was taken for granted by Plato, but is elaborately defended in our own day. During the intervening period epistemology has been largely occupied with difficulties inherent in the representative theory, and

which attributes to being a dependence upon the activity of mind. It is of the utmost importance to keep these two meanings clear. In the preferred sense Plato is a realist, and so opposed to idealism.

The term *idealism* is further confused on account of its employment in literature and common speech to denote the control of ideals. Although this is a kindred meaning, the student of philosophy will gain little or no help from it, and will avoid confusion if he distinguishes the term in its technical use and permits it in that capacity to acquire an independent meaning.

from that discussion there has emerged the theory of *idealism*,[17] the great rival theory to that of realism.

§ 70. The representative theory contains at least one obvious difficulty. If the thinker be **The Relation of Knowledge to its Object According to Idealism.** confined to his ideas, and if the reality be at the same time beyond these ideas, how can he ever verify their report? Indeed, what can it mean that an idea should be true of that which belongs to a wholly different category? How under such circumstances can that which is a part of the idea be attributed with any certainty to the object? Once grant that you know only your ideas, and the object reduces to an unknown x, which you retain to account for the outward pointing or reference of the ideas, but which is not missed if neglected. The obvious though radical theory of idealism is almost inevitably the next step. Why assume that there is any object other than the state of mind, since all positive content belongs to that realm? The eighteenth century English philosopher, Bishop Berkeley, was accused by his contemporaries of wilful eccentricity, and even madness, for his boldness in accepting this argument and drawing this conclusion:

[17] See *note*, p. 173.

"The table I write on I say exists; that is, I see and feel it: and if I were out of my study I should say it existed; meaning thereby that if I was in my study I might perceive it, or that some other spirit actually does perceive it. There was an odor—that is, it was smelt; there was a sound—that is, it was heard; a color or figure, and it was perceived by sight or touch. This is all that I can understand by these and the like expressions. For as to what is said of the *absolute* existence of unthinking things, without any relation to their being perceived, that is to me perfectly unintelligible. Their *esse* is *percipi;* nor is it possible that they should have any existence out of the minds or thinking thing which perceives them." [18]

§ 71. In this paragraph Berkeley maintains that it is essential to things, or at any rate to their

Phenomenalism, Spiritualism, and Panpsychism. qualities, that they *be perceived.* This principle when expressed as an epistemological or metaphysical generalization, is called *phenomenalism.* But in another phase of his thought Berkeley emphasizes the *perceiver,* or *spirit.* The theory which maintains that the only real substances are these active selves, with their powers and their states, has been called somewhat vaguely by the name of *spiritualism.*[19] Philosophically it shows a strong tendency to de-

[18] Berkeley: *Principles of Human Knowledge,* Part I, Fraser's edition, p. 259.
[19] To be distinguished from the religious sect which bears the same name.

velop into either *panpsychism* or *transcendentalism*. The former is radically empirical. Its classic representative is the German pessimist Schopenhauer, who defined reality in terms of will because that term signified to him most eloquently *the directly felt nature of the self*. This immediate revelation of the true inwardness of being serves as the key to an " intuitive interpretation " of the gradations of nature, and will finally awaken a sense of the presence of the universal Will.

§ 72. *Transcendentalism*, or *absolute idealism*, on the other hand, emphasizes the *rational activity*, rather than the bare subjectivity, *of the self*. The term " transcendental " has become associated with this type of idealism through Kant, whose favorite form of argument, the " transcendental deduction," was an analysis of experience with a view to discovering the categories, or formal principles of thought, implied in its meaning. From the Kantian method arose the conception of a standard or *absolute mind* for the standard experience. This mind is transcendental not in the sense of being alien, but in the sense of exceeding the human mind in the direction of what this means and strives to be. It is the ideal or normal mind, in which the true

Transcendentalism, or Absolute Idealism.

reality is contained, with all the chaos of finite experience compounded and redeemed. There is no being but the absolute, the one all-inclusive spiritual life, in whom all things are inherent, and whose perfection is the virtual implication of all purposive activities.

" God's life . . . sees the one plan fulfilled through all the manifold lives, the single consciousness winning its purpose by virtue of all the ideas, of all the individual selves, and of all the lives. No finite view is wholly illusory. Every finite intent taken precisely in its wholeness is fulfilled in the Absolute. The least life is not neglected, the most fleeting act is a recognized part of the world's meaning. You are for the divine view all that you know yourself at this instant to be. But you are also infinitely more. The preciousness of your present purposes to yourself is only a hint of that preciousness which in the end links their meaning to the entire realm of Being." [20]

The fruitfulness of the philosopher's reflective doubt concerning his own powers is now evident. Problems are raised which are not merely urgent in themselves, but which present wholly new alternatives to the metaphysician. Rationalism and empiricism, realism and idealism, are doctrines which, though springing from the epistemological query concerning the possibility of knowledge, may

[20] Quoted from Professor Josiah Royce's *The World and the Individual, First Series*, pp. 426–427.

determine an entire philosophical system.   They bear upon every question of metaphysics, whether the fundamental conception of being, or the problems of the world's unity, origin, and significance for human life.

CHAPTER VII

§ 73. THERE are three sets of problems whose
general philosophical importance depends upon the
The Normative place which metaphysics assigns to the
Sciences. *human critical faculties.* Man passes
judgment upon that which claims to be *true, beautiful,* or *good,* thus referring to ideals and standards that define these values. Attempts to make
these ideals explicit, and to formulate principles
which regulate their attainment, have resulted in
the development of the three so-called *normative
sciences: logic, æsthetics,* and *ethics.* These sciences are said to owe their origin to the Socratic
method, and it is indeed certain that their problem is closely related to the general rationalistic
attitude.[1] In Plato's dialogue, "Protagoras,"
one may observe the manner of the inception
of both ethics and logic. The question at issue
between Socrates and the master sophist Pro-

---

[1] Cf. § 68.

tagoras, is concerning the possibility of teaching virtue. Protagoras conducts his side of the
discussion with the customary rhetorical flourish,
expounding in set speeches the tradition and usage
in which such a possibility is accepted. Socrates,
on the other hand, conceives the issue quite differ-
ently. One can neither affirm nor deny anything
of virtue unless one knows *what is meant by it*.
Even the possession of such a meaning was scarcely
recognized by Protagoras, who was led by Socrates's questions to attribute to the various virtues an external grouping analogous to that of the
parts of the face. But Socrates shows that since
justice, temperance, courage, and the like, are admittedly similar in that they are all virtues, they
must have in common some essence, which is virtue in general. This he seeks to define in the
terms, *virtue is knowledge*. The interest which
Socrates here shows in the reduction of the ordinary moral judgments to a system centering in
some single fundamental principle, is the ethical
interest. But this is at the same time a particular application of the general rationalistic method
of definition, and of the general rationalistic postulate that one knows nothing until one can form
unitary and determinate conceptions. The recog-

nition which Socrates thus gives to criteria of
knowledge is an expression of the logical interest.
In a certain sense, indeed, the whole labor of Socrates was in the cause of the logical interest. For
he sought to demonstrate that belief is not necessarily knowledge; that belief may or may not be
true. In order that it shall be true, and constitute knowledge, it must be well-grounded, and
accompanied by an understanding of its object.
Socrates thus set the problem of logic, the discovery, namely, of those characters by virtue of the
possession of which belief is knowledge.

§ 74. Logic deals with the ground of belief, and
thus distinguishes itself from the psychological ac-
The Affilia- count of the elements of the believing
tions
of Logic. state.[2] But it is not possible sharply
to sunder psychology and logic. This is due to
the fact that the general principles which make
belief true, may be regarded quite independently
of this fact. They then become *the most general
truth*, belonging to the absolute, archetypal realm,
or to the mind of God.[3] When the general principles of certainty are so regarded, logic can be

[2] The Socratic distinction between the logical and the
psychological treatment of belief finds its best expression in
Plato's *Gorgias*, especially, 454, 455. Cf. also § 29.

[3] Thus, e. g. Hegel. See § 179. Cf. also §§ 199, 200.

distinguished from metaphysics only by adding to the study of the general principles themselves, the study of the special conditions (mainly psychological) under which they may be realized among men.   In the history of human thought the name of logic belongs to the study of this *attainment* of truth, as the terms æsthetics and ethics belong to the studies of the attainment of beauty and goodness.[4]   It is evident that logic will have a peculiar importance for the rationalist. For the empiricist, proposing to report upon things as they are given, will tend on the whole to maintain that knowledge has no properties save those which are given to it by its special subject-matter.   One cannot, in short, define any absolute relationship between the normative sciences and the other branches of philosophy.

§ 75. *Logic is the formulation, as independently as possible of special subject-matter, of that which* conditions *truth in belief.* Since logic is concerned with truth only in so far as it is predicated of belief, and since belief in so far as true is knowledge, logic can be defined as the formulation of the most general principles of knowledge. The principles so for-

Logic Deals with the Most General Conditions of Truth in Belief.

[4] Cf. § 84.

mulated would be those virtually used to *justify* belief or to disprove the imputation of error.

§ 76. What is called *formal logic* is animated with the hope of extracting these formulations

The Parts of Formal Logic. Definition, Self-evidence, Inference, and Observation.

directly from an analysis of the procedure of thought. The most general logical principles which have appeared in the historical development of formal logic are *definition, self-evidence, inference*, and *observation*. Each of these has been given special study, and each has given rise to special issues.

Definition has to do with the *formation of concepts*, or determinate and unequivocal meanings. The universality of such concepts, and their consequent relation to particular things, was, as we have seen, investigated at a very early date, and gave rise to the great realistic-nominalistic controversy.[5] A large part of the logical discussion in the Platonic dialogues is an outgrowth of the earlier " eristic," a form of disputation in favor with the sophists, and consisting in the adroit use of ambiguity.[6] It is natural that in its first conscious self-criticism thought should discover the need of definite terms. The perpetual importance of defi-

[5] See § 69, *note*.

[6] The reader will find a good illustration of eristic in Plato's *Euthydemus*, 275.

nition has been largely due to the great prestige in modern philosophy of the method of geometry, which was regarded by Descartes and Spinoza as the model for systems of necessary truth.

Self-evidence is the principle according to which *conviction of truth follows directly from an understanding of meaning.* In the practice of his intellectual midwifery, Socrates presupposed that thought is capable of bringing forth its own certainties. And rationalism has at all times regarded truth as ultimately accredited by internal marks recognizable by reason. Such truth arrived at antecedent to acquaintance with instances is called *a priori*, as distinguished from *a posteriori* knowledge, or observation after the fact. There can be no principles of self-evidence, but logicians have always been more or less concerned with the enumeration of alleged self-evident principles, notably those of *contradiction* and *identity*. A philosophical interest in the mathematical method has led to a logical study of axioms, but with a view rather to their fruitfulness than their intrinsic truth. Indeed, the interest in self-evident truth has always been subordinate to the interest in systematic truth, and the discovery of first principles most commonly serves to determine the relative

priority of definite concepts, or the correct point
of departure for a series of inferences.

The greater part of the famous Aristotelian
logic consists in a study of *inference,* or *the
derivation of new knowledge from old knowledge.*
Aristotle sought to set down and classify every
method of advancing from premises. The most
important form of inference which he defined was
the *syllogism,* a scheme of reasoning to a conclusion by means of two premises having one term in
common. From the premises " all men are mortal " and " Socrates is a man," one may conclude
that " Socrates is mortal." This is an instance
not only of the syllogism in general, but of its
most important " mood," the subsumption of a
particular case under a general rule. Since the
decline of Aristotle's influence in philosophy there
has been a notable decrease of interest in the different forms of inference; though its fundamental
importance as the very bone and sinew of *reasoning* or *deductive thinking* has never been chal-
lenged. Its loss of preëminence is in part due to
the growth of empiricism, stimulated by the writings of Lord Bacon in the seventeenth century,
and fostered by the subsequent development of experimental science.

Observation is the fundamental logical principle of empiricism. For a radical empiricism, knowledge would consist of descriptive generalizations based upon the summation of instances. That branch of logic which deals with *the advance from individual instances to general principles*, is called *inductive logic*. It has resulted in the announcement of canons of accuracy and freedom from preconception, and in the methodological study of hypothesis, experiment, and verification. Rules for observation directed to the end of discovering causes, constitute the most famous part of the epoch-making logic of J. S. Mills.[7]

§ 77. There are two significant tendencies in contemporary logic. *Theories of the judgment* have arisen in the course of an attempt to define the least complexity that must be present in order that thought shall come within the range of truth and error. It is evident that no one either knows or is in error until he takes some attitude which lays claim to knowledge. Denoting by the term *judgment* this minimum of complexity in knowledge, an important question arises as to the sense in which the

Present Tendencies. Theory of the Judgment.

[7] The reader can find these rules, and the detail of the traditional formal logic, in any elementary text-book, such as, e. g., Jevons: *Elements of Logic*.

judgment involves the subject, predicate, and copula that are commonly present in its propositional form.

§ 78. But a more important logical development has been due to the recent analysis of definite

Priority of Concepts.
accredited systems of knowledge. The study of the fundamental conceptions of mathematics and mechanics, together with an examination of the systematic structure of these sciences, furnishes the most notable cases. There are two senses in which such studies may be regarded as logical. In the first place, in so far as they bring to light the inner coherence of any body of truth, the kind of evidence upon which it rests, and the type of formal perfection which it seeks, they differ from formal logic only in that they derive their criteria from cases, rather than from the direct analysis of the procedure of thought. And since formal logic must itself make experiments, this difference is not a radical one. The study of cases tends chiefly to enrich *methodology*, or the knowledge of the special criteria of special sciences. In the second place, such studies serve to define the relatively few simple truths which are common to the relatively many complex truths. A study of the foundations of arithmetic reveals

more elementary conceptions, such as *class* and *order*, that must be employed in the very definition of number itself, and so are implied in every numerical calculation.   It appears similarly that the axioms of geometry are special axioms which involve the acceptance of more general axioms or indefinables.[8]   Logic in this sense, then, is the enumeration of conceptions and principles in the order of their indispensableness to knowledge. And while it must be observed that the most general conceptions and principles of knowledge are not necessarily those most significant for the existent world, nevertheless the careful analysis which such an enumeration involves is scarcely less fruitful for metaphysics than for logic.

§ 79. *Æsthetics is the formulation, as independently as possible of special subject-matter,*

Aesthetics Deals with the Most General Conditions of Beauty. Subjectivistic and Formalistic Tendencies.

of that which conditions beauty.   As logic commonly refers to a judgment of truth, so æsthetics at any rate *refers* to a judgment implied in appreciation. But while it is generally admitted that truth itself is by no means limited to the form of the judgment, the contrary is frequently main-

[8] What is called "the algebra of logic" seeks to obtain an unequivocal symbolic expression for these truths.

tained with reference to beauty. The aphorism, *De gustibus non est disputandum,* expresses a common opinion to the effect that beauty is not a property belonging to the object of which it is predicated, but a property generated by the appreciative consciousness. According to this opinion there can be no beauty except in the case of an object's presence in an individual experience. Investigators must of necessity refuse to leave individual caprice in complete possession of the field, but they have in many cases occupied themselves entirely with the *state of æsthetic enjoyment* in the hope of discovering its constant factors. The opposing tendency defines certain *formal characters which the beautiful object must possess.* Evidently the latter school will attribute a more profound philosophical importance to the conception of beauty, since for them it is a principle that obtains in the world of being. This was the first notable contention, that of Plato. But even with the emphasis laid upon the subjective aspect of the æsthetic experience, great metaphysical importance may be attached to it, where, as in the case of the German Romanticists, reality is deliberately construed as a spiritual life which is to be appreciated rather than understood.

As in the case of logic, a strong impulse has manifested itself in æsthetics to deal with groups of objects that lie within its province, rather than directly with its concepts and principles. The first special treatise on æsthetics, the "Poetics" of Aristotle, belongs to this type of inquiry, as does all criticism of art in so far as it aims at the formulation of general principles.

§ 80. *Ethics,* the oldest and most popular of the normative sciences, *is the formulation, as independently as possible of special subject-matter, of that which conditions goodness of conduct.* Ethics is commonly concerned with goodness only in so far as it is predicated of conduct, or of character, which is a more or less permanent disposition to conduct. Since conduct, in so far as good, is said to constitute moral goodness, ethics may be defined as the formulation of the general principles of *morality.* The principles so formulated would be those virtually employed to *justify* conduct, or to disprove the imputation of immorality.

Ethics Deals with the Most General Conditions of Moral Goodness.

§ 81. The student of this science is confronted with a very considerable diversity of method and differentiation of problems. The earliest and most profound opposition of

Conceptions of the Good. Hedonism.

doctrine in ethics arose from the differences of interpretation of which the teaching of Socrates is capable. His doctrine is, as we have seen, verbally expressed in the proposition, *virtue is knowledge*. Socrates was primarily concerned to show that there is no real living without an understanding of the significance of life. To live well is to know the end of life, the good of it all, and to govern action with reference to that end. Virtue is therefore the practical wisdom that enables one to live consistently with his real intention. But what is the real intention, the end or good of life? In the " Protagoras," where Plato represents Socrates as expounding his position, virtue is interpreted to mean prudence, or foresight of pleasurable and painful consequences. He who knows, possesses all virtue in that he is qualified to adapt himself to the real situation and to gain the end of pleasure. All men, indeed, seek pleasure, but only virtuous men seek it wisely and well.

"And do you, Protagoras, like the rest of the world, call some pleasant things evil and some painful things good?—for I am rather disposed to say that things are good in as far as they are pleasant, if they have no consequences of another sort, and in as far as they are painful they are bad."[9]

[9] Plato: *Protagoras*, 351.   Translation by Jowett.

According to this view painful things are good only when they lead eventually to pleasure, and pleasant things evil only when their painful consequences outweigh their pleasantness. Hence moral differences reduce to differences of skill in the universal quest for pleasure, and *sensible gratification is the ultimate standard of moral value.* This ancient doctrine, known as *hedonism*, expressing as it does a part of life that will not suffer itself for long to be denied, is one of the great perennial tendencies of ethical thought. In the course of many centuries it has passed through a number of phases, varying its conception of pleasure from the tranquillity of the wise man to the sensuous titillations of the sybarite, and from the individualism of the latter to the universalism of the humanitarian. But in every case it shows a respect for the natural man, praising morality for its disciplinary and instrumental value in the service of such human wants as are the outgrowth of the animal instinct of self-preservation.

§ 82. But if a man's life be regarded as a truer representation of his ideals than is his spoken **Rationalism.** theory, there is little to identify Socrates with the hedonists. At the conclusion of the defence of his own life, which Plato puts into his mouth in the well-known " Apology," he speaks thus :

" When my sons are grown up, I would ask you, O my friends, to punish them; and I would have you trouble them, as I have troubled you, if the seem to care about riches, or anything, more than about virtue; or if they pretend to be something when they are really nothing,— then reprove them, as I have reproved you, for not caring about that for which they ought to care, and thinking that they are something when they are really nothing." [10]

It is plain that the man Socrates cared little for the pleasurable or painful consequences of his acts, provided they were worthy of the high calling of human nature. A man's virtue would now seem to possess an intrinsic nobility. If knowledge be virtue, then on this basis it must be because knowledge is itself excellent. Virtue as knowledge contributes to the good by constituting it. We meet here with the *rationalistic* strain in ethics. It praises conduct for the *inherent worth which it may possess if it express that reason* which the Stoics called " *the ruling part*." The riches of wisdom consist for the hedonist in their purchase of pleasure. For the rationalist, on the other hand, wisdom is not coin, but itself the very substance of value.

§ 83. Rationalism has undergone modifications

[10] Plato: *Apology*, 41. Translation by Jowett.

even more significant than those of hedonism, **Eudæmonism and Pietism. Rigorism and Intuitionism.** and involving at least one radically new group of conceptions. Among the Greeks rationalism and hedonism alike are *eudæmonistic*. They aim to portray *the fulness of life* that makes " the happy man." In the ethics of Aristotle, whose synthetic mind weaves together these different strands, the Greek ideal finds its most complete expression as " the high-minded man," with all his powers and trappings. But the great spiritual transformation which accompanied the decline of Greek culture and the rise of Christianity, brought with it a new moral sensibility, which finds in man no virtue of himself, but only through the grace of God.

"And the virtues themselves," says St. Augustine, " if they bear no relation to God, are in truth vices rather than virtues; for although they are regarded by many as truly moral when they are desired as ends in themselves and not for the sake of something else, they are, nevertheless, inflated and arrogant, and therefore not to be viewed as virtues but as vices." [11]

The new ideal is that of renunciation, obedience, and resignation. Ethically this expresses itself in *pietism*. Virtue is good neither in itself nor on account of its consequences, but because it is con-

[11] Quoted by Paulsen in his *System of Ethics*. Translation by Thilly, p. 69.

formable to the will of God.   The extreme inwardness of this ideal is characteristic of an age that
despaired of attainment, whether of pleasure or
knowledge.   To all, even the persecuted, it is permitted to obey, and so gain entrance into the
kingdom of the children of God.   But as every
special study tends to rely upon its own conceptions, pietism, involving as it does a relation to
God, is replaced by *rigorism* and *intuitionism*.
The former doctrine defines virtue in terms of the
inner attitude which it expresses.   It must be done
in the spirit of dutifulness, *because one ought,* and
through sheer respect for the law which one's
moral nature affirms.   *Intuitionism* has attempted
to deal with the source of the moral law by defining conscience as a *special faculty* or sense, qualified to pass directly upon moral questions, and
deserving of implicit obediences.   It is characteristic of this whole tendency to look for the spring
of virtuous living, not in a good which such living
obtains, but in a law to which its owes obedience.

§ 84. This third general ethical tendency has
thus been of the greatest importance in emphasiz-

Duty and
Freedom.
Ethics and
Metaphysics.

ing the *consciousness of duty,* and has
brought both hedonism and rationalism
to a recognition of its fundamental im-

portance.   Ethics must deal not only with the
moral ideal, but also with the ground of its appeal
to the individual, and his obligation to pursue it.
In connection with this recognition of moral responsibility, the problem of human *freedom* has
come to be regarded in the light of an inevitable
point of contact between ethics and metaphysics.
That which is absolutely binding upon the human
will can be determined only in view of some
theory of its ultimate nature.   On this account
the rationalistic and hedonistic motives are no
longer abstractly sundered, as in the days of the
Stoics and Epicureans, but tend to be absorbed in
broader philosophical tendencies.   Hedonism appears as the sequel to naturalism; or, more rarely,
as part of a theistic system whose morality is
divine legislation enforced by an appeal to motives
of pleasure and pain.   Rationalism, on the other
hand, tends to be absorbed in rationalistic or idealistic philosophies, where man's rational nature is
construed as his bond of kinship with the universe.

Ethics has exhibited from the beginning a tendency to universalize its conceptions and take the
central place in metaphysics.   Thus with Plato
good conduct was but a special case of goodness,
the good being the most general principle of

reality.[12]   In modern times Fichte and his school
have founded an ethical metaphysics upon the conception of duty.[13]   In these cases ethics can be distinguished from metaphysics only by adding to
the study of the good or of duty, a study of the
special physical, psychological, and social conditions under which goodness and dutifulness may
obtain in human life.   It is possible to attach the
name of ethics, and we have seen the same to be
true of logic, either to a realm of ideal truth or
to that realm wherein the ideal is realized in
humanity.

§ 85. A systematic study of ethics requires that
the *virtues*, or types of moral practice, shall be
The Virtues, interpreted in the light of the central
Customs, and
Institutions. conception of good, or of conscience.
Justice, temperance, wisdom, and *courage* were
praised by the Greeks.   Christianity added *self-
sacrifice, humility, purity,* and *benevolence*.   These
and other virtues have been defined, justified, and
co-ordinated with the aid of a standard of moral
value or a canon of duty.

There is in modern ethics a pronounced tendency, parallel to those already noted in logic and
æsthetics, to study such phenomena belonging to

---

[12] Cf. § 160.   [13] Cf. § 177.

its field as have become historically established. A very considerable investigation of *custom, institutions,* and other social forces has led to a contact of ethics with anthropology and sociology scarcely less significant than that with metaphysics.

§ 86. In that part of his philosophy in which he deals with faith, the great German philosopher

The Problems of Religion. The Special Interests of Faith. Kant mentions God, Freedom, and Immortality as the three pre-eminent religious interests. Religion, as we have seen, sets up a social relationship between man and that massive drift of things which determines his destiny. Of the two terms of this relation, God signifies the latter, while freedom and immortality are prerogatives which religion bestows upon the former. Man, viewed from the stand-point of religion as an object of special interest to the universe, is said to have a soul; and by virtue of this soul he is said to be free and immortal, when thought of as having a life in certain senses independent of its immediate natural environment. The attempt to make this faith theoretically intelligible has led to the philosophical disciplines known as *theology* and *psychology.*[14]

[14] Concerning the duty of philosophy to religion in these

§ 87. *Theology,* as a branch of philosophy, deals with *the proof and the nature of God.* Since

Theology Deals with the Nature and Proof of God. "God" is not primarily a theoretical conception, the proof of God is not properly a philosophical problem. Historically, this task has been assumed as a legacy from Christian apologetics; and it has involved, at any rate so far as European philosophy is concerned, the definition of ultimate being in such spiritual terms as make possible the relation with man postulated in Christianity. For this it has been regarded as sufficient to ascribe to the world an underlying unity capable of bearing the predicates of perfection, omnipotence, and omniscience. Each proof of God has defined him pre-eminently in terms of some one of these his attributes.

§ 88. The *ontological* proof of God held the foremost place in philosophy's contribution to

The Ontological Proof of God. Christianity up to the eighteenth century. This proof *infers the existence from the ideal* of God, and so approaches the nature of God through the attribute of perfection. It owes the form in which it was accepted in the Middle Ages and Renaissance to St. Anselm,

matters, Cf. Descartes: *Meditations, Dedication.* Translation by Veitch, p. 81.

Archbishop of Canterbury at the close of the eleventh century. He argued from the idea of a most perfect being to its existence, on the ground that non-existence, or existence only in idea, would contradict its perfection. It is evident that the force of this argument depends upon the necessity of the idea of God. The argument was accepted in Scholastic Philosophy[15] largely because of the virtual acceptance of this necessity. Mediæval thought was under the dominance of the philosophical ideas of Plato and Aristotle, and through them rationalism had come to be the unquestioned starting-point for all thought. For Plato reality and rationality meant one and the same thing, so that the ultimate reality was the highest principle of rationality, which he conceived to be the idea of the good. In the case of Aristotle the ideal of rationality was conceived to determine the course of the cosmical evolution as its immanent final cause. But in itself it was beyond the world, or transcendent. For Plato perfection itself is reality, whereas for Aristotle perfection determines the hierarchical order of natural substances. The latter theory, more suitable to the uses of Chris-

---

[15] The school-philosophy that flourished from the eleventh to the fifteenth century, under the authority of the church.

tianity, because it distinguished between God and the world, was incorporated into the great school systems. But both theories contain the essence of the ontological proof of God. In thought one seeks the perfect truth, and posits it as at once the culmination of insight and the meaning of life. The ideal of God is therefore a necessary idea, because implied in all the effort of thought as the object capable of finally satisfying it. St. Anselm adds little to the force of this argument, and does much to obscure its real significance.

In stating the ontological argument the term perfection has been expressly emphasized, because it may be taken to embrace both truth and goodness. Owing to a habit of thought, due in the main to Plato, it was long customary to regard degrees of truth and goodness as interchangeable, and as equivalent to degrees of reality. The *ens realissimum* was in its completeness the highest object both of the faculty of cognition and of the moral will. But even in the scholastic period these two different aspects of the ideal were clearly recognized, and led to sharply divergent tendencies. More recently they have been divided and embodied in separate arguments. *The epistemological* argument *defines God in terms of that abso-*

lute truth which is referred to in every judgment. Under the influence of idealism this absolute truth has taken the form of a universal mind, or all-embracing standard experience, called more briefly the absolute. The *ethical* argument, on the other hand, conceives God as *the perfect goodness implied in the moral struggle,* or *the power through which goodness is made to triumph in the universe* to the justification of moral faith. While the former of these arguments identifies God with being, the latter defines God in terms of the intent or outcome of being. Thus, while the epistemological argument does not distinguish God and the world, the latter does so, assuming that independent reality can be attributed to the stages of a process and to the purpose that dominates it.

§ 89. The *cosmological* proof of God approaches him through the attribute of creative omnipotence.

The Cosmo- The common principle of causal ex-
logical Proof
of God. planation refers the origin of natural events to similar antecedent events. But there must be some *first cause* from which the whole series is derived, a cause which is ultimate, sufficient to itself, and the responsible author of the world. Because God's function as creator was a part of the Christian teaching, and because expla-

nation by causes is habitual with common sense, this argument has had great vogue. But in philosophy it has declined in importance, chiefly because it has been absorbed in arguments which deal with the *kind* of causality proper to a first cause or world-ground. The argument that follows is a case in point.

§ 90. The *teleological* proof argues that the world can owe its origin only to an *intelligent first cause.* The evidence for this is fur-

The Teleological Proof of God.

nished by the cunning contrivances and beneficent adaptations of nature. These could not have come about through chance or the working of mechanical forces, but only through the foresight of a rational will. This argument originally infers God from the character of nature and history; and the extension of mechanical principles to organic and social phenomena, especially as stimulated by Darwin's principle of natural selection, has tended greatly to diminish its importance. When, on the other hand, for nature and history there are substituted the intellectual and moral activities themselves, and the inference is made to the ideal which they imply, the teleological argument merges into the ontological. But the old-fashioned statement of it remains in the form of religious faith, and in this capacity it has had the approval even of Hume and Kant, the philosophers who have contributed most forcibly to its overthrow as a demonstration of God. They agree that the *acknowledgment* of God in nature and history is the sequel to a theistic belief, and an inevitable attitude on the part of the religious consciousness.

§ 91. Another group of ideas belonging to philosophical theology consists of three generalizations

God and the World. Theism and Pantheism.

respecting God's relation to the world, known as *theism, pantheism,* and *deism.* Although, theoretically, these are corollaries of the different arguments for God, two of them, theism and pantheism, owe their importance to their rivalry as religious tendencies. *Theism* emphasizes that attitude to God which recognizes in him an historical personage, in some sense distinct from both the world and man, which are his works and yet stand in an external relationship to him. It expresses the spirit of ethical and monotheistic religion, and is therefore the natural belief of the Christian. *Pantheism* appears in primitive religion as an animistic or polytheistic sense of the presence of a divine principle diffused throughout nature. But it figures most notably

in the history of religions, in the highly reflective
Brahmanism of India. In sharp opposition to
Christianity, this religion preaches the indivisible
unity of the world and the illusoriness of the individual's sense of his own independent reality.
In spite of the fact that such a doctrine is alien
to the spirit of Christianity, it enters into Christian theology through the influence of philosophy.
The theoretical idea of God tends, as we have seen,
to the identification of him with the world as its
most real principle. Or it bestows upon him a
nature so logical and formal, and so far removed
from the characters of humanity, as to forbid his
entering into personal or social relations. Such
reflections concerning God find their religious expression in a mystical sense of unity, which has in
many cases either entirely replaced or profoundly
modified the theistic strain in Christianity. In
current philosophy pantheism appears in the epistemological argument which identifies God with
being; while the chief bulwark of theism is the
ethical argument, with its provision for a distinction between the actual world and ideal principle
of evolution.

§ 92. While theism and pantheism appear to be
permanent phases in the philosophy of religion,

deism is the peculiar product of the eighteenth cen-
Deism.   tury. It is based upon a repudia-
tion of supernaturalism and " enthusiasm," on the
one hand, and a literal acceptance of the cosmological and teleological proofs on the other. Religions, like all else, were required, in this epoch
of clear thinking, to submit to the canons of experimental observation and practical common sense.
These authorize only a *natural religion*, the acknowledgment in pious living of a God who, having contrived this natural world, has given it over
to the rule, not of priests and prophets, but of
natural law. The artificiality of its conception of
God, and the calculating spirit of its piety, make
deism a much less genuine expression of the religious experience than either the moral chivalry
of theism or the intellectual and mystical exaltation of pantheism.

§ 93. The systematic development of philosophy
leads to the inclusion of conceptions of God within
Metaphysics   the problem of metaphysics, and the
and Theology. subordination of the proof of God to
the determination of the fundamental principle of
reality. There will always remain, however, an
outstanding theological discipline, whose function
it is to interpret worship, or the living religious

attitude, in terms of the theoretical principles of philosophy.

§ 94. *Psychology is the theory of the soul.* As we have already seen, the rise of scepticism directs

Psychology is the Theory of the Soul.
attention from the object of thought to the thinker, and so emphasizes the self as a field for theoretical investigation. But the original and the dominating interest in the self is a practical one. The precept, γνῶθι σεαυτόν, has its deepest justification in the concern for the salvation of one's soul. In primitive and half-instinctive belief the self is recognized in practical relations. In its animistic phase this belief admitted of such relations with all living creatures, and extended the conception of life very generally to natural processes. Thus in the beginning the self was doubtless indistinguishable from the vital principle. In the first treatise on psychology, the "περὶ Ψυχῆς" of Aristotle, this interpretation finds a place in theoretical philosophy. For Aristotle the soul is the *entelechy* of the body—that function or activity which makes a man of it. He recognized, furthermore, three stages in this activity: the nutritive, sensitive, and rational souls, or the vegetable, animal, and distinctively human natures, respectively. The rational soul, in its

own proper activity, is man's highest prerogative, the soul to be saved. By virtue of it man rises above bodily conditions, and lays hold on the divine and eternal. But Plato, who, as we have seen, was ever ready to grant reality to the ideal apart from the circumstances of its particular embodiment, had already undertaken to demonstrate the immortality of the soul on the ground of its distinctive nature.[16] According to his way of thinking, the soul's essentially moral nature made it incapable of destruction through the operation of natural causes. It is evident, then, that there were already ideas in vogue capable of interpreting the Christian teaching concerning the existence of a soul, or of an inner essence of man capable of being made an object of divine interest.

§ 95. The immediate effect of Christianity was to introduce into philosophy as one of its cardinal

Spiritual Substance

doctrines the theory of a spiritual being, constituting the true self of the individual, and separable from the body. The difference recognized in Plato and Aristotle between the divine spark and the appetitive and perceptual parts of human nature was now emphasized. The former (frequently called the " spirit," to distin-

[16] Especially in the *Phœdo.*

guish it from the lower soul) was defined as a
substance having the attributes of thought and
will. The fundamental argument for its existence
was the immediate appeal to self-consciousness;
and it was further defined as indestructible on
the ground of its being utterly discontinuous and
incommensurable with its material environment.
This theory survives at the present day in the conception of pure activity, but on the whole the attributes of the soul have superseded its substance.

§ 96. *Intellectualism and voluntarism* are the
two rival possibilities of emphasis when the soul is
Intellectualism defined in terms of its known activities.
and Voluntar-
ism.   Wherever the essence of personality is
in question, as also occurs in the case of theology,
thought and will present their respective claims
to the place of first importance. *Intellectualism
would make will merely the concluding phase of
thought, while voluntarism would reduce thought
to one of the interests of a general appetency.* It
is evident that idealistic theories will be much
concerned with this question of priority. It is
also true, though less evident, that intellectualism,
since it emphasizes the general and objective
features of the mind, tends to subordinate the
individual to the universal; while voluntarism,

emphasizing desire and action, is relatively individualistic, and so, since there are many individuals, also pluralistic.[17]

§ 97. The question of the *freedom of the will* furnishes a favorite controversial topic in philos-

Freedom of the Will. Necessitarianism, Determinism, and Indeterminism. ophy. For the interest at stake is no less than the individual's responsibility before man and God for his good or bad works. It bears alike upon science, religion, and philosophy, and is at the same time a question of most fundamental practical importance. But this diffusion of the problem has led to so considerable a complication of it that it becomes necessary in outlining it to define two issues. In the first place, the concept of freedom is designed to express generally the distinction between man and the rest of nature. To make man in all respects *the product and creature of his natural environment* would be to deny freedom and accept the radically *necessitarian* doctrine. The question still remains, however, as to the causes which dominate man. He may be free from nature, and yet be ruled by God, or by distinctively spiritual causes, such as ideas or character. Where in general the will is regarded as submitting only to a

[17] Schopenhauer is a notable exception. Cf. §§ 135, 138.

spiritual causation proper to its own realm, the conception is best named *determinism;* though in the tradition of philosophy it is held to be a doctrine of freedom, because contrasted with the necessitarianism above defined. There remains *indeterminism,* which attributes to the will a spontaneity that makes possible the *direct presence to it of genuine alternatives.* The issue may here coincide with that between intellectualism and voluntarism. If, *e.g.,* in God's act of creation, his ideals and standards are prior to his fiat, his conduct is determined; whereas it is free in the radical or indeterministic sense if his ideals themselves are due to his sheer will. This theory involves at a certain point in action the absence of cause. On this account the free will is often identified with *chance,* in which case it loses its distinction from nature, and we have swung round the circle.

§ 98. There is similar complexity in the problem concerning *immortality.* Were the extreme Immortality. claims of naturalism to be established, Survival and Eternalism. there would be no ground whatsoever upon which to maintain the immortality of man, mere dust returning unto dust. The philosophical concept of immortality is due to the supposition that the quintessence of the individual's nature is divine.[18]   But several possibilities are at this point open to us.   The first would maintain the survival after death of a recognizable and discrete personality.   Another would suppose a preservation after death, through being taken up into the life of God.   Still another, the theory commonly maintained on the ground of rationalistic and idealistic metaphysics, would deny that immortality has to do with life after death, and affirm that it signifies the perpetual membership of the human individual in a realm of eternity through the truth or virtue that is in him.   But this interpretation evidently leaves open the question of the immortality of that which is distinctive and personal in human nature.

§ 99.   So far we have followed the fortunes only of the "spirit" of man.   What of that lower soul
The Natural Science of Psychology. Its Problems and Method. through which he is identified with the fortunes of his body?   When philosophy gradually ceased, in the sixteenth and seventeenth centuries, to be " the handmaid of religion," there arose a renewed interest in that part of human nature lying between the strictly

[18] It is interesting, however, to observe that current spiritualistic theories maintain a naturalistic theory of immortality, verifiable, it is alleged, in certain extraordinary empirical observations.

physiological functions, on the one hand, and thought and will on the other. Descartes and Spinoza analyzed what they called the " passions," meaning such states of mind as are conditioned by a concern for the interests of the body. At a later period, certain English philosophers, following Locke, traced the dependence of ideas upon the senses. Their method was that of *introspection*, or the direct examination by the individual of his own ideas, and for the sake of noting their origin and composition from simple factors. The lineal descendants of these same English philosophers defined more carefully the process of *association*, whereby the complexity and sequence of ideas are brought about, and made certain conjectures as to its dependence upon properties and transactions in the physical brain. These are the three main philosophical sources of what has now grown to be the separate *natural science of psychology*. It will be noted that there are two characteristics which all of these studies have in common. They deal with the experience of the individual as composing his own private history, and tend to attribute the specific course which this private history takes to bodily conditions. It is only recently that these investigations have ac-

quired sufficient unity and exclusiveness of aim to
warrant their being regarded as a special science.
But such is now so far the case that the psychologist of this type pursues his way quite independently of philosophy. It is true his research has
advanced considerably beyond his understanding
of its province. But it is generally recognized
that he must examine those very *factors of subjectivity* which the natural scientist otherwise
seeks to evade, and, furthermore, that he must seek
to *provide for them in nature.* He treats the inner
life in what Locke called " the plain historical
method," that is to say, instead of interpreting
and defining its ideas, he analyzes and reports
upon its content. He would not seek to justify a
moral judgment, as would ethics, or to criticise
the cogency of thought, as would logic; but only
to describe the actual state as he found it. In
order to make his data commensurable with the
phenomena of nature, he discovers or defines bodily conditions for the subjective content which he
analyzes. His fundamental principle of method
is the postulate of *psycho-physical parallelism,* according to which he assumes a *state of brain or
nervous system for every state of mind.* But in
adopting a province and a method the psychologist

foregoes finality of truth after the manner of all natural science. He deals admittedly with an aspect of experience, and his conclusions are no more adequate to the nature of the self than they are to the nature of outer objects. An admirable reference to this abstract division of experience occurs in Külpe's " Introduction to Philosophy ":

" For the developed consciousness, as for the naive, every experience is an unitary whole; and it is only the habit of abstract reflection upon experience that makes the objective and subjective worlds seem to fall apart as originally different forms of existence. Just as a plane curve can be represented in analytical geometry as the function of two variables, the abscissæ and the ordinates, without prejudice to the unitary course of the curve itself, so the world of human experience may be reduced to a subjective and an objective factor, without prejudice to its real coherence." [19]

§ 100. The problems of psychology, like those of theology, tend to disappear as independent philo-

Psychology and Philosophy. sophical topics. The ultimate nature of the self will continue to interest philosophers—more deeply, perhaps, than any aspect of experience—but their conception of it will be a corollary of their metaphysics and epistemology. The remainder of the field of the old philosophical psychology, the introspective and experimental

[19] Translation by Pillsbury and Titchener, p. 59,

analysis of special states of mind, is already the province of a natural science which is becoming more and more free from the stand-point and method of philosophy.

§ 101. Reminding ourselves anew that philosophical problems cannot be treated in isolation

Transition from Classification by Problems to Classification by Doctrines. Naturalism. Subjectivism. Absolute Idealism. Absolute Realism.
from one another, we shall hereinafter seek to become acquainted with general stand-points that give systematic unity to the issues which have been enumerated. Such stand-points are not clearly defined by those who occupy them, and they afford no clear-cut classification of all historical philosophical philosophies. But system-making in philosophy is commonly due to the moving in an individual mind of some most significant idea; and certain of these ideas have reappeared so frequently as to define more or less clearly marked tendencies, or continuous strands, out of which the history of thought is forever weaving itself. Such is clearly the case with *naturalism*. From the beginning until now there have been men whose philosophy is a summation of the natural sciences, whose entire thought is based upon an acceptance of the methods and the fundamental conceptions

of these disciplines. This tendency stands in the history of thought for the conviction that the visible and tangible world which interacts with the body is veritable reality. This philosophy is realistic and empirical to an extent entirely determined by its belief concerning being. But while naturalism is only secondarily epistemological, *subjectivism* and *absolute idealism* have their very source in the self-examination and the self-criticism of thought. Subjectivism signifies the conviction that the knower cannot escape himself. If reality is to be kept within the range of possible knowledge, it must be defined in terms of the processes or states of selves. *Absolute idealism* arises from a union of this epistemological motive with a recognition of what are regarded as the logical necessities to which reality must submit. Reality must be both knowledge and rational knowledge; the object, in short, of an absolute mind, which shall be at once all-containing and systematic. This rationalistic motive was, however, not originally associated with an idealistic epistemology, but with the common-sense principle that being is discovered and not constituted by thought. Such an *absolute realism* is, like naturalism, primarily metaphysical rather than epistemological; but, unlike naturalism, it seeks to define reality as a logical or ethical necessity.

Under these several divisions, then, we shall meet once more with the special problems of philosophy, but this time they will be ranged in an order that is determined by some central doctrine. They will appear as parts not of the general problem of philosophy, but of some definite system of philosophy.

PART III

SYSTEMS OF PHILOSOPHY

CHAPTER VIII

NATURALISM [1]

§ 102. THE meaning conveyed by any philosophical term consists largely of the distinctions
which it suggests. Its peculiar qual-
ity, like the physiognomy of the battle-
scarred veteran, is a composite of the controversies
which it has survived. There is, therefore, an
almost unavoidable confusion attendant upon the
denomination of any early phase of philosophy as
materialism. But in the historical beginnings of
thought, as also in the common-sense of all ages,
there is at any rate present a very essential strand
of this theory. The naive habit of mind which,
in the sixth century before Christ, prompted successive Greek thinkers to define reality in terms

The General Meaning of Materialism.

[1] PRELIMINARY NOTE. — By *naturalism* is meant that
system of philosophy which defines the universe in the
terms of *natural science*. In its dogmatic phase, wherein it
maintains that *being is corporeal*, it is called *materialism*.
In its critical phase, wherein it makes the general assertion
that the natural sciences constitute the only *possible knowledge*, whatever be the nature of reality itself, it is called
positivism, agnosticism, or simply *naturalism*.

of water, air, and fire, is in this respect one with
that exhibited in Dr. Samuel Johnson's smiting
the ground with his stick in curt refutation of
Bishop Berkeley's idea-philosophy. There is a
theoretical instinct, not accidental or perverse, but
springing from the very life-preserving equipment
of the organism, which attributes reality to *tangible space-filling things encountered by the body.*
For obvious reasons of self-interest the organism
is first of all endowed with a sense of contact, and
the more delicate senses enter into its practical
economy as means of anticipating or avoiding
contact. From such practical expectations concerning the proximity of that which may press
upon, injure, or displace the body, arise the first
crude judgments of reality. And these are at the
same time the nucleus of naive philosophy and
the germinal phase of materialism.

§ 103. The first philosophical movement among
the Greeks was a series of attempts to reduce the
Corporeal   tangible world to unity, and of these
Being.   the conception offered by Anaximander
is of marked interest in its bearing upon the development of materialism. This philosopher is
remarkable for having *defined* his first principle,
instead of having chosen it from among the dif-

ferent elements already distinguished by common-sense. He thought the unity of nature to consist in its periodic evolution from and return into one infinite sum of material (τὸ ἄπειρον), which, much in the manner of the "nebula" of modern science, is conceived as both indeterminate in its actual state and infinitely rich in its potentiality. The conception of matter, the most familiar commonplace of science, begins to be recognizable. It has here reached the point of signifying a common substance for all tangible things, a substance that in its own general and omnipresent nature is without the special marks that distinguish these tangible things from one another. And in so far the philosophy of Anaximander is materialistic.

§ 104. But the earliest thinkers are said to be *hylozoists,* rather than strict materialists, because Corporeal of their failure to make certain distinc-Processes. Hylozoism and tions in connection with the *processes* Mechanism. of matter. The term hylozoism unites with the conception of the formless material of the world (ὕλη), that of an animating power to which its formations and transformations are due. Hylozoism itself was not a deliberate synthesis of these two conceptions, but a primitive practical tendency to universalize the conception of life.

Such " animism " instinctively associates with an object's bulk and hardness a capacity for locomotion and general initiative. And the material principles defined by the philosophers retain this vague and comprehensive attribute as a matter of course, until it is distinguished and separated through attempts to understand it.

That aspect of natural process which was most impressive to Greek minds of the reflective type was the alternation of " generation and decay." In full accord with his more ancient master, Epicurus, the Latin poet Lucretius writes:

" Thus neither can death-dealing motions keep the mastery always, nor entomb existence forevermore; nor, on the other hand, can the birth and increase giving motions of things preserve them always after they are born. Thus the war of first beginnings waged from eternity is carried on with dubious issue: now here, now there, the life-bringing elements of things get the mastery and are o'ermastered in turn: with the funeral wail blends the cry which babies raise when they enter the borders of light; and no night ever followed day, nor morning night, that heard not, mingling with the sickly infant's cries, wailings of the attendants on death and black funeral." [2]

In a similar vein, the earliest conceptions of natural evolution attributed it to the coworking of

[2] Lucretius: *De Rerum Natura*, Bk. II, lines 569–580. Translation by Munro.

two principles, that of Love or union and that of
Hate or dissolution. The process is here distinguished from the material of nature, but is still
described in the language of practical life. A
distinction between two aspects of vital phenomena
is the next step. These may be regarded in respect
either of the motion and change which attend them,
or the rationality which informs them. Life is
both effective and significant. Although neither
of these ideas ever wholly ceases to be animistic,
they may nevertheless be applied quite independently of one another. The one reduces the primitive animistic world to the lower end of its scale,
the other construes it in terms of a purposive utility commensurable with that of human action.
Now it is with *mechanism*, the former of these
diverging ways, that the development of materialism is identified. For this philosophy a thing
need have no value to justify its existence, nor any
acting intelligence to which it may owe its origin.
Its bulk and position are sufficient for its being,
and the operation of forces capable of integrating,
dividing, or moving it is sufficient for its derivation and history. In short, there is no rhyme or
reason at the heart of things, but only actual matter distributed by sheer force. With this elimina-

tion of the element of purposiveness from the hylozoistic world, the content and process of nature are fitted to one another. Matter is that which is moved by force, and force is the determining principle of the motions of matter. Materialism is now definitely equipped with its fundamental conceptions.

§ 105. The central conceptions of materialism as a philosophical theory differ from those em- ployed in the physical sciences only in what is demanded of them. The sci- entist reports upon physical phenomena without accepting any further responsibility, while those who like Lucretius maintain a physical meta- physics, must, like him, prove that " the minute bodies of matter from everlasting continually up- hold the sum of things." But, though they employ them in their own way, materialists and all other exponents of naturalism derive their central con- ceptions from the physical sciences, and so reflect the historical development through which these sciences have passed. To certain historical phases of physical science, in so far as these bear directly upon the meaning of naturalism, we now turn.

Materialism and Physical Science.

§ 106. From the earliest times down to the present day the groundwork of materialism has most commonly been cast in the form of an *atomic theory*. Democritus, the first system-builder of

The Development of the Conceptions of Physical Science. Space and Matter.

this school, adopted the conception of indivisible particles (*ἄτομοι*), impenetrable in their occupancy of space, and varying among themselves only in form, order, and position. To provide for the motion that distributes them he conceived them as separated from one another by empty space. From this it follows that the void is as real as matter, or, as Democritus himself is reputed to have said, "thing is not more real than no-thing."

But atomism has not been by any means universally regarded as the most satisfactory conception of the relation between space and matter. Not only does it require two kinds of being, with the different attributes of extension and hardness, respectively,[3] but it would also seem to be experimentally inadequate in the case of the more subtle physical processes, such as light. The former of these is a speculative consideration, and as such had no little weight with the French philosopher Descartes, whose divisions and definitions so profoundly affected the course of thought in these

[3] The reader will find an interesting account of these opposing views in Locke's chapter on *Space*, in his *Essay Concerning Human Understanding*.

matters after the sixteenth century. Holding also
" that a vacuum or space in which there is absolutely no body is repugnant to reason," and that
an indivisible space-filling particle is self-contra-
dictory, he was led to *identify space and matter;*
that is, to make matter as indispensable to space
as space to matter. There is, then, but one kind
of corporeal being, whose attribute is extension,
and whose modes are motion and rest. The most
famous application of the mechanical conceptions
which he bases upon this first principle, is his
theory of the planets, which are conceived to be
embedded in a transparent medium, and to move
with it, vortex fashion, about the sun.[4]

But the conception of the space-filling continuity
of material substance owes its prominence at the
present time to the experimental hypothesis of
ether. This substance, originally conceived to
occupy the intermolecular spaces and to serve as
a medium for the propagation of undulations, is
now regarded by many physicists as replacing
matter. " It is the great hope of science at the
present day," says a contemporary exponent of
naturalism, " that hard and heavy matter will be

---

[4] Descartes distinguished his theory from that of Democritus in the *Principles of Philosophy*, Part IV, § ccii.

shown to be ether in motion." [5] Such a theory
would reduce bodies to the relative displacements
of parts of a continuous substance, which would
be first of all defined as spacial, and would possess such further properties as special scientific
hypotheses might require.

Two broadly contrasting theories thus appear:
that which defines matter as a continuous substance coextensive with space; and that which defines it as a discrete substance divided by empty
space. But both theories are seriously affected by
the peculiarly significant development of the conception of force.

§ 107. In the Cartesian system the cause of
motion was pressure within a plenum. But in the
seventeenth century this notion encountered the system of Newton, a system
which seemed to involve action at a
distance. In the year 1728 Voltaire
wrote from London:

Motion and its Cause. Development and Extension of the Conception of Force.

"When a Frenchman arrives in London, he finds a
very great change, in philosophy as well as in most other
things. In Paris he left the world all full of matter;
here he finds absolute vacua. At Paris the universe is
seen filled up with ethereal vortices, while here the same

[5] Pearson: *Grammar of Science*, pp. 259–260. Cf. *ibid.*,
Chap. VII, entire.

space is occupied with the play of the invisible forces of gravitation. In Paris the earth is painted for us longish like an egg, and in London it is oblate like a melon. At Paris the pressure of the moon causes the ebb and flow of tides; in England, on the other hand, the sea gravitates toward the moon, so that at the same time when the Parisians demand high water of the moon, the gentlemen of London require an ebb."[6]

But these differences are not matters of taste, nor even rival hypotheses upon an equal footing. The Newtonian system of mechanics, the consummation of a development initiated by Galileo, differed from the vortex theory of Descartes as exact science differs from speculation and unverified conjecture. And this difference of method carried with it eventually certain profound differences of content, distinguishing the Newtonian theory even from that of Democritus, with which it had so much in common. Although Democritus had sought to avoid the element of purposiveness in the older hylozoism by referring the motions of bodies as far as possible to the impact of other bodies, he nevertheless attributed these motions ultimately to *weight*, signifying thereby a certain *downward disposition*. Now it is true that in his general belief Newton himself is not free from hylozoism. He thought of the motions of the

[6] Quoted in Ueberweg: *History of Philosophy*, II, p. 124.

planets themselves as initiated and quickened by a power emanating ultimately from God. They are " impressed by an intelligent Agent," and

" can be the effect of nothing else than the wisdom and skill of a powerful ever-living Agent who, being in all places, is more able by his will to move the bodies within his boundless uniform *sensorium*, and thereby to form and reform the parts of the universe, than we are by our will to move the parts of our own bodies." [7]

But by the side of these statements must be set his famous disclaimer, " *hypotheses non fingo.*" In his capacity of natural philosopher he did not seek to explain motions, but only to describe them. Disbelieving as he did in action at a distance, he saw no possibility of explanation short of a reference of them to God; but such " hypotheses " he thought to be no proper concern of science. As a consequence, the mathematical formulation of motions came, through him, to be regarded as the entire content of mechanics. The notion of an efficient cause of motion is still suggested by the term *force,* but even this term within the system of mechanics refers always to a definite amount of motion, or measurement of relative motion. And the same is true of *attraction, action,*

[7] Quoted from the *Opticks* of Newton by James Ward, in his *Naturalism and Agnosticism*, I, p. 43.

reaction, and the like. The further explanation
of motion, the definition of a virtue or potency
that produces it, first a neglected problem, then an
irrelevant problem, is finally, for a naturalistic
philosophy in which this progression is completed,
an insoluble problem. For the sequel to this
purely descriptive procedure on the part of science
is the disavowal of " metaphysics " by those who
will have no philosophy but science. Thus the
scientific conservatism of Newton has led to the
positivistic and agnostic phase of naturalism. But
a further treatment of this development must be
reserved until the issue of epistemology shall have
been definitely raised.

A different emphasis within the general mechanical scheme, attaching especial importance to the
conceptions of force and energy, has led to a rival
tendency in science and a contrasting type of naturalism. The mechanical hypotheses hitherto described are all of a simple and readily depicted
type. They suggest an imagery quite in accord
with common-sense and with observation of the
motions of great masses like the planets. Material
particles are conceived to move within a contain-
ing space; the motions of corpuscles, atoms, or the
minute parts of ether, differing only in degree

from those of visible bodies. The whole physical universe may be represented in the imagination as an aggregate of bodies participating in motions of extraordinary complexity, but of one type. But now let the emphasis be placed upon the determining causes rather than upon the moving bodies themselves. In other words, let the bodies be regarded as attributive and the forces as substantive. The result is a radical alteration of the mechanical scheme and the transcendence of common-sense imagery. This was one direction of outgrowth from the work of Newton. His force of gravitation prevailed between bodies separated by spaces of great magnitude. Certain of the followers of Newton, notably Cotes, accepting the formulas of the master but neglecting his allusions to the agency of God, accepted the principle of action at a distance. *Force, in short, was conceived to pervade space of itself.* But if force be granted this substantial and self-dependent character, what further need is there of matter as a separate form of entity? For does not the presence of matter consist essentially in resistance, itself a case of force? Such reflections as these led Boscovich and others to the radical departure of defining material particles *as centres of force.*

§ 108. But a more fruitful hypothesis of the same general order is due to the attention directed

The Development and Extension of the Conception of Energy.

to the conception of *energy*, or capacity for work, by experimental discoveries of the possibility of reciprocal transformations without loss, of motion, heat, electricity, and other processes. The principle of the conservation of energy affirms the quantitative constancy of that which is so transformed, measured, for example, in terms of capacity to move units of mass against gravity. The exponents of what is called " energetics " have in many cases come to regard that the quantity of which is so conserved, as a substantial reality whose forms and distributions compose nature. A contemporary scientist, whose synthetic and dogmatic habit of mind has made him eminent in the ranks of popular philosophy, writes as follows:

"Mechanical and chemical energy, sound and heat, light and electricity, are mutually convertible; they seem to be but different modes of one and the same fundamental force or *energy*. Thence follows the important thesis of the unity of all natural forces, or, as it may also be expressed, the 'monism of energy.'" [8]

[8] Haeckel: *Riddle of the Universe*. Translation by McCabe, p. 254.
The best systematic presentation of " energetics " is to be found in Ostwald's *Vorlesungen über Natur-Philosophie*.

The conception of energy seems, indeed, to afford an exceptional opportunity to naturalism. We have seen that the matter-motion theory was satisfied to ignore, or regard as insoluble, problems concerning the ultimate causes of things. Furthermore, as we shall presently see to better advantage, the more strictly materialistic type of naturalism must regard thought as an anomaly, and has no little difficulty with life. But the conception of energy is more adaptable, and hence better qualified to serve as a common denominator for various aspects of experience. The very readiness with which we can picture the corpuscular scheme is a source of embarrassment to the seeker after unity. That which is so distinct is bristling with incompatibilities. The most aggressive materialist hesitates to describe thought as a motion of bodies in space. Energy, on the other hand, exacts little if anything beyond the character of measurable power. Thought is at any rate in some sense a power, and to some degree measurable. Recent discoveries of the dependence of capacity for mental exertion upon physical vitality and measurements of chemical energy received into the system

Herbert Spencer, in his well-known *First Principles*, makes philosophical use of both "force" and "energy."

as food, and somehow exhausted by the activities
of thought, have lent plausibility to the hypothesis
of a universal energy of which physical and " psychical " processes are alike manifestations. And
the conception of energy seems capable not only
of unifying nature, but also of satisfying the
metaphysical demand for an efficient and moving
cause. This term, like " force " and " power," is
endowed with such a significance by common
sense. Indeed, naturalism would seem here to
have swung round toward its hylozoistic starting-
point. The exponent of energetics, like the naïve
animistic thinker, attributes to nature a power like
that which he feels welling up within himself.
When he acts upon the environment, like meets
like. Energetics, it is true, may obtain a definite
meaning for its central conception from the measurable behavior of external bodies, and a meaning
that may be quite free from vitalism or teleology.
But in his extension of the conception the author
of a philosophical energetics abandons this strict
meaning, and blends his thought even with a phase
of subjectivism, known as *panpsychism*.[9] This
theory regards the inward life of all nature as
homogeneous with an immediately felt activity or

[9] Cf. Chap. IX.

appetency, as energetics finds the inner life to be homogeneous with the forces of nature. Both owe their philosophical appeal to their apparent success in unifying the world upon a direct empirical basis, and to their provision for the practical sense of reality.

Such, in brief, are the main alternatives available for a naturalistic theory of being, in consequence of the historical development of the fundamental conceptions of natural science.

§ 109. We turn now to an examination of the manner in which naturalism, equipped with working principles, seeks to meet the special requirements of philosophy. The conception of the unity of nature is directly in the line of a purely scientific development, but naturalism takes the bold and radical step of regarding nature so unified as coextensive with the real, or at any rate knowable, universe. It will be remembered that among the early Greeks Anaxagoras had referred the creative and formative processes of nature to a non-natural or rational agency, which he called the *Nous*. The adventitious character of this principle, the external and almost purely nominal part which it played in the actual cosmology of Anaxagoras, betrayed it into the hands

The Claims of Naturalism.

of the atomists, with their more consistently naturalistic creed. Better, these maintain, the somewhat dogmatic extension of conceptions proved to
be successful in the description of nature, than a
vague dualism which can serve only to distract the
scientific attention and people the world with ob-
scurities. There is a remarkable passage in Lucretius in which atomism is thus written large and
inspired with cosmical eloquence:

" For verily not by design did the first-beginnings of
things station themselves each in its right place guided
by keen intelligence, nor did they bargain sooth to say
what motions each should assume, but because many in
number and shifting about in many ways throughout
the universe, they are driven and tormented by blows
during infinite time past, after trying motions and unions
of every kind at length they fall into arrangements such
as those out of which our sum of things has been formed,
and by which too it is preserved through many great
years, when once it has been thrown into the appropriate
motions, and causes the streams to replenish the greedy
sea with copious river waters, and the earth, fostered by
the heat of the sun, to renew its produce, and the race of
living things to come up and flourish, and the gliding
fires of ether to live: all which these several things could
in no wise bring to pass, unless a store of matter could
rise up from infinite space, out of which store they are
wont to make up in due season whatever has been lost." [10]

The prophecy of La Place, the great French
mathematician, voices the similar faith of the

[10] Lucretius: *Op. cit.*, Bk. I, lines 1021–1237.

eighteenth century in a mechanical understanding
of the universe:

"The human mind, in the perfection it has been able
to give to astronomy, affords a feeble outline of such an
intelligence.   Its discoveries in mechanics and in geometry, joined to that of universal gravitation, have brought
it within reach of comprehending in the same analytical
expressions the past and future states of the system of
the world." [11]

As for God, the creative and presiding intelligence,
La Place had " no need of any such hypothesis."

§ 110. But these are the boasts of Homeric
heroes before going into battle.   The moment

The Task of such a general position is assumed there
Naturalism. arise sundry difficulties in the application of naturalistic principles to special interests
and groups of facts.   It is one thing to project a
mechanical scheme in the large, but quite another
to make explicit provision within it for the origin
of nature, for life, for the human self with its
ideals, and for society with its institutions.   The
naturalistic method of meeting these problems involves a reduction all along the line in the direction of such categories as are derived from the
infra-organic world.   That which is not like the

[11] Quoted from La Place's essay on *Probability* by Ward:
Op. cit., I, p. 41.

planetary system must be construed as mechanical by indirection and subtlety.

§ 111. The origin of the present known natural world was the first philosophical question to be

The Origin of the Cosmos.

definitely met by science. The general form of solution which naturalism offers is anticipated in the most ancient theories of nature. These already suppose that the observed mechanical processes of the circular or periodic type, like the revolutions and rotations of the stars, are incidents in a historical mechanical process of a larger scale. Prior to the present fixed motions of the celestial bodies, the whole mass of cosmic matter participated in irregular motions analogous to present terrestrial redistributions. Such motions may be understood to have resulted in the integration of separate bodies, to which they at the same time imparted a rotary motion. It is such a hypothesis that Lucretius paints in his bold, impressionistic colors.

But the development of mechanics paved the way for a definite scientific theory, the so-called " nebular hypothesis," announced by La Place in 1796, and by the philosopher Kant at a still earlier date. Largely through the Newtonian principle of the parallelogram of forces, the present masses, orbits, and velocities were analyzed into a more primitive process of concentration within a nebulous or highly diffused aggregate of matter. And with the aid of the principle of the conservation of energy this theory appears to make possible the derivation of heat, light, and other apparently non-mechanical processes from the same original energy of motion.

But a persistently philosophical mind at once raises the question of the origin of this primeval nebula itself, with a definite organization and a vast potential energy that must, after all, be regarded as a part of nature rather than its source. Several courses are here open to naturalism. It may maintain that the question of ultimate origin is unanswerable; it may regard such a process of concentration as extending back through an infinitely long past; [12] or, and this is the favorite alternative for more constructive minds, the historical cosmical process may be included within a still higher type of periodic process, which is regarded as eternal. This last course has been followed in the well-known synthetic naturalism of Herbert Spencer. " Evolution," he says, " is the

[12] An interesting account and criticism of such a theory (Clifford's) is to be found in Royce's *Spirit of Modern Philosophy*, Lecture X.

progressive integration of matter and dissipation of motion." But such a process eventually runs down, and may be conceived as giving place to a counter-process of devolution which scatters the parts of matter and gathers another store of potential motion. The two processes in alternation will then constitute a cosmical system without beginning or end.

In such wise a sweeping survey of the physical universe may be thought in the terms of natural science. The uniformitarian method in geology, resolving the history of the crust of the earth into known processes, such as erosion and igneous fusion; [13] and spectral analysis, with its discoveries concerning the chemical constituents of distant bodies through the study of their light, have powerfully reënforced this effort of thought, and apparently completed an outline sketch of the universe in terms of infra-organic processes.

§ 112. But the cosmos must be made internally homogeneous in these same terms. There awaits

Life.
Natural
Selection.
solution, in the first place, the serious problem of the genesis and maintenance of *life* within a nature that is originally and ulti-

[13] This method replaced the old theory of " catastrophes" through the efforts of the English geologists, Hutton (1726–1797) and Lyell (1767–1849).

mately inorganic. The assimilation of the field of
biology and physiology to the mechanical cosmos
had made little real progress prior to the nineteenth century. Mechanical theories had, indeed,
been projected in the earliest age of philosophy,
and proposed anew in the seventeenth century.[14]
Nevertheless, the structural and functional teleology of the organism remained as apparently
irrefutable testimony to the inworking of some
principle other than that of mechanical necessity.
Indeed, the only fruitful method applicable to
organic phenomena was that which explained them
in terms of purposive adaptation. And it was its
provision for a mechanical interpretation of this
very principle that gave to the Darwinian *law of
natural selection*, promulgated in 1859 in the
" Origin of Species," so profound a significance
for naturalism. It threatened to reduce the last
stronghold of teleology, and completely to dispense
with the intelligent Author of nature.

Darwin's hypothesis sought to explain the origin
of animal species by survival under competitive
conditions of existence through the possession of
a structure suited to the environment. Only the

[14] Harvey's discovery of the circulation of the blood,
published in 1628, was regarded as a step in this direction.

most elementary organism need be presupposed, together with slight variations in the course of subsequent generations, and both may be conceived to arise mechanically. There will then result in surviving organisms a gradual accumulation of such variations as promote survival under the special conditions of the environment. Such a principle had been suggested as early as the time of Empedocles, but it remained for Darwin to establish it with an unanswerable array of observation and experimentation. If any organism whatsoever endowed with the power of generation be allowed to have somehow come to be, naturalism now promises to account for the whole subsequent history of organic phenomena and the origin of any known species.

§ 113. But what of life itself? The question of the derivation of organic from inorganic matter

Mechanical Physiology.

has proved insoluble by direct means, and the case of naturalism must here rest upon such facts as the chemical homogeneity of these two kinds of matter, and the conformity of physiological processes to more general physical laws. Organic matter differs from inorganic only through the presence of proteid, a peculiar product of known elements, which cannot be artificially produced, but which is by natural means perpetually dissolved into these elements without any discoverable residuum. Respiration may be studied as a case of aerodynamics, the circulation of the blood as a case of hydrodynamics, and the heat given off in the course of work done by the body as a case of thermodynamics. And although vitalistic theories still retain a place in physiology, as do teleological theories in biology, on the whole the naturalistic programme of a reduction of organic processes to the type of the inorganic tends to prevail.

§ 114. The history of naturalism shows that, as in the case of life, so also in the case of *mind,* its hypotheses were projected by the Greeks, but precisely formulated and verified only in the modern period of science. In the philosophy of Democritus the soul was itself an atom, finer, rounder, and smoother than the ordinary, but thoroughly a part of the mechanism of nature. The processes of the soul are construed as interactions between the soul and surrounding objects. In sensation, the thing perceived produces images by means of effluxes which impinge upon the soul-atom. These images are not true reports of the outer world, but must be revised by

Mind.
The Reduction to Sensation.

thought before its real atomic structure emerges. For this higher critical exercise of thought Democritus devised no special atomic genesis. The result may be expressed either as the invalidity of such operations of mind as he could provide for in his universe, or the irreducibility to his chosen first principles of the very thought which defined them. Later naturalism has generally sacrificed epistemology to cosmology, and reduced thought to sensation. Similarly, will has been regarded as a highly developed case of instinct. Knowledge and will, construed as sensation and instinct, may thus be interpreted in the naturalistic manner within the field of biology.

§ 115. But the actual content of sensation, and the actual feelings which attend upon the prompt-
Automatism. ings of instinct, still stubbornly testify to the presence in the universe of something belonging to a wholly different category from matter and motion. The attitude of naturalism in this crucial issue has never been fixed and unwavering, but there has gradually come to predominate a method of denying to the inner life all efficacy and real significance in the cosmos, while admitting its presence on the scene. It is a strange fact of history that Descartes, the French philosopher who

prided himself on having rid the soul of all
dependence on nature, should have greatly contributed to this method. But it is perhaps not so
strange when we consider that every dualism is,
after all, symmetrical, and that consequently whatever rids the soul of nature at the same time rids
nature of the soul. It was Descartes who first conceived the body and soul to be utterly distinct
substances. The corollary to this doctrine was his
automatism, applied in his own system to animals
other than man, but which those less concerned
with religious tradition and less firmly convinced
of the soul's originating activity were not slow to
apply universally. This theory conceived the vital
processes to take place quite regardless of any
inner consciousness, or even without its attendance.
To this radical theory the French materialists of
the eighteenth century were especially attracted.
With them the active soul of Descartes, the distinct
spiritual entity, disappeared. This latter author
had himself admitted a department of the self,
which he called the " passions," in which the
course and content of mind is determined by bodily conditions. Extending this conception to the
whole province of mind, they employed it to demonstrate the thorough-going subordination of mind

to body. La Mettrie, a physician and the author
of a book entitled " L'Homme Machine," was first
interested in this thesis by a fever delirium, and
afterward adduced anatomical and pathological
data in support of it. The angle from which he
views human life is well illustrated in the following:

" What would have sufficed in the case of Julius Cæsar,
of Seneca, of Petronius, to turn their fearlessness into
timidity or braggartry? An obstruction in the spleen,
the liver, or the *vena portæ*. For the imagination is
intimately connected with these viscera, and from them
arise all the curious phenomena of hypochondria and
hysteria. . . . 'A mere nothing, a little fibre, some
trifling thing that the most subtle anatomy cannot discover, would have made two idiots out of Erasmus and
Fontenelle.'" [15]

§ 116. The extreme claim that the soul is a
physical organ of the body, identical with the
brain, marked the culmination of this
militant materialism, so good an instance of that over-simplification and
whole-hearted conviction characteristic of the doc-
trinaire propagandism of France. Locke, the Eng-
lishman, had admitted that possibly the substance
which thinks is corporeal. In the letters of Vol-

Radical
Materialism.
Mind as an
Epiphenome-
non.

[15] From the account of La Mettrie in Lange: *History of
Materialism*. Translation by Thomas, II, pp. 67–68.

taire this thought has already found a more positive expression:

"I am body, and I think; more I do not know. Shall I then attribute to an unknown cause what I can so easily attribute to the only fruitful cause I am acquainted with? In fact, where is the man who, without an absurd godlessness, dare assert that it is impossible for the Creator to endow matter with thought and feeling?"[16]

Finally, Holbach, the great systematizer of this movement, takes the affair out of the hands of the Creator and definitively announces that "a sensitive soul is nothing but a human brain so constituted that it easily receives the motions communicated to it."[17]

This theory has been considerably tempered since the age of Holbach. Naturalism has latterly been less interested in identifying the soul with the body, and more interested in demonstrating its dependence upon specific bodily conditions, after the manner of La Mettrie. The so-called higher faculties, such as thought and will, have been related to central or *cortical* processes of the nervous system, processes of connection and complication which within the brain itself supplement the impulses and sensations congenitally and externally

[16] Quoted from Voltaire's London *Letter on the English*, by Lange: *Op. cit.*, II, p. 18.

[17] Quoted by Lange: *Op. cit.*, II, p. 113.

stimulated. The term " epiphenomenon " has been adopted to express the distinctness but entire dependence of the mind. Man is "a conscious automaton." The real course of nature passes through his nervous system, while consciousness attends upon its functions like a shadow, present but not efficient.[18]

§ 117. Holbach's " Système de la Nature," published in 1770, marks the culmination of the un-

Knowledge. Positivism and Agnosticism. equivocally materialistic form of naturalism. Its epistemological difficulties, always more or less in evidence, have since that day sufficed to discredit materialism, and to foster the growth of a critical and apologetic form of naturalism known as *positivism* or *agnosticism*. The modesty of this doctrine does not, it is true, strike very deep. For, although it disclaims knowledge of ultimate reality, it also forbids anyone else to have any. Knowledge, it affirms, can be of but one type, that which comprises the verifiable laws governing nature. All questions concerning

[18] The phrase " psycho-physical parallelism," current in psychology, may mean automatism of the kind expounded above, and may also mean dualism. It is used commonly as a methodological principle to signify that no causal relationship between mind and body, but one of *correspondence*, is to be looked for in empirical psychology. Cf. § 99.

first causes are futile, a stimulus only to excursions of fancy popularly mistaken for knowledge. The superior certainty and stability which attaches to natural science is to be permanently secured by the savant's steadfast refusal to be led away after the false gods of metaphysics.

But though this is sufficient ground for an agnostic policy, it does prove an agnostic theory. The latter has sprung from a closer analysis of knowledge, though it fails to make a very brave showing for thoroughness and consistency. The crucial point has already been brought within our view. The general principles of naturalism require that knowledge shall be reduced to sensations, or impressions of the environment upon the organism. But the environment and the sensations do not correspond. The environment is matter and motion, force and energy; the sensations are of motions, to be sure, but much more conspicuously of colors, sounds, odors, pleasures, and pains. Critically, this may be expressed by saying that since the larger part of sense-perception is so unmistakably subjective, and since all knowledge alike must be derived from this source, knowledge as a whole must be regarded as dealing only with appearances. There are at least three agnostic

methods progressing from this point. All agree
that the inner or essential reality is unfathomable.
But, in the first place, those most close to the
tradition of materialism maintain that the most
significant appearances, the primary qualities, are
those which compose a purely quantitative and
corporeal world. The inner essence of things may
at any rate be *approached* by a monism of matter
or of energy. This theory is epistemological only
to the extent of moderating its claims in the hope
of lessening its responsibility. Another agnosticism places all sense qualities on a par, but would
regard physics and psychology as complementary
reports upon the two distinct series of phenomena
in which the underlying reality expresses itself.
This theory is epistemological to the extent of
granting knowledge, viewed as perception, as good
a standing in the universe as that which is accorded
to its object. But such a dualism tends almost
irresistibly to relapse into materialistic monism,
because of the fundamental place of physical conceptions in the system of the sciences. Finally,
in another and a more radical phase of agnosticism,
we find an attempt to make full provision for the
legitimate problems of epistemology. The only
datum, the only existent accessible to knowledge,

is said to be the sensation, or state of consciousness. In the words of Huxley:

".What, after all, do we know of this terrible 'matter' except as a name for the unknown and hypothetical cause of states of our own consciousness? And what do we know of that 'spirit' over whose threatened extinction by matter a great lamentation is arising, . . . except that it is also a name for an unknown and hypothetical cause, or condition, of states of consciousness?" [19]

The physical world is now to be regarded as a construction which does not assimilate to itself the content of sensations, but enables one to anticipate them. The sensation signifies a contact to which science can provide a key for practical guidance.

§ 118. This last phase of naturalism is an attempt to state a pure and consistent experimental-

Experimen-   ism, a workable theory of the routine of
talism.   sensations. But it commonly falls into
the error of the vicious circle. The hypothetical cause of sensations is said to be matter. From this point of view the sensation is a complex, comprising elaborate physical and physiological processes. But these processes themselves, on the other hand, are said to be analyzable into sensations. Now two such methods of analysis cannot be equally ultimate. If all of reality is finally reducible to

⁹ Quoted by Ward: *Op. cit.*, I, p. 18.

sensations, then the term sensation must be used
in a new sense to connote a self-subsistent being,
and can no longer refer merely to a function of
certain physiological processes. The issue of this
would be some form of idealism or of the experi-
ence-philosophy that is now coming so rapidly to
the front.[20] But while it is true that idealism
has sometimes been intended, and that a radically
new philosophy of experience has sometimes been
closely approached, those, nevertheless, who have
developed experimentalism from the naturalistic
stand-point have in reality achieved only a thinly
disguised materialism. For *the very ground of
their agnosticism is materialistic.*[21] Knowledge
of reality itself is said to be unattainable, because
knowledge, in order to come within the order of
nature, must be regarded as reducible to sensation;
and because sensation itself, when regarded as a
part of nature, is only a physiological process, a
special phenomenon, in no way qualified to be
knowledge that is true of reality.

§ 119. Perhaps, after all, it would be as fair to
the spirit of naturalism to relieve it of responsibil-

[20] There are times when Huxley, *e. g.*, would seem to be
on the verge of the Berkeleyan idealism. Cf. Chap. IX.

[21] For the case of Karl Pearson, read his *Grammar of
Science*, Chap. II.

ity for an epistemology. It has never thoroughly reckoned with this problem. It has deliberately **Naturalistic** selected from among the elements of ex-**Epistemology not Systematic.** perience, and been so highly construc- tive in its method as to forfeit its claim to pure empiricism; and, on the other hand, has, in this same selection of categories and in its insistence upon the test of experiment, fallen short of a thor- ough-going rationalism. While, on the one hand, it defines and constructs, it does so, on the other hand, within the field of perception and with con- stant reference to the test of perception. The ex- planation and justification of this procedure is to be found in the aim of natural science rather than in that of philosophy. It is this special interest, rather than the general problem of being, that de- termines the order of its categories. Naturalism as an account of reality is acceptable only so far as its success in satisfying specific demands obtains for it a certain logical immunity. These demands are unquestionably valid and fundamental, but they are not coextensive with the demand for truth. They coincide rather with the immediate practical need of a formulation of the spacial and temporal changes that confront the will. Hence naturalism is acceptable to common-sense as an account of

what the every-day attitude to the environment
treats as its object. Naturalism is common-sense
about the " outer world," revised and brought up
to date with the aid of the results of science. Its
deepest spring is the organic instinct for the reality
of the tangible, the vital recognition of the significance of that which is on the plane of interaction
with the body.

§ 120. Oddly enough, although common-sense is
ready to intrust to naturalism the description of
General   the situation of life, it prefers to deal
Ethical
Stand-point.   otherwise with its ideals. Indeed, common-sense is not without a certain suspicion that
naturalism is the advocate of moral reversion. It
is recognized as the prophecy of the brute majority
of life, of those considerations of expediency and
pleasure that are the warrant for its secular moods
rather than for its sustaining ideals. And that
strand of life is indeed its special province. For
the naturalistic method of reduction must find the
key to human action among those practical conditions that are common to man and his inferiors
in the scale of being. In short, human life,
like all life, must be construed as the adjustment
of the organism to its natural environment for

the sake of preservation and economic advancement.

§ 121. Early in Greek philosophy this general idea of life was picturesquely interpreted in two
Cynicism and Cyrenaicism. contrasting ways, those of the Cynic and the Cyrenaic. Both of these wise men postulated the spiritual indifference of the universe at large, and looked only to the *contact* of life with its immediate environment. But while the one hoped only to hedge himself about, the other sought confidently the gratification of his sensibilities. The figure of the Cynic is the more familiar. Diogenes of the tub practised self-mortification until his dermal and spiritual callousness were alike impervious. From behind his protective sheath he could without affectation despise both nature and society. He could reckon himself more blessed than Alexander, because, with demand reduced to the minimum, he could be sure of a surplus of supply. Having renounced all goods save the bare necessities of life, he could neglect both promises and threats and be played upon by no one. He was securely intrenched within himself, an unfurnished habitation, but the citadel of a king. The Cyrenaic, on the other hand, did not seek to make impervious the surface

of contact with nature and society, but sought to heighten its sensibility, that it might become a medium of pleasurable feeling. For the inspiration with which it may be pursued this ideal has nowhere been more eloquently set forth than in the pages of Walter Pater, who styles himself " the new Cyrenaic."

" Not the fruit of experience, but experience itself, is the end. A counted number of pulses only is given to us of a variegated, dramatic life. How may we see in them all that is to be seen in them by the finest senses? How shall we pass most swiftly from point to point, and be present always at the focus where the greatest number of vital forces unite in their purest energy?

To burn always with this hard, gemlike flame, to maintain this ecstacy, is success in life. . . . While all melts under our feet, we may well catch at any exquisite passion, or any contribution to knowledge that seems by a lifted horizon to set the spirit free for a moment, or any stirring of the senses, strange dyes, strange colors, and curious odors, or work of the artist's hands, or the face of one's friend. Not to discriminate every moment some passionate attitude in those about us, and in the brilliancy of their gifts some tragic dividing of forces on their ways, is, on this short day of frost and sun, to sleep before evening." [22]

§ 122. In the course of modern philosophy the ethics of naturalism has undergone a transforma-

[22] Pater: *The Renaissance*, pp. 249–250.

tion and development that equip it much more formidably for its competition with rival theories.

Development of Utilitarianism. Evolutionary Conception of Social Relations. If the Cynic and Cyrenaic philosophies of life seem too egoistic and narrow in outlook, this inadequacy has been largely overcome through the modern conception of the relation of the individual to society. Man is regarded as so dependent upon social relations that it is both natural and rational for him to govern his actions with a concern for the community. There was a time when this relation of dependence was viewed as external, a barter of goods between the individual and society, sanctioned by an implied contract. Thomas Hobbes, whose unblushing materialism and egoism stimulated by opposition the whole development of English ethics, conceived morality to consist in rules of action which condition the stability of the state, and so secure for the individual that " peace " which self-interest teaches him is essential to his welfare.

" And therefore so long a man is in the condition of mere nature, which is a condition of war, as private appetite is the measure of good and evil: and consequently all men agree on this, that peace is good, and therefore also the ways or means of peace, which, as I have showed before, are 'justice,' 'gratitude,' modesty,' 'equity,' 'mercy,' and the rest of the laws of Nature, are good; that is to say, 'moral virtues'; and their contrary 'vices,' evil." [23]

Jeremy Bentham, the apostle of utilitarianism in the eighteenth century, defined political and social sanctions through which the individual could purchase security and good repute with action conducive to the common welfare. But the nineteenth century has understood the matter better—and the idea of an evolution under conditions that select and reject, is here again the illuminating thought. No individual, evolutionary naturalism maintains, has survived the perils of life without possessing as an inalienable part of his nature, congenital like his egoism, certain impulses and instinctive desires in the interest of the community as a whole. The latest generation of a race whose perpetuation has been conditioned by a capacity to sustain social relations and make common cause against a more external environment, *is* moral, and does not adopt morality in the course of a calculating egoism. Conscience is the racial instinct of self-preservation uttering itself in the individual member, who draws his very life-blood from the greater organism.

§ 123. This latest word of naturalistic ethics has

[23] Hobbes: *Leviathan*, Chap. XV.

not won acceptance as the last word in ethics, and
this in spite of its indubitable truth within its scope.

Naturalistic Ethics not Systematic. For the deeper ethical interest seeks not
so much to account for the moral nature
as to construe and justify its promptings. The
evolutionary theory reveals the genesis of conscience, and demonstrates its continuity with nature, but this falls as far short of realizing the purpose of ethical study as a history of the natural
genesis of thought would fall short of logic. Indeed, naturalism shows here, as in the realm of
epistemology, a persistent failure to appreciate the
central problem. Its acceptance as a philosophy,
we are again reminded, can be accounted for only
on the score of its genuinely rudimentary character. As a rudimentary phase of thought it
is both indispensable and inadequate. It is the
philosophy of instinct, which should in normal
development precede a philosophy of reason, in
which it is eventually assimilated and supplemented.

§ 124. There is, finally, an inspiration for life
which this philosophy of naturalism may convey—

Naturalism as Antagonistic to Religion. atheism, its detractors would call it, but
none the less a faith and a spiritual ex-
altation that spring from its summing up of truth.

It is well first to realize that which is dispiriting in it, its failure to provide for the freedom, immortality, and moral providence of the more sanguine faith.

"For what is man looked at from this point of view? . . . Man, so far as natural science by itself is able to teach us, is no longer the final cause of the universe, the Heaven-descended heir of all the ages. His very existence is an accident, his story a brief and transitory episode in the life of one of the meanest of the planets. Of the combination of causes which first converted a dead organic compound into the living progenitors of humanity, science, indeed, as yet knows nothing. It is enough that from such beginnings famine, disease, and mutual slaughter, fit nurses of the future lords of creation, have gradually evolved, after infinite travail, a race with conscience enough to feel that it is vile, and intelligence enough to know that it is insignificant. . . . We sound the future, and learn that after a period, long compared with the individual life, but short indeed compared with the divisions of time open to our investigation, the energies of our system will decay, the glory of the sun will be dimmed, and the earth, tideless and inert, will no longer tolerate the race which has for a moment disturbed its solitude. Man will go down into the pit, and all his thoughts will perish. The uneasy consciousness, which in this obscure corner has for a brief space broken the contented silence of the universe, will be at rest. Matter will know itself no longer. 'Imperishable monuments' and 'immortal deeds,' death itself, and love stronger than death, will be as though they had never been. Nor will anything that *is* be better or be worse for all that the labor, genius, devo-

tion, and suffering of man have striven through countless generations to effect." [24]

§ 125. But though our philosopher must accept
the truth of this terrible picture, he is not left

Naturalism as the Basis for a Religion of Service, Wonder, and Renunciation. without spiritual resources. The abstract religion provided for the agnostic
faithful by Herbert Spencer does not,
it is true, afford any nourishment to the
religious nature. He would have men look for a
deep spring of life in the negative idea of mystery,
the apotheosis of ignorance, while religious faith to
live at all must lay hold upon reality. But there
does spring from naturalism a positive religion,
whose fundamental motives are those of service,
wonder, and renunciation: service of humanity in
the present, wonder at the natural truth, and renunciation of a universe keyed to vibrate with
human ideals.

"Have you," writes Charles Ferguson, "had dreams
of Nirvana and sickly visions and raptures? Have you
imagined that the end of your life is to be absorbed back
into the life of God, and to flee the earth and forget all?
Or do you want to walk on air, or fly on wings, or build a
heavenly city in the clouds? Come, let us take our kit
on our shoulders, and go out and build the city *here*." [25]

[24] Quoted from Balfour: *Foundations of Belief*, pp. 29–31.
[25] Ferguson: *Religion of Democracy*, p. 10.

For Haeckel " natural religion " is such as

" the astonishment with which we gaze upon the starry heavens and the microscopic life in a drop of water, the awe with which we trace the marvellous working of energy in the motion of matter, the reverence with which we grasp the universal dominance of the law of substance throughout the universe." [26]

There is a deeper and a sincerer note in the stout, forlorn humanism of Huxley:

" That which lies before the human race is a constant struggle to maintain and improve, in opposition to the State of Nature, the State of Art of an organized polity; in which, and by which, man may develop a worthy civilization, capable of maintaining and constantly improving itself, until the evolution of our globe shall have entered so far upon its downward course that the cosmic process resumes its sway; and, once more, the State of Nature prevails over the surface of our planet." [27]

[26] Haeckel: *Op. cit.*, p. 344.
[27] Huxley: *Evolution and Ethics*, p. 45. *Collected Essays,* Vol. IX.

CHAPTER IX

SUBJECTIVISM [1]

§ 126. WHEN, in the year 1710, Bishop Berkeley maintained the thesis of empirical idealism,

Subjectivism Originally Associated with Relativism and Scepticism.

having rediscovered it and announced it with a justifiable sense of originality, he provoked a kind of critical judgment that was keenly annoying if not entirely surprising to him. In refuting the conception of material substance and demonstrating the dependence of being upon mind, he at once sought, as he did repeatedly in later years, to establish the world of practical belief, and so to reconcile metaphysics and common-sense. Yet he found himself hailed as a fool and a sceptic. In answer to an inquiry

[1] PRELIMINARY NOTE. By *Subjectivism* is meant that system of philosophy which construes the universe in accordance with the epistemological principle that *all knowledge is of its own states or activities*. In so far as subjectivism reduces reality to *states of knowledge,* such as *perceptions* or *ideas*, it is *phenomenalism.* In so far as it reduces reality to a more *internal active principle* such as *spirit* or *will*, it is *spiritualism*.

concerning the reception of his book in London, his friend Sir John Percival wrote as follows:

" I did but name the subject matter of your book of *Principles* to some ingenious friends of mine and they immediately treated it with ridicule, at the same time refusing to read it, which I have not yet got one to do. A physician of my acquaintance undertook to discover your person, and argued you must needs be mad, and that you ought to take remedies. A bishop pitied you, that a desire of starting something new should put you upon such an undertaking. Another told me that you are not gone so far as another gentleman in town, who asserts not only that there is no such thing as Matter, but that we ourselves have no being at all." [2]

There can be no doubt but that the idea of the dependence of real things upon their appearance to the individual is a paradox to common-sense. It is a paradox because it seems to reverse the theoretical instinct itself, and to define the real in those very terms which disciplined thought learns to neglect. In the early history of thought the nature of the thinker himself is recognized as that which is likely to distort truth rather than that which conditions it. When the wise man, the devotee of truth, first makes his appearance, his authority is acknowledged because he has renounced himself. As witness of the universal

[2] Berkeley: *Complete Works*, Vol. I, p. 352. Fraser's edition.

being he purges himself of whatever is peculiar to his own individuality, or even to his human nature. In the aloofness of his meditation he escapes the cloud of opinion and prejudice that obscures the vision of the common man. In short, the element of belief dependent upon the thinker himself is the dross which must be refined away in order to obtain the pure truth. When, then, in the critical epoch of the Greek sophists, Protagoras declares that there is no belief that is not of this character, his philosophy is promptly recognized as scepticism. Protagoras argues that sense qualities are clearly dependent upon the actual operations of the senses, and that all knowledge reduces ultimately to these terms.

"The senses are variously named hearing, seeing, smelling; there is the sense of heat, cold, pleasure, pain, desire, fear, and many more which are named, as well as innumerable others which have no name; *with each of them there is born an object of sense,*—all sorts of colors born with all sorts of sight and sounds in like manner with hearing, and other objects with the other senses." [3]

If the objects are " born with " the senses, it follows that they are born with and appertain to the individual perceiver.

[3] Plato: *Theaetetus*, 156. Translation by Jowett. The italics are mine.

" Either show, if you can, that our sensations are not
relative and individual, or, if you admit that they are
individual, prove that this does not involve the consequence that the appearance becomes, or, if you like to
say, is to the individual only." [4]

The same motif is thus rendered by Walter Pater
in the Conclusion of his " Renaissance " :

"At first sight experience seems to bury us under a
flood of external objects, pressing upon us with a sharp
and importunate reality, calling us out of ourselves in a
thousand forms of action. But when reflexion begins
to act upon those objects they are dissipated under its
influence; the cohesive force seems suspended like a
trick of magic; each object is loosed into a group of
impressions—color, odor, texture—in the mind of the
observer. . . . Experience, already reduced to a
swarm of impressions, is ringed round for each one of
us by that thick wall of personality through which no
real voice has ever pierced on its way to us, or from us to
that which we can only conjecture to be without. Every
one of these impressions is the impression of the individual in his isolation, each mind keeping as a solitary
prisoner its own dream of a world."

The Protagorean generalization is due to the reflection that all experience is some individual experience, that no subject of discourse escapes the
imputation of belonging to some individual's private history. The individual must start with his
own experiences and ideas, and he can never get

[4] Plato: *Op. cit.*, 166.

beyond them, for he cannot see outside his own vision, or even think outside his own mind. The scepticism of this theory is explicit, and the formulas of Protagoras—the famous " *Man is the measure of all things*," and the more exact formula, " *The truth is what appears to each man at each time* " [5]—have been the articles of scepticism throughout the history of thought.

§ 127. There is, therefore, nothing really surprising in the reception accorded the " new philosophy " of Bishop Berkeley. A scep-

Phenomenalism and Spiritualism.

tical relativism is the earliest phase of subjectivism, and its avoidance at once becomes the most urgent problem of any philosophy which proposes to proceed forth from this principle. And this problem Berkeley meets with great adroitness and a wise recognition of difficulties. But his sanguine temperament and speculative interest impel him to what he regards as the extension of his first principle, the reintroduction of the conception of substance under the form of spirit, and of the objective order of nature under the form of the mind of God. In short, there are two motives at work in him, side by side: the epistemological motive, restricting reality to perceptions

⁵ ἀληθὲς ὃ ἑκάστῳ ἑκάστοτε δοκεῖ.

and thoughts, and the metaphysical-religious motive, leading him eventually to the definition of
reality in terms of perceiving and thinking spirits.
And from the time of Berkeley these two principles, *phenomenalism* and *spiritualism,* have remained as distinct and alternating phases of
subjectivism. The former is its critical and
dialectical conception, the latter its constructive
and practical conception.

§ 128. As *phenomenalism* has its classic statement and proof in the writings of Berkeley, we

Phenomenal-
ism as Main-
tained by
Berkeley.
The Problem
Inherited from
Descartes
and Locke.

shall do well to return to these. The
fact that this philosopher wished to be
regarded as the prophet of common-
sense has already been mentioned. This
purpose reveals itself explicitly in the
series of "Dialogues between Hylas and Philonous." The form in which Berkeley here advances
his thesis is further determined by the manner in
which the lines were drawn in his day of thought.
The world of enlightened public opinion was then
threefold, consisting of God, physical nature, and
the soul. In the early years of the seventeenth
century Descartes had sharply distinguished between the two substances—mind, with its attribute of thought; and body, with its attribute of

extension—and divided the finite world between them. God was regarded as the infinite and sustaining cause of both. Stated in the terms of epistemology, the object of clear thinking is the physical cosmos, the subject of clear thinking the immortal soul. The realm of perception, wherein the mind is subjected to the body, embarrasses the Cartesian system, and has no clear title to any place in it. And without attaching cognitive importance to this realm, the system is utterly dogmatic in its epistemology.[6] For what one substance thinks, must be assumed to be somehow true of another quite independent substance without any medium of communication. Now between Descartes and Berkeley appeared the sober and questioning " Essay Concerning Human Understanding," by John Locke. This is an interesting combination (they cannot be said to blend) of traditional metaphysics and revolutionary epistemology. The universe still consists of God, the immortal thinking soul, and a corporeal nature, the object of its thought. But, except for certain proofs of God and self, knowledge is entirely reduced to the perceptual type, to sensations, or ideas directly imparted to the mind by the objects

[6] For another issue out of this situation, cf. §§ 185–187.

themselves.   To escape dogmatism it is maintained that the real is what is *observed to be present*.   But Locke thinks the qualities so discovered
belong in part to the perceiver and in part to
the substance outside the mind.   Color is a case
of the former, a " secondary quality " ; and extension a case of the latter, a " primary quality."
And evidently the above empirical test of knowledge is not equally well met in these two cases.
When I see a red object I know that red exists,
for it is observed to be present, and I make no
claim for it beyond the present.   But when I note
that the red object is square, I am supposed to
know a property that will continue to exist in the
object after I have closed my eyes or turned to
something else.   Here my claim exceeds my observation, and the empirical principle adopted at
the outset would seem to be violated.   Berkeley
develops his philosophy from this criticism.   His
refutation of material substance is intended as a
full acceptance of the implications of the new empirical epistemology.   Knowledge is to be all of
the perceptual type, where what is known is
directly presented; and, in conformity with this
principle, being is to be restricted to the content
of the living pulses of experience.

§ 129. Berkeley, then, beginning with the three-fold world of Descartes and of common-sense,

The Refutation of Material Substance. proposes to apply Locke's theory of knowledge to the discomfiture of corporeal nature. It was a radical doctrine, because it meant for him and for his contemporaries the denial of all finite objects outside the mind. But at the same time it meant a restoration of the homogeneity of experience, the reëstablishment of the qualitative world of everyday living, and so had its basis of appeal to common-sense. The encounter between Hylas, the advocate of the traditional philosophy, and Philonous, who represents the author himself, begins with an exchange of the charge of innovation.

Hyl. I am glad to find there was nothing in the accounts I heard of you.

Phil. Pray, what were those?

Hyl. You were represented, in last night's conversation, as one who maintained the most extravagant opinion that ever entered into the mind of man, to wit, that there is no such thing as *material substance* in the world.

Phil. That there is no such thing as what *philosophers* call *material substance*, I am seriously persuaded: but if I were made to see anything absurd or sceptical in this, I should then have the same reason to renounce this that I imagine I have now to reject the contrary opinion.

Hyl. What! can anything be more fantastical, more

repugnant to Common-Sense, or a more manifest piece of Scepticism, than to believe there is no such thing as *matter?*

Phil. Softly, good Hylas. What if it should prove that you, who hold there is, are, by virtue of that opinion, a greater sceptic, and maintain more paradoxes and repugnances to Common-Sense, than I who believe no such thing?[7]

Philonous now proceeds with his case. Beginning by obtaining from Hylas the admission that pleasure and pain are essentially relative and subjective, he argues that sensations such as heat, since they are inseparable from these feelings, must be similarly regarded. And he is about to annex other qualities in turn to this core of subjectivity, when Hylas enters a general demurrer:

" Hold, Philonous, I now see what it was deluded me all this time. You asked me whether heat and cold, sweetness and bitterness, were not particular sorts of pleasure and pain; to which I answered simply that they were. Whereas I should have thus distinguished:— those qualities as perceived by us, are pleasures or pains; but not as existing in the external objects. We must not therefore conclude absolutely, that there is no heat in the fire, or sweetness in the sugar, but only that heat or sweetness, as perceived by us, are not in the fire or sugar."[8]

[7] Berkeley: *Op. cit.*, Vol. I, pp. 380-381.
[8] *Ibid.*, p. 389.

§ 130. Here the argument touches upon profound issues. Philonous now assumes the extreme

The Applica-
tion of the
Epistemologi-
cal Principle. empirical contention *that knowledge
applies only to its own psychological
moment, that its object in no way extends beyond that individual situation which we
call the state of knowing.* The full import of such
an epistemology Berkeley never recognized, but he
is clearly employing it here, and the overthrow of
Hylas is inevitable so long as he does not challenge
it or turn it against his opponent. This, however,
as a protagonist of Berkeley's own making, he fails
to do, and he plays into Philonous's hands by admitting that what is known only in perception
must for that reason *consist* in perception. He
frankly owns " that it is vain to stand out any
longer," that " colors, sounds, tastes, in a word,
all those termed *secondary qualities,* have certainly
no existence without the mind." [9]

Hylas has now arrived at the distinction between primary and secondary qualities. " Extension, Figure, Solidity, Gravity, Motion, and Rest "
are the attributes of an external substance which
is the cause of sensations. But the same epistemological principle readily reduces these also to

• Ibid., p. 397.

dependence on mind, for, like the secondary qualities, their content is given only in perception.
Hylas is then driven to defend a general material
substratum, which is the cause of ideas, but to
which none of the definite content of these ideas
can be attributed. In short, he has put all the
content of knowledge on the one side, and admitted
its inseparability from the perceiving spirit, and
left the being of things standing empty and forlorn on the other. This amounts, as Philonous re-
minds him, to the denial of the reality of the
known world.

"You are therefore, by your principles, forced to
deny the *reality* of sensible things; since you made it to
consist in an absolute existence exterior to the mind.
That is to say, you are a downright sceptic. So I have
gained my point, which was to show your principles led
to Scepticism."[10]

§ 131. Having advanced the direct empiricist
argument for phenomenalism, Berkeley now gives
The Refuta-   the rationalistic motive an opportunity
tion of a
Conceived   to express itself in the queries of Hylas
Corporeal
World.   as to whether there be not an "absolute
extension," somehow abstracted by thought from
the relativities of perception. Is there not at least
a *conceivable* world independent of perception?

[10] *Ibid.*, p. 418.

The answers of Philonous throw much light upon the Berkeleyan position. He admits that thought is capable of separating the primary from the secondary qualities in certain *operations*, but at the same time denies that this is forming an idea of them as separate.

"I acknowledge, Hylas, it is not difficult to form general propositions and reasonings about those qualities, without mentioning any other; and, in this sense, to consider or treat of them abstractedly. But, how doth it follow that, because I can pronounce the word *motion* by itself, I can form the idea of it in my mind exclusive of body? or, because theorems may be made of extension and figures, without any mention of *great* or *small*, or any other sensible mode or quality, that therefore it is possible such an abstract idea of extension, without any particular size or figure, or sensible quality, should be distinctly formed, and apprehended by the mind? Mathematicians treat of quantity, without regarding what other sensible qualities it is attended with, as being altogether indifferent to their demonstrations. But, when laying aside the words, they contemplate the bare ideas, I believe you will find, they are not the pure abstracted ideas of extension." [11]

Berkeley denies that we have ideas of pure extension or motion, because, although we do actually *deal* with these and find them intelligible, we can never obtain a state of mind in which they appear as the content. He applies this psychological test

[11] *Ibid.*, pp. 403–404.

because of his adherence to the general empirical postulate that knowledge is limited to the individual content of its own individual states. " It is a universally received maxim," he says, " that *everything which exists is particular*." Now the truth of mathematical reckoning is not particular, but is valid wherever the conditions to which it refers are fulfilled. Mathematical reckoning, if it is to be particular, must be regarded as a particular act or state of some thinker. Its truth must then be construed as relative to the interests of the thinker, as a symbolism which has an instrumental rather than a purely cognitive value. This conclusion cannot be disputed short of a radical stand against the general epistemological principle to which Berkeley is so far true, the principle that the reality which is known in any state of thinking or perceiving is the state itself.

§ 132. This concludes the purely phenomenalistic strain of Berkeley's thought. He has taken

The Transition to Spiritualism. the immediate apprehension of sensible objects in a state of mind centring about the pleasure and pain of an individual, to be the norm of knowledge. He has further maintained that knowledge cannot escape the particularity of its own states. The result is that the universe is composed of private perceptions and ideas. Strictly on the basis of what has preceded, Hylas is justified in regarding this conclusion as no less sceptical than that to which his own position had been reduced; for while he had been compelled to admit that the real is unknowable, Philonous has apparently defined the knowable as relative to the individual. But the supplementary metaphysics which had hitherto been kept in the background is now revealed. It is maintained that though perceptions know no external world, they do nevertheless reveal a spiritual substance of which they are the states. Although it has hitherto been argued that the *esse* of things is in their *percipi*, this is now replaced by the more fundamental principle that the *esse* of things is in their *percipere* or *velle*. The real world consists not in perceptions, but in perceivers.

§ 133. Now it is at once evident that the epistemological theory which has been Berkeley's dia-

Further Attempts to Maintain Phenomenalism. lectical weapon in the foregoing argument is no longer available. And those who have cared more for this theory than for metaphysical speculation have attempted to stop at this point, and so to construe phenomenalism as to make it self-sufficient on its own grounds.   Such attempts are so instructive as to make it worth our while to review them before proceeding with the development of the spiritualistic motive in subjectivism.

The world is to be regarded as made up of sense-perceptions, ideas, or phenomena.   What is to be accepted as the fundamental category which gives to all of these terms their subjectivistic significance?   So far there seems to be nothing in view save the principle of relativity.   The type to which these were reduced was that of the peculiar or unsharable experience best represented by an individual's pleasure and pain.   But relativity will not work as a general principle of being.   It consigns the individual to his private mind, and cannot provide for the validity of knowledge enough even to maintain itself.   Some other course, then, must be followed.   Perception may be given a psycho-physical definition, which employs physical terms as fundamental; [12] but this flagrantly contradicts the phenomenalistic first principle.   Or, reality may be regarded as so stamped with its marks as to insure the proprietorship of thought. But this definition of certain objective entities of

[12] Cf. Pearson: *Grammar of Science*, Chap. II.   See above, § 118.

mind, of beings attributed to intelligence because
of their intrinsic intelligibility, is inconsistent
with empiricism, if indeed it does not lead eventually to a realism of the Platonic type.[13]   Finally,
and most commonly, the terms of phenomenalism
have been retained after their orignal meaning has
been suffered to lapse.   The "impressions" of
Hume, e. g., are the remnant of the Berkeleyan
world with the spirit stricken out.   There is no
longer any point in calling them impressions, for
they now mean only elements or qualities.   As a
consequence this outgrowth of the Berkeleyanism
epistemology is at present merging into a realistic
philosophy of experience.[14]   Any one, then, of
these three may be the last state of one who undertakes to remain exclusively faithful to the phenomenalistic aspect of Berkeleyanism, embodied in
the principle *esse est percipi.*

[13] See Chap. XI.   Cf. also § 140.
[14] The same may be said of the "permanent possibilities of
sensation," proposed by J. S. Mill.   Such possibilities outside of actual perception are either nothing or things such
as they are known to be *in* perception.   In either case they are
not perceptions.

In Ernst Mach's *Analysis of Sensations,* the reader will
find an interesting transition from sensationalism to realism
through the substitution of the term *Bestandtheil* for *Empfindung.*   (See Translation by Williams, pp. 18–20.)   See
below, § 207.

Berkeley's
Spiritualism.
Immediate
Knowledge of
the Perceiver.
§ 134. Let us now follow the fortunes of the other phase of subjectivism— that which develops the conception of the perceiver rather than the perceived. When Berkeley holds that

" all the choir of heaven and furniture of the Earth, in a word, all those bodies which compose the mighty frame of the world, have not any subsistence without a Mind,"

his thought has transcended the epistemology with which he overthrew the conception of material substance, in two directions. For neither mind of the finite type nor mind of the divine type is perceived. But the first of these may yet be regarded as a direct empirical datum, even though sharply distinguished from an object of perception. In the third dialogue, Philonous thus expounds this new kind of knowledge:

" I own I have properly no *idea*, either of God or any other spirit; for these being active, cannot be represented by things perfectly inert, as our ideas are. I do nevertheless know that I, who am a spirit or thinking substance, exist as certainly as I know my ideas exist. Farther, I know what I mean by the terms *I* and *myself;* and I know this immediately or intuitively, though I do not perceive it as I perceive a triangle, a color, or a sound." [15]

[15] Berkeley: *Op. cit.*, p. 447.

The knowledge here provided for may be regarded as empirical because the reality in question is an individual present in the moment of the knowledge. Particular acts of perception are said directly to reveal not only perceptual objects, but perceiving subjects. And the conception of spiritual substance, once accredited, may then be extended to account for social relations and to fill in the nature of God. The latter extension, in so far as it attributes such further predicates as universality and infinity, implies still a third epistemology, and threatens to pass over into rationalism. But the knowledge of one's fellow-men may, it is claimed, be regarded as immediate, like the knowledge of one's self. Perceptual and volitional activity has a sense for itself and also a sense for other like activity. The self is both self-conscious and socially conscious in an immediate experience of the same type.

§ 135. But this general spiritualistic conception is developed with less singleness of purpose in Berkeley than among the *voluntarists* and *panpsychists* who spring from Schopenhauer, the orientalist, pessimist, and mystic among the German Kantians of the early nineteenth century. His great

Schopenhauer's Spiritualism, or Voluntarism. Immediate Knowledge of the Will.

book, " Die Welt als Wille und Vorstellung,"
opens with the phenomenalistic contention that
" the world is my idea." It soon appears, however, that the " my " is more profoundly significant than the " idea." Nature is my creation,
due to the working within me of certain fixed
principles of thought, such as space, time, and
causality. But nature, just because it is my creation, is less than me: is but a manifestation of the
true being for which I must look *within* myself.
But this inner self cannot be made an object of
thought, for that would be only to create another
term of nature. The will itself, from which such
creation springs, is " that which is most immediate " in one's consciousness, and " makes itself
known in a direct manner in its particular acts."
The term *will* is used by Schopenhauer as a general term covering the whole dynamics of life, instinct and desire, as well as volition. It is that
sense of life-preserving and life-enhancing appetency which is the conscious accompaniment of
struggle. With its aid the inwardness of the whole
world may now be apprehended.

" Whoever has now gained from all these expositions
a knowledge *in abstracto*, and therefore clear and certain,
of what everyone knows directly *in concreto, i. e.*, as

feeling, a knowledge that his will is the real inner nature of his phenomenal being, . . . and that his will is that which is most immediate in his consciousness, . . . will find that of itself it affords him the key to the knowledge of the inmost being of the whole of nature; for he now transfers it to all those phenomena which are not given to him, like his own phenomenal existence, both in direct and indirect knowledge, but only in the latter, thus merely one-sidedly as *idea* alone." [16]

The heart of reality is thus known by an "intuitive interpretation," which begins at home in the individual's own heart.

§ 136. The panpsychist follows the same course of reflection. There is an outwardness and an **Panpsychism.** inwardness of nature, corresponding to the knower's body on the one hand, and his feeling or will on the other. With this principle in hand one may pass down the whole scale of being and discover no breach of continuity. Such an interpretation of nature has been well set forth by a contemporary writer, who quotes the following from the botanist, C. v. Naegeli:

" Sensation is clearly connected with the reflex actions of higher animals. We are obliged to concede it to the other animals also, and we have no grounds for denying it to plants and inorganic bodies. The sensation arouses in us a condition of comfort and discomfort. In general,

[16] Schopenhauer: *The World as Will and Idea.* Translation by Haldane and Kemp, Vol. I, p. 141.

the feeling of pleasure arises when the natural impulses are satisfied, the feeling of pain when they are not satisfied. Since all material processes are composed of movements of molecules and elementary atoms, pleasure and pain must have their seat in these particles. . . . Thus the same mental thread runs through all material phenomena. The human mind is nothing but the highest devolpment on our earth of the mental processes which universally animate and move nature." [17]

According to panpsychism, then, physical nature is the manifestation of an *appetency or bare consciousness generalized from the thinker's awareness of his most intimate self.* Such appetency or bare consciousness is the essential or substantial state of that which appears as physical nature.

§ 137. We must now turn to the efforts which this doctrine has made to maintain itself against

The Inherent Difficulty in Spiritualism. No Provision for Objective Knowledge.

the sceptical trend of its own epistemology. For precisely as in the case of phenomenalism its dialectical principle threatens to be self-destructive. Immediate presence is still the test of knowledge. But does not immediate presence connote relativity and inadequacy, at best; an initial phase of knowledge that must be supplemented and cor-

[17] Quoted from Naegeli: *Die Mechanisch-physiologische Theorie der Abstammungslehre,* by Friedrich Paulsen, in his *Introduction to Philosophy.* Translation by Thilly, p. 103.

rected before objective reality and valid truth
are apprehended? Does not the individuality of
the individual thinker connote the very maximum
of error? Indeed, spiritualism would seem to have
exceeded even Protagoreanism itself, and to have
passed from scepticism to deliberate nihilism. The
object of knowledge is no longer even, as with the
phenomenalist, the thinker's thought, but only his
thinking. And if the thinker's thought is relative
to him, then the thinker's act of thinking is the
very vanishing-point of relativity, the negative
term of a negating relation. How is a real, a
self-subsistent world to be composed of such? Im-
pelled by a half-conscious realization of the hope-
lessness of this situation, the exponent of spiritualism has sought to universalize his conception;
to define an *absolute or ultimate spirit* other than
the individual thinker, though known in and
through him. But it is clear that this development
of spiritualism, like all of the speculative procedure of subjectivism, threatens to exceed the scope
of the original principle of knowledge. There is
a strong presumption against the possibility of
introducing a knowledge of God by the way of
the particular presentations of an individual consciousness.

§ 138. Schopenhauer must be credited with a genuine effort to accept the metaphysical conse-

Schopen-
hauer's At-
tempt to
Universalize
Subjectivism.
Mysticism.

quences of his epistemology. His epistemology, as we have seen, defined knowledge as centripetal. The object of real knowledge is identical with the subject of knowledge. If I am to know the universal will, therefore, I must in knowing become that will. And this Schopenhauer maintains. The innermost heart of the individual into which he may retreat, even from his private will, is—the universal. But there is another way of arriving at the same knowledge. In contemplation I may become absorbed in principles and laws, rather than be diverted by the particular spacial and temporal objects, until (and this is peculiarly true of the æsthetic experience) my interest no longer distinguishes itself, but coincides with truth. In other words, abstract thinking and pure willing are not opposite extremes, but adjacent points on the deeper or transcendent circle of experience. One may reach this part of the circle by moving in either of two directions that at the start are directly opposite: by turning in upon the subject or by utterly giving one's self up to the object. Reality obtains no definition by this means. Philosophy, for Schopenhauer, is rather a programme for realizing the state in which I will the universal and know the universal will. The final theory of knowledge, then, is mysticism, reality directly apprehended in a supreme and incommunicable experience, direct and vivid, like perception, and at the same time universal, like thought. But the empiricism with which Schopenhauer began, the appeal to a familiar experience of self as will, has meanwhile been forgotten. The idea as object of my perception, and the will as its subject were in the beginning regarded as common and verifiable items of experience. But who, save the occasional philosopher, knows a universal will? Nor have attempts to avoid mysticism, while retaining Schopenhauer's first principle, been successful. Certain voluntarists and panpsychists have attempted to do without the universal will, and define the world solely in terms of the many individual wills. But, as Schopenhauer himself pointed out, individual wills cannot be distinguished except in terms of something other than will, such as space and time. The same is true if for will there be substituted inner feeling or consciousness. Within this category individuals can be distinguished only as points of view, which to be comparable at all must

contain common objects, or be defined in terms
of a system of relations like that of the physical
world or that of an ethical community. The conception of pure will or pure feeling inevitably attaches to itself that of an undivided unity, if for
no other reason because there is no ground for distinction. And such a unity, a will or consciousness that is no particular act or idea, can be known
only in the unique experience which mysticism
provides.

§ 139. The way of Schopenhauer is the way of
one who adheres to the belief that what the thinker
Objective   knows must always be a part of himself,
Spiritualism.   his state or his activity. From this
point of view the important element of being, its
very essence or substance, is not any definable
nature but an immediate relation to the knower.
The consequence is that the universe in the last
analysis can only be defined as a supreme state or
activity into which the individual's consciousness
may develop. Spiritualism has, however, other
interests, interests which may be quite independent
of epistemology. It is speculatively interested in
a kind of being which it defines as spiritual, and
in terms of which it proposes to define the universe.
Such procedure is radically different from the

epistemological criticism which led Berkeley to maintain that the *esse* of objects is in their *percipi,* or Schopenhauer to maintain that " the world is my idea," or that led both of these philosophers to find a deeper reality in immediately intuited self-activity. For now it is proposed to *understand* spirit, discover its properties, and to acknowledge it only where these properties appear. I may now know spirit as an object; which in its properties, to be sure, is quite different from matter, but which like matter is capable of subsisting quite independently of my knowledge. This is a metaphysical spiritualism quite distinct from epistemological spiritualism, and by no means easily made consistent therewith. Indeed, it exhibits an almost irrepressible tendency to overstep the bounds both of empiricism and subjectivism, an historical connection with which alone justifies its introduction in the present chapter.

§ 140. To return again to the instructive example of Bishop Berkeley, we find him proving God from the evidence of him in experience, or the need of him to support the claims of experience.

Berkeley's Conception of God as Cause, Goodness and Order.

" But, whatever power I may have over my own thoughts, I find the ideas actually perceived by Sense have not a like dependence on *my* will.   When in broad daylight I open my eyes, it is not in my power to choose whether I shall see or no, or to determine what particular objects shall present themselves to my view: and so likewise as to the hearing and other senses; the ideas imprinted on them are not creatures of *my* will.   There is therefore some other Will or Spirit that produces them.

The ideas of Sense are more strong, lively, and distinct than those of the Imagination; they have likewise a steadiness, order, and coherence, and are not excited at random, as those which are the effects of human wills often are, but in a regular train or series—the admirable connection whereof sufficiently testifies the wisdom and benevolence of its Author.   Now the set rules, or established methods, wherein the Mind we depend on excites in us the ideas of Sense, are called *the laws of nature.*" [18]

Of the attributes of experience here in question, independence or " steadiness " is not regarded as *prima facie* evidence of spirit, but rather as an aspect of experience for which some cause is necessary.   But it is assumed that the power to " produce," with which such a cause must be endowed, is the peculiar prerogative of spirit, and that this cause gives further evidence of its spiritual nature, of its eminently spiritual nature, in the orderliness and the goodness of its effects.

" The force that produces, the intellect that orders, the goodness that perfects all things is the Supreme Being." [19]

[18] Berkeley: *Op. cit.*, p. 273.
[19] *Op. cit.*, Vol. I, pp. 272–273.

That spirit is possessed of causal efficacy, Berkeley has in an earlier passage proved by a direct appeal to the individual's sense of power.

"I find I can excite ideas in my mind at pleasure, and vary and shift the scene as oft as I think fit. It is no more than *willing*, and straightway this or that idea arises in my fancy; and by the same power it is obliterated and makes way for another. This making and unmaking of ideas doth very properly denominate the mind active. Thus much is certain and grounded on experience: but when we talk of unthinking agents, or of exciting ideas exclusive of volition, we only amuse ourselves with words." [20]

Although Berkeley is here in general agreement with a very considerable variety of philosophical views, it will be readily observed that this doctrine tends to lapse into mysticism whenever it is retained in its purity. Berkeley himself admitted that there was no " idea " of such power. And philosophers will as a rule either obtain an idea corresponding to a term or amend the term— always excepting the mystical appeal to an inarticulate and indefinable experience. Hence pure power revealed in an ineffable immediate experience tends to give place to kinds of power to which some definite meaning may be attached. The energy of physics, defined by measurable quan-

[20] *Op. cit.*, Vol. III, p. 278.

titative equivalence, is a case in point. The idealistic trend is in another direction, power coming
to signify ethical or logical connection. Similarly, in the later philosophy of Berkeley himself,
God is known by the nature of his activity rather
than by the fact of his activity; and we are said
" to account for a thing, when we show that it
is so best." God's power, in short, becomes indistinguishable from his universality attended with
the attributes of goodness and orderliness. But
this means that the analogy of the human spirit,
conscious of its own activity, is no longer the basis
of the argument. By the divine will is now meant
ethical principles, rather than the " here am I
willing " of the empirical consciousness. Similarly the divine mind is defined in terms of logical
principles, such as coherence and order, rather
than in terms of the " here am I thinking " of the
finite knower himself. But enough has been said
to make it plain that this is no longer the stand-
point of empirio-idealism. Indeed, in his last
philosophical writing, the " Siris," Berkeley is so
far removed from the principles of knowledge
which made him at once the disciple and the critic
of Locke, as to pronounce himself the devotee of
Platonism and the prophet of transcendentalism.

The former strain appears in his conclusion that
" the *principles* of science are neither objects of
sense nor imagination; and that intellect and reason are alone the sure guides to truth." [21]   His
transcendentalism appears in his belief that such
principles, participating in the vital unity of the
Individual Purpose, constitute the meaning and so
the substantial essence of the universe.

§ 141. Such then are the various paths which
lead from subjectivism to other types of philos-

The General Tendency of Subjectivism to Transcend Itself. ophy, demonstrating the peculiar apti-
tude of the former for departing from
its first principle. Beginning with the
relativity of all knowable reality to the individual
knower, it undertakes to conceive reality in one or
the other of the terms of this relation, as particular state of knowledge or as individual subject of
knowledge.   But these terms develop an intrinsic
nature of their own, and become respectively
empirical datum, and *logical* or *ethical principle*.
In either case the subjectivistic principle of knowledge has been abandoned. Those whose speculative interest in a definable objective world has been
less strong than their attachment to this principle,
have either accepted the imputation of scepticism,

[21] *Op. cit.*, Vol. III, p. 249.

or had recourse to the radical epistemological doctrine of mysticism.

§ 142. Since the essence of subjectivism is epistemological rather than metaphysical, its prac-

Ethical Theories. Relativism.

tical and religious implications are various. The ethical theories which are corollary to the tendencies expounded above, range from extreme egoism to a mystical universalism. The close connection between the former and relativism is evident, and the form of egoism most consistent with epistemological relativism is to be found among those same Sophists who first maintained this latter doctrine. If we may believe Plato, the Sophists sought to create for their individual pupils an *appearance* of good. In the " Theaetetus," Socrates is represented as speaking thus on behalf of Protagoras:

" And I am far from saying that wisdom and the wise man have no existence; but I say that the wise man is he who makes the evils which are and appear to a man, into goods which are and appear to him. . . . I say that they (the wise men) are the physicians of the human body, and the husbandmen of plants—for the husbandmen also take away the evil and disordered sensations of plants, and infuse into them good and healthy sensations as well as true ones; and the wise and good rhetoricians make the good instead of the evil seem just to states; for whatever appears to be just and fair to a state, while sanctioned by a state, is just and fair to it; but the teacher of wisdom causes the good to take the place of the evil, both in appearance and in reality." [22]

As truth is indistinguishable from the appearance of truth to the individual, so good is indistinguishable from a particular seeming good. The supreme moral value according to this plan of life is the agreeable feeling tone of that dream world to which the individual is forever consigned. The possible perfection of an experience which is " reduced to a swarm of impressions," and " ringed round " for each one of us by a " thick wall of personality " has been brilliantly depicted in the passage already quoted from Walter Pater, in whom the naturalistic and subjectivistic motives unite.[23] If all my experience is strictly my own, then my good must likewise be my own. And if all of my experience is valid only in its instants of immediacy, then my best good must likewise consist in some " exquisite passion," or stirring of the senses.

§ 143. But for Schopenhauer the internal world opens out into the boundless and unfathomable sea of the universal will. If I retire from the world upon my own pri-

Pessimism and
Self-denial.

[22] Plato: *Theaetetus*, 167.   Translation by Jowett.
[23] See § 121.

vate feelings, I am still short of the true life, for
I am asserting myself against the world. I should
seek a sense of unison with a world whose deeper
heart-beats I may learn to feel and adopt as the
rhythm of my own. The folly of willing for one's
private self is the ground of Schopenhauer's
pessimism.

"All *willing* arises from want, therefore from deficiency, and therefore from suffering. The satisfaction
of a wish ends it; yet for one wish that is satisfied there
remain at least ten which are denied. Further, the
desire lasts long, the demands are infinite; the satisfaction is short and scantily measured out. But even the
final satisfaction is itself only apparent; every satisfied
wish at once makes room for a new one, both are illusions;
the one is known to be so, the other not yet. No at-
tained object of desire can give lasting satisfaction, but
merely a fleeting gratification; it is like the alms thrown
to the beggar, that keeps him alive to-day that his misery
may be prolonged till the morrow. . . . The subject
of willing is thus constantly stretched on the revolving
wheel of Ixion, pours water into the sieve of the Danaids,
is the ever-longing Tantalus."[24]

The escape from this torture and self-deception is
possible through the same mystical experience, the
same blending with the universe that conditions
knowledge.

§ 144. But though pleasant dreaming be the

[24] Schopenhauer: *Op. cit.* Translation by Haldane and
Kemp, Vol. I, pp. 253–254.

most consistent practical sequel to a subjectivistic epistemology, its *individualism* presents another

The Ethics of Welfare. basis for life with quite different possibilities of emphasis. It may develop into an aggressive egoism of the type represented by the sophist Thrasymachus, in his proclamation that "might is right, justice the interest of the stronger." [25] But more commonly it is tempered by a conception of social interest, and serves as the champion of action against contemplation. The gospel of action is always individualistic. It requires of the individual a sense of his independence, and of the real virtue of his initiative. Hence those voluntarists who emphasize the many individual wills and decline to reduce them, after the manner of Schopenhauer, to a universal, may be said to afford a direct justification of it. It is true that this practical realism threatens the tenability of an epistemological idealism, but the two have been united, and because of their common emphasis upon the individual such procedure is not entirely inconsequential. Friedrich Paulsen, whose panpsychism has already been cited, is an excellent case in point. The only good, he maintains, is " welfare," the fulfilment of those natural

[25] See Plato: *Republic*, Bk. I, 338.

desires which both distinguish the individual and
signify his continuity with all grades of being.

"The goal at which the will aims does not consist in
a maximum of pleasurable feelings, but in the normal
exercise of the vital functions for which the species is
predisposed. In the case of man the mode of life is on
the whole determined by the nature of the historical
unity from which the individual evolves as a member.
Here the objective content of life, after which the will
strives, also enters into consciousness with the progressive evolution of presentation; the type of life becomes
a conscious ideal of life."[26]

Here, contrary to the teaching of Schopenhauer,
the good consists in individual attainment, the
extension and fulfilment of the *distinct* interests
that arise from the common fund of nature. To
be and to do to the uttermost, to realize the maximum from nature's investment in one's special
capacities and powers—this is indeed the first
principle of a morality of action.

§ 145. But a type of ethics still further removed from the initial relativism has been adopted
The Ethical and more or less successfully assimi-
Community. lated by subjectivistic philosophies.
Accepting Berkeley's spirits, with their indefinite
capacities, and likewise the stability of the ideal
principles that underlie a God-administered world,

[26] Paulsen: *Op. cit.*, p. 423.

and morality becomes the obedience which the individual renders to the law. The individual, free to act in his own right, coöperates with the purposes of the general spiritual community, whose laws are worthy of obedience though not coercive. The recognition of such a spiritual citizenship, entailing opportunities, duties, and obligations, rather than thraldom, partakes of the truth as well as the inadequacy of common-sense.

§ 146. As for religion, at least two distinct practical appreciations of the universe have been historically associated with this chapter in philosophy. The one of these is the mysticism of Schopenhauer, the religious sequel to a universalistic voluntarism. Schopenhauer's ethics, his very philosophy, is religion. For the good and the true are alike attainable only through identification with the Absolute Will. This consummation of life, transcending practical and theoretical differences, engulfing and effacing all qualities and all values, is like the Nirvâna of the Orient—a positive ideal only for one who has appraised the apparent world at its real value.

The Religion of Mysticism.

"Rather do we freely acknowledge that what remains after the entire abolition of will is for all those who are still full of will certainly nothing; but, conversely, to those in whom the will has turned and has denied itself, this our world, which is so real, with all its suns and milky-ways—is nothing." [27]

§ 147. From the union of the two motives of voluntarism and individualism springs another

The Religion of Individual Coöperation with God. and a more familiar type of religion, that of coöperative spiritual endeavor. In the religion of Schopenhauer the soul must utterly lose itself for the sake of peace; here the soul must persist in its own being and activity for the sake of the progressive goodness of the world. For Schopenhauer God is the universal solution, in which all motions cease and all differences disappear; here God is the General of moral forces. The deeper and more significant universe is

"a society of rational agents, acting under the eye of Providence, concurring in one design to promote the common benefit of the whole, and conforming their actions to the established laws and order of the Divine parental wisdom: wherein each particular agent shall not consider himself apart, but as the member of a great City, whose author and founder is God: in which the civil laws are no other than the rules of virtue and the duties of religion: and where everyone's true interest is combined with his duty." [28]

[27] Schopenhauer: *Op. cit.* Translation by Haldane and Kemp, p. 532.

[28] Berkeley: *Op. cit.*, Vol. II, p. 138.

But so uncompromising an optimism is not essential to this religion. Its distinction lies rather in its acceptance of the manifest plurality of souls, and its appeal to the faith that is engendered by service.[29] As William James has said:

" Even God's being is sacred from ours. To coöperate with his creation by the best and rightest response seems all he wants of us. In such coöperation with his purposes, not in any chimerical speculative conquest of him, not in any theoretical drinking of him up, must lie the real meaning of our destiny." [30]

[29] For an interesting characterization of this type of religion, cf. Royce: *Spirit of Modern Philosophy*, p. 46.

[30] James: *The Will to Believe*, p. 141.

CHAPTER X

ABSOLUTE REALISM [1]

§ 148. No one has understood better than the philosopher himself that he cannot hope to be popu-

The Philosopher's Task, and the Philosopher's Object, or the Absolute. lar with men of practical common-sense. Indeed, it has commonly been a matter of pride with him. The classic representation of the philosopher's faith in himself is to be found in Plato's "Republic." The philosopher is there portrayed in the famous cave simile as one who having seen the light itself can no longer distinguish the shadows which are apparent to those who sit perpetually in the twilight. Within the cave of shadows he is indeed less at his ease than those who have never seen the sun. But since he knows the source of the shadows, his knowledge surrounds

---

[1] By *Absolute Realism* is meant that system of philosophy which defines the universe as the *absolute being*, implied in knowledge as its final object, but assumed to be independent of knowledge. In the *Spinozistic* system this absolute being is conceived under the form of *substance*, or self-sufficiency; in *Platonism* under the form of *perfection;* and in the *Aristotelian* system under the form of *a hierarchy of substances.*

306

that of the shadow connoisseurs. And his equanimity need not suffer from the contempt of those whom he understands better than they understand themselves. The history of philosophy is due to the dogged persistence with which the philosopher has taken himself seriously and endured the poor opinion of the world. But the pride of the philosopher has done more than perpetuate the philosophical outlook and problem; it has led to the formulation of a definite philosophical conception, and of two great philosophical doctrines. The conception is that of the *absolute;* and the doctrines are that of the *absolute being,* and that of the *absolute self* or *mind.* The former of these doctrines is the topic of the present chapter.

Among the early Greeks the rôle of the philosopher was one of superlative dignity. In point of knowledge he was less easily satisfied than other men. He thought beyond immediate practical problems, devoting himself to a profounder reflection, that could not but induce in him a sense of superior intellectual worth. The familiar was not binding upon him, for his thought was emancipated from routine and superficiality. Furthermore his intellectual courage and resolution did not permit him to indulge in triviality, doubt, or paradox. He sought his own with a faith that could not be denied. Even Heraclitus the Dark, who was also called " the Weeping Philosopher," because he found at the very heart of nature that transiency which the philosophical mind seeks to escape, felt himself to be exalted as well as isolated by that insight. But this sentiment of personal aloofness led at once to a division of experience. He who knows truly belongs to another and more abiding world. As there is a philosophical way of thought, there is a philosophical way of life, and *a philosophical object*. Since the philosopher and the common man do not see alike, the terms of their experience are incommensurable. In Parmenides the Eleatic this motive is most strikingly exhibited. There is a *Way of Truth* which diverges from the *Way of Opinion*. The philosopher walks the former way alone. And there is an object of truth, accessible only to one who takes this way of truth. Parmenides finds this object to be the content of pure affirmation.

"One path only is left for us to speak of, namely, that *It is*. In it are very many tokens that what is, is uncreated and indestructible, alone, complete, immovable, and without end. Nor was it ever, nor will it be; for now *it is*, all at once, a continuous one." [2]

        [2] Burnet: *Early Greek Philosophy*, p. 185.

The philosophy of Parmenides, commonly called the Eleatic Philosophy, is notable for this emergence of the pure concept of *absolute being* as the final object of knowledge. The philosopher aims to discover that which is, and so turns away from that which is not or that which ceases to be. The negative and transient aspects of experience only hinder him in his search for the eternal. It was the great Eleatic insight to realize that the outcome of thought is thus predetermined; that the answer to philosophy is contained in the question of philosophy. The philosopher, in that he resolutely avoids all partiality, relativity, and superficiality, must affirm a complete, universal, and ultimate being as the very object of that perfect knowledge which he means to possess. This object is known in the history of these philosophies as the *infinite* or *absolute*.[3]

§ 149. The Eleatic reasons somewhat as follows. The philosopher seeks to know what is. **The Eleatic Conception of Being.** The object of his knowledge will then contain as its primary and essential predicate, that of being. It is a step further to *define* being in terms of this essential predicate.

[3] When contrasted with the temporal realm of " generation and decay," this ultimate object is often called the *eternal.*

Parmenides thinks of being as a power or strength, a positive self-maintenance to which all affirmations refer. The remainder of the Eleatic philosophy is the analysis of this concept and the proof of its implications. Being must persist through all change, and span all chasms. Before being there can be only nothing, which is the same as to say that so far as being is concerned there is no before. Similarly there can be no after or beyond. There can be no motion, change, or division of being, because being will be in all parts of every division, and in all stages of every process. Hence being is "uncreated and indestructible, alone, complete, immovable, and without end."

The argument turns upon the application to being as a whole of the meaning and the implications of *only being*. Being is the affirmative or positive. From that *alone*, one can derive only such properties as eternity or unity. For generation and decay and plurality may belong to that which is *also* affirmative and positive, but not to that which is affirmative and positive *only*. The Eleatic philosophy is due, then, to the determination to derive the whole of reality from the bare necessity of being, to cut down reality to what flows entirely from the assertion of its only known nec-

essary aspect, that of being. We meet here in its
simplest form a persistent rationalistic motive, the
attempt to derive the universe from the isolation
and analysis of its most universal character. As
in the case of every well-defined philosophy, this
motive is always attended by a " besetting " problem. Here it is the accounting for what, empirically at least, is alien to that universal character.
And this difficulty is emphasized rather than resolved by Parmenides in his designation of a limbo
of opinion, " in which is no true belief at all," to
which the manifold of common experience with
all its irrelevancies can be relegated.

§ 150. The Eleatic philosophy, enriched and
supplemented, appears many centuries later in the
Spinoza's
Conception
of Substance.
rigorous rationalism of Spinoza.[4] With
Spinoza philosophy is a demonstration
of necessities after the manner of geometry.
Reality is to be set forth in theorems derived from
fundamental axioms and definitions. As in the
case of Parmenides, these necessities are the implications of the very problem of being. The philosopher's problem is made to solve itself. But
for Spinoza that problem is more definite and
more pregnant. The problematic being must not

[4] Holland, 1632–1677.

only be, but must be *sufficient to itself*. What the philosopher seeks to know is primarily an intrinsic entity. Its nature must be independent of other natures, and my knowledge of it independent of my knowledge of anything else. Reality is something which need not be sought further. So construed, being is in Spinoza's philosophy termed *substance*. It will be seen that to define substance is to affirm the existence of it, for substance is so defined as to embody the very qualification for existence. Whatever exists exists under the form of substance, as that "which is in itself, and is conceived through itself: in other words, that of which a conception can be formed independently of any other conception." [5]

§ 151. There remains but one further funda-mental thesis for the establishment of the Spino-zistic philosophy, the thesis which main-tains the exclusive existence of the one "absolutely infinite being," or God. The exclusive existence of God follows from his existence, because of the exhaustiveness of his nature. His is the nature "consisting in infinite attributes, of which each expresses eternal and infinite essentiality." He will contain all

Spinoza's Proof of God, the Infinite Substance. The Modes and the Attributes.

[5] Spinoza: *Ethics*, Part I. Translation by Elwes, p. 45.

meaning, and all possible meaning, within his fixed
and necessary constitution. It is evident that if
such a God exist, nothing can fall outside of him.
One such substance must be the only substance.
But upon what grounds are we to assert God's
existence?

To proceed further with Spinoza's philosophy
we must introduce two terms which are scarcely
less fundamental in his system than that of substance. The one of these is " attribute," by which
he means *kind* or general property; the other is
" mode," by which he means *case* or individual
thing. Spinoza's proof of God consists in showing that no single mode, single attribute, or finite
group of modes or attributes, can be a substance;
but only an infinite system of all modes of all attributes. Translated into common speech this
means that neither kinds nor cases, nor special
groups of either, can stand alone and be of themselves, but only the unity of all possible cases of
all possible kinds.

The argument concerning the possible substantiality of the case or individual thing is relatively
simple. Suppose an attribute or kind, A, of which
there are cases am_1, am_2, am_3, etc. The number
of cases is never involved in the nature of the

kind, as is seen for example in the fact that the definition of triangle prescribes no special number of individual triangles. Hence am_1, am_2, am_3, etc., must be explained by something outside of their nature: Their being cases of A does not account for their existing severally. This is Spinoza's statement of the argument that individual events, such as motions or sensations, are not self-dependent, but belong to a context of like events which are mutually dependent.

The question of the attribute is more difficult. Why may not an attribute as a complete domain of interdependent events, itself be independent or substantial? Spinoza's predecessor, Descartes, had maintained precisely that thesis in behalf of the domain of thought and the domain of space. Spinoza's answer rests upon the famous ontological argument, inherited from scholasticism and generally accepted in the first period of modern philosophy. The evidence of existence, he declares, is clear and distinct conceivability.

"For a person to say that he has a clear and distinct—that is, a true—idea of a substance, but that he is not sure whether such substance exists, would be the same as if he said that he had a true idea, but was not sure whether or no it was false."[6]

[6] *Ibid.*, p. 49.

Now we can form a clear and distinct idea of an
absolutely infinite being that shall have all possible
attributes. This idea is a well-recognized standard and object of reference for thought. But it is
a conception which is highly qualified, not only
through its clearness and distinctness, but also
through its abundance of content. It affirms itself
therefore with a certainty that surpasses any other
certainty, because it is supported by each and
every other certainty, and even by the residuum
of possibility. If any intelligible meaning be
permitted to affirm itself, so much the more irresistible is the claim of this infinitely rich meaning. Since every attribute contributes to its validity, the being with infinite attributes is infinitely
or absolutely valid. The conclusion of the argument is now obvious. If the being constituted by
the infinite attributes exists, it swallows up all
possibilities and exists exclusively.

§ 152. The vulnerable point in Spinoza's argument can thus be expressed: that which is important is questionable, and that which
is unquestionable is of doubtful importance. Have I indeed a clear and
distinct idea of an absolutely infinite being?
The answer turns upon the meaning of the

The Limits of
Spinoza's
Argument
for God.

phrase " idea of." It is true I can add to such meaning as I apprehend the thought of possible other meaning, and suppose the whole to have a definiteness and systematic unity like that of the triangle. But such an idea is problematic. I am compelled to use the term " possible," and so to confess the failure of definite content to measure up to my idea. My idea of an absolutely infinite being is like my idea of a universal language: I can think *of* it, but I cannot *think it out,* for lack of data or because of the conflicting testimony of other data. If I mean the infinity of my being to be a term of inclusiveness, and to insist that the all must be, and that there can be nothing not included in the all, I can scarcely be denied. But it is reasonable to doubt the importance of such a truth. If, on the other hand, I mean that my infinite being shall have the compactness and organic unity of a triangle, I must admit that such a being is indeed problematic. The degree to which the meaning of the part is dependent upon the meaning of the whole, or the degree to which the geometrical analogy is to be preferred to the analogy of aggregates, like the events within a year, is a problem that falls quite outside Spinoza's fundamental arguments.

§ 153. But the advance of Spinoza over the Eleatics must not be lost sight of. The modern **Spinoza's Provision for the Finite.** philosopher has so conceived being as to provide for parts within an individual unity. The geometrical analogy is a most illuminating one, for it enables us to understand how manyness may be indispensable to a being that is essentially unitary. The triangle as triangle is one. But it could not be such without sides and angles. The unity is equally necessary to the parts, for sides and angles of a triangle could not be such without an arrangement governed by the nature triangle. The whole of nature may be similarly conceived: as the reciprocal necessity of *natura naturans,* or nature defined in respect of its unity, and *natura naturata,* or nature specified in detail. There is some promise here of a reconciliation of the *Way of Opinion* with the *Way of Truth.* Opinion would be a gathering of detail, truth a comprehension of the intelligible unity. Both would be provided for through the consideration that whatever is complete and necessary must be made up of incompletenesses that are necessary to it.

§ 154. This consideration, however, does not receive its most effective formulation in Spinoza.

THE APPROACH TO PHILOSOPHY

The isolation of the parts, the actual severalty and irrelevance of the modes, still presents a grave

Transition to Teleological Conceptions. problem. Is there a kind of whole to which not only parts but fragments, or parts in their very incompleteness, are indispensable? This would seem to be true of a *progression* or *development,* since that would require both perfection as its end, and degrees of imperfection as its stages. Spinoza was prevented from making much of this idea by his rejection of the principle of *teleology.* He regarded appreciation or valuation as a projection of personal bias. " Nature has no particular goal in view," and " final causes are mere human figments." " The perfection of things is to be reckoned only from their own nature and power." [7] The philosophical method which Spinoza here repudiates, the interpretation of the world in moral terms, is *Platonism,* an independent and profoundly important movement, belonging to the same general realistic type with Eleaticism and Spinozism. Absolute being is again the fundamental conception. Here, however, it is conceived that being is primarily not affirmation or self-sufficiency, but the *good* or *ideal.* There are few great metaphysical systems that have not

[7] *Ibid.*, pp. 77, 81.

been deeply influenced by Platonism; hence the importance of understanding it in its purity. To this end we must return again to the early Greek conception of the philosopher; for Platonism, like Eleaticism, is a sequel to the philosopher's self-consciousness.

§ 155. Although the first Greek philosophers, such men as Thales, Heraclitus, Parmenides, and **Early Greek Philosophers not Self-critical.** Empedocles, were clearly aware of their distinction and high calling, it by no means follows that they were good judges of themselves. Their sense of intellectual power was unsuspecting; and they praised philosophy without definitely raising the question of its meaning. They were like unskilled players who try all the stops and scales of an organ, and know that somehow they can make a music that exceeds the noises, monotones or simple melodies of those who play upon lesser instruments. They knew their power rather than their instrument or their art. The first philosophers, in short, were self-conscious but not self-critical.

§ 156. The immediately succeeding phase in the history of Greek philosophy was a curtailment, but only in the most superficial sense a criticism, of the activity of the philosopher. In the Periclean

Curtailment of Philosophy in the Age of the Sophists. Age philosophy suffered more from inattention than from refutation. The scepticism of the sophists, who were the knowing men of this age, was not so much conviction as indisposition. They failed to recognize the old philosophical problem; it did not *appeal* to them as a genuine problem. The sophists were the intellectual men of an age of *humanism, individualism,* and *secularism.* These were years in which the circle of human society, the state with its institutions, citizenship with its manifold activities and interests, bounded the horizon of thought. What need to look beyond? Life was not a problem, but an abundant opportunity and a sense of capacity. The world was not a mystery, but a place of entertainment and a sphere of action. Of this the sophists were faithful witnesses. In their love of novelty, irreverence, impressionism, elegance of speech, and above all in their praise of individual efficiency, they preached and pandered to their age. Their public, though it loved to abuse them, was the greatest sophist of them all—brilliant and capricious, incomparably rich in all but wisdom. The majority belonged to what

Plato called " the sight-loving, art-loving, busy class." This is an age, then, when the man of practical common-sense is preëminent, and the philosopher with his dark sayings has passed away. The pride of wisdom has given way to the pride of power and the pride of cleverness. The many men pursue the many goods of life, and there is no spirit among them all who, sitting apart in contemplation, wonders at the meaning of the whole.

§ 157. But in their midst there moved a strange prophet, whom they mistook for one of themselves. **Socrates and the Self-criticism of the Philosopher.** Socrates was not one who prayed in the wilderness, but a man of the streets and the market-place, who talked rather more incessantly than the rest, and apparently with less right. He did not testify to the truth, but pleaded ignorance in extenuation of an exasperating habit of asking questions. There was, however, a humor and a method in his innocence that arrested attention. He was a formidable adversary in discussion from his very irresponsibility; and he was especially successful with the more rhetorical sophists because he chose his own weapons, and substituted critical analysis, question and answer, for the long speeches to which these teachers were habituated by their profession. He appeared to be governed by an insatiable inquisitiveness, and a somewhat malicious desire to discredit those who spoke with authority.

But to those who knew him better, and especially to Plato, who knew him best, Socrates was at once the sweetest and most compelling spirit of his age. There was a kind of truth in the quality of his character. He was perhaps *the first of all reverent men*. In the presence of conceit his self-deprecia- tion was ironical, but in another presence it was most genuine, and his deepest spring of thought and action. This other presence was his own ideal. Socrates was sincerely humble because, ex- pecting so much of philosophy, he saw his own de- ficiency. Unlike the unskilled player, he did not seek to *make* music; but he loved music, and knew that such music as is indeed music was beyond his power. On the other hand he was well aware of his superiority to those in whom self-satisfaction was possible because they had no conception of the ideal. Of such he could say in truth that they did not know enough even to realize the extent of their ignorance. The world has long been famil- iar with the vivid portrayal of the Socratic con- sciousness which is contained in Plato's " Apol- ogy." Socrates had set out in life with the opinion

that his was an age of exceptional enlightenment.
But as he came to know men he found that after
all no one of them really knew what he was about.
Each "sight-loving, art-loving, busy" man was
quite blind to the meaning of life.   While he was
capable of practical achievement, his judgments
concerning the real virtue of his achievements
were conventional and ungrounded, a mere reflection of tradition and opinion.   When asked concerning the meaning of life, or the ground of his
opinions, he was thrown into confusion or aggra-
vated to meaningless reiteration.   Such men, Socrates reflected, were both unwise and confirmed
in their folly through being unconscious of it.
Because he knew that vanity is vanity, that opinion is indeed mere opinion, Socrates felt himself
to be the wisest man in a generation of dogged
unwisdom.

§ 158. It is scarcely necessary to point out that
this insight, however negatively it be used, is a
revelation of positive knowledge.   Heraclitus and Parmenides claimed to
know; Socrates disclaimed knowledge
for reasons.   Like all real criticism this is at once
a confounding of error and a prophecy of truth.
The truth so discovered is indeed not ordinary

Socrates's
Self-criticism
a Prophecy
of Truth.

truth concerning historical or physical things, but not on that account less significant and necessary. This truth, it will also be admitted, is virtually rather than actually set forth by Socrates himself. He knew that life has some meaning which those who live with conviction desire at heart to realize, and that knowledge has principles with which those who speak with conviction intend to be consistent. There is, in short, a rational life and a rational discourse. Furthermore, a rational life will be a life wisely directed to the end of the good; and a rational discourse one constructed with reference to the real natures of things, and the necessities which flow from these natures. But Socrates did not conclusively define either the meaning of life or the form of perfect knowledge. He testified to the necessity of some such truths, and his testimony demonstrated both the blindness of his contemporaries and also his own deficiency.

§ 159. The character and method of Socrates have their best foil in the sophists, but their

The Historical Preparation for Plato.
bearing on the earlier philosophers is for our purposes even more instructive. Unlike Socrates these philosophers had not made a study of the task of the philosopher. They *were* philosophers—" spectators of all time and all ex-

istence "; but they were precritical or dogmatic
philosophers, to whom it had not occurred to define
the requirements of philosophy. They knew no
perfect knowledge other than their own actual
knowledge. They defined being and interpreted
life without reflecting upon the quality of the
knowledge whose object is being, or the quality of
insight that would indeed be practical wisdom.
But when through Socrates the whole philosophical
prospect is again revealed after the period of
humanistic concentration, it is as an ideal whose
possibilities, whose necessities, are conceived before they are realized. Socrates celebrates the rôle
of the philosopher without assigning it to himself.
The new philosophical object is the philosopher
himself; and the new insight a knowledge of
knowledge itself. These three types of intellectual
procedure, dogmatic speculation concerning being,
humanistic interest in life, and the self-criticism of
thought, form the historical preparation for Plato,
the philosopher who defined being a the ideal of
thought, and upon this ground interpreted life.

There is no more striking case in history of the
subtle continuity of thought than the relation
between Plato and his master Socrates. The
wonder of it is due to the absence of any formula-

tion of doctrine on the part of Socrates himself. He only lived and talked; and yet Plato created a system of philosophy in which he is faithfully embodied. The form of embodiment is the dialogue, in which the talking of Socrates is perpetuated and conducted to profounder issues, and in which his life is both rendered and interpreted. But as the vehicle of Plato's thought preserves and makes perfect the Socratic method, so the thought itself begins with the Socratic motive and remains to the end an expression of it. The presentiment of perfect knowledge which distinguished Socrates from his contemporaries becomes in Plato the clear vision of a realm of ideal truth.

§ 160. Plato begins his philosophy with the philosopher and the philosopher's interest. The

Platonism: Reality as the Absolute Ideal or Good.

philosopher is a lover, who like all lovers longs for the beautiful. But he is the supreme lover, for he loves not the individual beautiful object but the Absolute Beauty itself. He is a lover too in that he does not possess, but somehow apprehends his object from afar. Though imperfect, he seeks perfection; though standing like all his fellows in the twilight of half-reality, he faces toward the sun. Now it is the fundamental proposition of the Pla-

tonic philosophy that reality is the sun itself, or
the perfection whose possession every wise thinker
covets, whose presence would satisfy every longing of experience. The real is that beloved object
which is "truly beautiful, delicate, perfect, and
blessed." There is both a serious ground for such
an affirmation and an important truth in its meaning. The ground is the evident incompleteness of
every special judgment concerning experience.
We understand only in part, and we know that we
understand only in part. What we discover is
real enough for practical purposes, but even common-sense questions the true reality of its objects.
Special judgments seem to terminate our thought
abruptly and arbitrarily. We give "the best
answer we can," but such answers do not come as
the completion of our thinking. Our thought is
in some sense surely a seeking, and it would appear
that we are not permitted to rest and be satisfied
at any stage of it. If we do so we are like the
sophists—blind to our own ignorance. But it is
equally true that our thought is straightforward
and progressive. We are not permitted to return
to earlier stages, but must push on to that which is
not less, but more, than what we have as yet found.
There is good hope, then, of understanding what

the ideal may be from our knowledge of the direction which it impels us to follow.

But to understand Plato's conception of the
progression of experience we must again catch up
the Socratic strain which he weaves into every
theme. For Socrates, student of life and mankind, all objects were objects of interest, and all
interests practical interests. One is ignorant
when one does not know the good of things; opin-
ionative when one rates things by conventional
standards; wise when one knows their real good.
In Platonism this practical interpretation of experience appears in the principle that the object
of perfect knowledge is *the good*. The nature of
things which one seeks to know better is the good
of things, the absolute being which is the goal of
all thinking is the very good itself. Plato does
not use the term good in any merely utilitarian
sense. Indeed it is very significant that for Plato
there is no cleavage between theoretical and practical interests. To be morally good is to know the
good, to set one's heart on the true object of affec-
tion; and to be theoretically sound is to understand
perfection. The good itself is the end of every
aim, that in which all interests converge. Hence
it cannot be defined, as might a special good, in

terms of the fulfilment of a set of concrete conditions, but only in terms of the sense or direction of all purposes. The following passage occurs in the " Symposium ":

"The true order of going or being led by others to the things of love, is to use the beauties of earth as steps along which he mounts upward for the sake of that other beauty, going from one to two, and from two to all fair forms, and from fair forms to fair actions, and from fair actions to fair notions, until from fair notions he arrives at the notion of absolute beauty, and at last knows what the essence of beauty is."[8]

§ 161. There is, then, a " true order of going," and an order that leads from one to many, from thence to forms, from thence to morality, and from thence to the general objects of thought or *the ideas*. In the " Republic," where the proper education of the philosopher is in question, it is proposed that he shall study arithmetic, geometry, astronomy, and dialectic. Thus in each case mathematics is the first advance in knowledge, and dialectic the nearest to perfection. Most of Plato's examples are drawn from mathematics. This science replaces the variety and vagueness of the forms of experience with *clear, unitary, definite,* and *eternal* natures,

The Progression of Experience toward God.

---

[8] Plato: *Symposium*, 211. Translation by Jowett.

such as the number and the geometrical figure. Thus certain individual things are approximately triangular, but subject to alteration, and indefinitely many. On the other hand the triangle as defined by geometry is the fixed and unequivocal nature or idea which such experiences suggest; and the philosophical mind will at once pass to it from these. But the mathematical objects are themselves not thoroughly understood when understood only in mathematical terms, for the foundations of mathematics are arbitrary. And the same is true of all the so-called special sciences. Even the scientists themselves, says Plato,

"only dream about being, but never can behold the waking reality so long as they leave the hypotheses they use unexamined, and are unable to give an account of them. For when a man knows not his own first principle, and when the conclusion and intermediate steps are also constructed out of he knows not what, how can he imagine that such a conventional statement will ever become science?"[9]

Within the science of dialectics we are to understand the connections and sequences of ideas themselves, in the hope of eliminating every arbitrariness and conventionality within a system of truth that is pure and self-luminous rationality. To

[9] Plato: *Republic*, 533. Translation by Jowett.

this science, which is the great interest of his later years, Plato contributes only incomplete studies and experiments. We must be satisfied with the playful answer with which, in the " Republic," he replies to Glaucon's entreaty that " he proceed at once from the prelude or preamble to the chief strain, and describe that in like manner ": " Dear Glaucon, you will not be able to follow me here, though I would do my best."

But a philosophical system has been projected. The real is that perfect significance or meaning which thought and every interest suggests, and toward which there is in experience an appreciable movement. It is this significance which makes things what they really are, and which constitutes our understanding of them. In itself it transcends the steps which lead to it; " for God," says Plato, " mingles not with men." But it is nevertheless the meaning of human life. And this we can readily conceive. The last word may transform the sentence from nonsense into sense, and it would be true to say that its sense mingles not with nonsense. Similarly the last touch of the brush may transform an inchoate mass of color into a picture, disarray into an object of beauty; and its beauty mingles not with ugliness. So life, when it finally realizes itself, obtains a new and incommensurable quality of perfection in which humanity is transformed into deity. There is frankly no provision for imperfection in such a world. In his later writings Plato sounds his characteristic note less frequently, and permits the ideal to create a cosmos through the admixture of matter. But in his moment of inspiration, the Platonist will have no sense for the imperfect. It is the darkness behind his back, or the twilight through which he passes on his way to the light. He will use even the beauties of earth only " as steps along which he mounts upward for the sake of that other beauty."

§ 162. We have met, then, with two distinct philosophical doctrines which arise from the con-

Aristotle's Hierarchy of Substances in Relation to Platonism. ception of the *absolute,* or the philosopher's peculiar object: the doctrine of the *absolute being* or *substance,* and that of the *absolute ideal* or *good.* Both doctrines are realistic in that they assume reality to be demonstrated or revealed, rather than created, by knowledge. Both are rationalistic in that they develop a system of philosophy from the problem of philosophy, or deduce a definition of reality from the conception of reality. There remains a third doctrine of the same type—the philosophy of Aristotle, the most elaborately constructed system of Greek antiquity, and the most potent influence exerted upon the Scholastic Philosophy of the long mediæval period. This philosophy was rehabilitated in the eighteenth century by Leibniz, the brilliant librarian of the court of Hanover. The extraordinary comprehensiveness of Aristotle's philosophy makes it quite impossible to render here even a general account of it. There is scarcely any human discipline that does not to some extent draw upon it. We are concerned only with the central principles of the metaphysics.

Upon the common ground of rationalism and realism, Plato and Aristotle are complementary in temper, method, and principle. Plato's is the genius of inspiration and fertility, Aristotle's the genius of erudition, mastery, and synthesis. In form, Plato's is the gift of expression, Aristotle's the gift of arrangement. Plato was born and bred an aristocrat, and became the lover of the best—the uncompromising purist; Aristotle is middle-class, and limitlessly wide, hospitable, and patient in his interests. Thus while both are speculative and acute, Plato's mind is intensive

and profound, Aristotle's extensive and orderly.
It was inevitable, then, that Aristotle should find
Plato one-sided. The philosophy of the ideal is
not worldly enough to be true. It is a religion
rather than a theory of reality. Aristotle, however, would not renounce it, but construe it that
it may better provide for nature and history.
This is the significance of his new terminology.
Matter, to which Plato reluctantly concedes some
room as a principle of degradation in the universe, is now admitted to good standing. *Matter* or material is indispensable to being as
its potentiality or that out of which it is constituted. The ideal, on the other hand, loses its exclusive title to the predicate of reality, and becomes
the *form,* or the determinate nature which exists
only in its particular embodiments. The being
or *substance* is the concrete individual, of which
these are the abstracted aspects. Aristotle's
" form," like Plato's " idea," is a teleological principle. The essential nature of the object is its
perfection. It is furthermore essential to the object that it should strive after a higher perfection.
With Aristotle, however, the reality is not the
consummation of the process, the highest perfection in and for itself, but the very hierarchy of

objects that ascends toward it. The highest perfection, or God, is not itself coextensive with
being, but the final cause of being—that on account
of which the whole progression of events takes
place. Reality is the development with all of its
ascending stages from the maximum of potentiality, or matter, to the maximum of actuality, or
God the pure form.

§ 163. To understand the virtue of this philosophy as a basis for the reconciliation of different
interests, we must recall the relation
between Plato and Spinoza. Their
characteristic difference appears to the
best advantage in connection with
mathematical truth. Both regarded geometry as
the best model for philosophical thinking, but for
different reasons. Spinoza prized geometry for
its necessity, and proposed to extend it. His
philosophy is the attempt to formulate a geometry
of being, which shall set forth the inevitable certainties of the universe. Plato, on the other
hand, prized geometry rather for its definition of
types, for its knowledge of pure or perfect natures
such as the circle and triangle, which in immediate experience are only approximated. His
philosophy defines reality similarly as the absolute

The Aristote-
lian Philos-
ophy as a
Reconcilia-
tion of Plato-
nism and
Spinozism.

perfection. Applied to nature Spinozism is mechanical, and looks for necessary laws, while Platonism is teleological, and looks for adaptation and significance. Aristotle's position is intermediate. With Plato he affirms that the good is the ultimate principle. But this very principle is conceived to govern a universe of substances, each of which maintains its own proper being, and all of which are reciprocally determined in their changes. Final causes dominate nature, but work through efficient causes. Reality is not pure perfection, as in Platonism, nor the indifferent necessity, as in Spinozism, but the system of beings necessary to the complete progression toward the highest perfection. The Aristotelian philosophy promises, then, to overcome both the hard realism of Parmenides and Spinoza, and also the supernaturalism of Plato.

§ 164. But it promises, furthermore, to remedy the defect common to these two doctrines, the very

Leibniz's Application of the Conception of Development to the Problem of Imperfection.

besetting problem of this whole type of philosophy. That problem, as has been seen, is to provide for the imperfect within the perfect, for the temporal incidents of nature and history within the eternal being. Many absolutist philosophers have declared the explanation of this realm to be impossible, and have contented themselves with calling it the realm of opinion or appearance. And this realm of opinion or appearance has been used as a proof of the absolute. Zeno, the pupil of Parmenides, was the first to elaborate what have since come to be known as the paradoxes of the empirical world. Most of these paradoxes turn upon the infinite extension and divisibility of space and time. Zeno was especially interested in the difficulty of conceiving motion, which involves both space and time, and thought himself to have demonstrated its absurdity and impossibility.[10] His argument is thus the complement of Parmenides's argument for the indivisible and unchanging substance. Now the method which Zeno here adopts may be extended to cover the whole realm of nature and history. We should then be dialectically driven from this realm to take refuge in absolute being. But the empirical world is not destroyed by disparagement, and cannot long lack champions even among the absolutists themselves. The reconciliation of nature and history with the absolute being became the special interest of Leibniz, the great modern Aristotelian. As a scientist and

[10] See Burnet: *Op. cit.*, pp. 322–333.

man of affairs, he was profoundly dissatisfied with Spinoza's resolution of nature, the human individual, and the human society into the universal being. He became an advocate of individualism while retaining the general aim and method of rationalism.

Like Aristotle, Leibniz attributes reality to individual substances, which he calls " monads "; and like Aristotle he conceives these monads to compose an ascending order, with God, the monad of monads, as its dominating goal.

" Furthermore, every substance is like an entire world and like a mirror of God, or indeed of the whole world which it portrays, each one in its own fashion; almost as the same city is variously represented according to the various situations of him who is regarding it. Thus the universe is multiplied in some sort as many times as there are substances, and the glory of God is multiplied in the same way by as many wholly different representations of his works."[11]

The very " glory of God," then, requires the innumerable finite individuals with all their characteristic imperfections, that the universe may lack no possible shade or quality of perspective.

§ 165. But the besetting problem is in fact not

[11] Leibniz: *Discourse on Metaphysics*. Translation by Montgomery, p. 15.

In so far as the monads are spiritual this doctrine tends to be subjectivistic. Cf. Chap. IX.

solved, and is one of the chief incentives to that
other philosophy of absolutism which defines an

The Problem of Imperfection Remains Unsolved. absolute spirit or mind. Both Aristotle
and Leibniz undertake to make the
perfection which determines the order
of the hierarchy of substances, at the same time
the responsible author of the whole hierarchy. In
this case the dilemma is plain. If the divine form
or the divine monad be other than the stages that
lead up to it, these latter cannot be essential to it,
for God is by definition absolutely self-sufficient.
If, on the other hand, God is identical with the
development in its entirety, then two quite incommensurable standards of perfection determine the
supremacy of the divine nature, that of the whole
and that of the highest parts of the whole. The
union of these two and the definition of a perfection which may be at once the development and its
goal, is the task of absolute idealism.

§ 166. Of the two fundamental questions of
epistemology, absolute realism answers the one

Absolute Realism in Epistemology. Rationalism. explicitly, the other implicitly. As respects *the source of the most valid
knowledge,* Parmenides, Plato, Aristotle, Spinoza are all agreed: true knowledge is

the work of reason, of pure intellection. Plato
is the great exponent of dialectic, or the reciprocal
affinities and necessities of ideas. Aristotle is the
founder of deductive logic. Spinoza proposes to
consider even " human actions and desires " as
though he were " concerned with lines, planes, and
solids." Empirical data may be the occasion, but
cannot be the ground of the highest knowledge.
According to Leibniz,

" it seems that necessary truths, such as we find in pure
mathematics, and especially in arithmetic and geometry,
must have principles whose proof does not depend upon
instances, nor, consequently, upon the witness of the
senses, although without the senses it would never have
come into our heads to think of them." [12]

§ 167. The answers which these philosophies
give to the question of *the relation between the*
The Relation *state of knowledge and its object,* divide
of Thought
and its Object them into two groups. Among the an-
in Absolute
Realism.   cients reason is regarded as the means
of emancipation from the limitations of the private mind. " The sleeping turn aside each into
a world of his own," but " the waking "—the wise
men—" have one and the same world." What the
individual knows belongs to himself only in so

[12] Leibniz: *New Essays on the Human Understanding.*
Translation by Latta, p. 363.

far as it is inadequate. Hence for Plato the ideas are not the attributes of a mind, but that self-subsistent truth to which, in its moments of insight, a mind may have access. Opinion is " my own," the truth is being. The position of Aristotle is equally clear. "Actual knowledge," he maintains, " is identical with its object."

Spinoza and Leibniz belong to another age. Modern philosophy began with a new emphasis upon self-consciousness. In his celebrated argument—" I think, hence I am " (*cogito ergo sum*) —Descartes established the independent and substantial reality of the thinking activity. The " I think " is recognized as in itself a fundamental being, known intuitively to the thinker himself. Now although Spinoza and Leibniz are finally determined by the same motives that obtain in the cases of Plato and Aristotle, they must reckon with this new distinction between the thinker and his object. The result in the case of Spinoza is the doctrine of " parallelism," in which mind is defined as an " infinite attribute " of substance, an aspect or phase coextensive with the whole of being. The result in the case of Leibniz is his doctrine of " representation " and " preëstablished harmony," whereby each monadic substance is in itself an active spiritual entity, and belongs to the universe through its knowledge of a specific stage of the development of the universe. But both Spinoza and Leibniz subordinate such conceptions as these to the fundamental identity that pervades the whole. With Spinoza the attributes belong to the same absolute substance, and with Leibniz the monads represent the one universe. And with both, finally, the perfection of knowledge, or the knowledge of God, is indistinguishable from its object, God himself. The epistemological subtleties peculiar to these philosophers are not stable doctrines, but render inevitable either a return to the simpler and bolder realism of the Greeks, or a passing over into the more radical and systematic doctrine of absolute idealism.

§ 168. We have met with two general motives, both of which are subordinated to the doctrine of

The Stoic and Spinozistic Ethics of Necessity.

an absolute being postulated and sought by philosophy. The one of these motives leads to the conception of the absolutely necessary and immutable substance, the other to the conception of a consummate perfection. There is an *interpretation of life* appropriate to each of these conceptions. Both agree in regarding life seriously, in defining reason or philosophy as the highest human activity, and in emphasizing the identity of the individual's good with the good of the universe. But there are striking differences of tone and spirit.

Although the metaphysics of the Stoics have various affiliations, the Stoic code of morality is the true practical sequel to the Eleatic-Spinozistic view of the world. The Stoic is one who has set his affections on the eternal being. He asks nothing of it for himself, but identifies himself with it. The saving grace is a sense of reality. The virtuous man is not one who remakes the world, or draws upon it for his private uses; even less one who rails against it, or complains that it has used him ill. He is rather one who recognizes that there is but one really valid claim, that of the universe itself. But he not only submits to this claim on account of its superiority; he makes it his own. The discipline of Stoicism is the regulation of the individual will to the end that it may coincide with the universal will. There is a part of man by virtue of which he is satisfied with what things are, whatever they be. That part, designated by the Stoics as " the ruling part," is the reason. In so far as man seeks to

understand the laws and natures which actually
prevail, he cannot be discontented with anything
whatsoever that may be known to him.

" For, in so far as we are intelligent beings, we cannot
desire anything save that which is necessary, nor yield
absolute acquiescence to anything, save to that which is
true: wherefore, in so far as we have a right understanding of these things, the endeavor of the better part of ourselves is in harmony with the order of nature as a whole." [13]

In agreement with this teaching of Spinoza's is the
famous Stoic formula to the effect that " nothing
can happen contrary to the will of the wise man,"
who is free through his very acquiescence.   If reason be the proper " ruling part," the first step in
the moral life is the subordination of the appetitive nature and the enthronement of reason.   One
who is himself rational will then recognize the
fellowship of all rational beings, and the unitary
and beneficent rationality of the entire universe.
The highest morality is thus already upon the
plane of religion.

§ 169. With Spinoza and the Stoics, the per-
fection of the individual is reduced to what the
The Platonic   universe requires of him. The good
Ethics of
Perfection.   man is willing to be whatever he must

[13] Spinoza: *Op. cit.*, Part IV. Translation by Elwes,
p. 243.

be, for the sake of the whole with which through reason he is enabled to identify himself. With Plato and Aristotle the perfection of the individual himself is commended, that the universe may abound in perfection. The good man is the ideal man—the expression of the type. And how different the quality of a morality in keeping with this principle! The virtues which Plato enumerates—temperance, courage, wisdom, and justice—compose a consummate human nature. He is thinking not of the necessities but of the possibilities of life. Knowledge of the truth will indeed be the best of human living, but knowledge is not prized because it can reconcile man to his limitations; it is the very overflowing of his cup of life. The youth are to

"dwell in the land of health, amid fair sights and sounds; and beauty, the effluence of fair works, will visit the eye and ear, like a healthful breeze from a purer region, and insensibly draw the soul even in childhood into harmony with the beauty of reason."[4]

Aristotle's account of human perfection is more circumstantial and more prosaic. "The function of man is an activity of soul in accordance with reason," and his happiness or well-being will con-

[4] Plato: *Op. cit.*, 401.

sist in the fulness of rational living. But such
fulness requires a sphere of life that will call forth
and exercise the highest human capacities. Aristotle frankly pronounces " external goods " to be
indispensable, and happiness to be therefore " a
gift of the gods." The rational man will acquire
a certain exquisiteness or finesse of action, a
" mean " of conduct; and this virtue will be diver-
sified through the various relations into which he
must enter, and the different situations which he
must meet. He will be not merely brave, temperate, and just, as Plato would have him, but liberal,
magnificent, gentle, truthful, witty, friendly, and
in all self-respecting or high-minded. In addition to these strictly moral virtues, he will possess
the intellectual virtues of prudence and wisdom,
the resources of art and science; and will finally
possess the gift of insight, or intuitive reason.
Speculation will be his highest activity, and the
mark of his kinship with the gods who dwell in
the perpetual contemplation of the truth.

The Religion   § 170. Aristotle's ethics expresses the
of Fulfilment,
and the Re-   buoyancy of the ancient world, when
ligion of Re-
nunciation.   the individual does not feel himself
oppressed by the eternal reality, but rejoices in it.
He is not too conscious of his sufferings to be

disinterested in his admiration and wonder. It is this which distinguishes the religion of Plato and Aristotle from that of the Stoics and Spinoza. With both alike, religion consists not in making the world, but in contemplating it; not in coöperating with God, but in worshipping him. Plato and Aristotle, however, do not find any antagonism between the ways of God and the natural interests of men. God does not differ from men save in his exalted perfection. The contemplation and worship of him comes as the final and highest stage of a life which is organic and continuous throughout. The love of God is the natural love when it has found its true object.

" For he who has been instructed thus far in the things of love, and who has learned to see the beautiful in due order and succession, when he comes toward the end will suddenly perceive a nature of wondrous beauty— and this, Socrates, is that final cause of all our former toils, which in the first place is everlasting—not growing and decaying, or waxing and waning; in the next place not fair in one point of view and foul in another, . . . or in the likeness of a face or hands or any other part of the bodily frame, or in any form of speech or knowledge, nor existing in any other being; . . . but beauty only, absolute, separate, simple, and everlasting, which without diminution and without increase, or any change, is imparted to the ever-growing and perishing beauties of all other things."[15]

[15] Plato: *Symposium*, 210–211. Translation by Jowett.

The religion of Spinoza is the religion of one who has renounced the favor of the universe. He was deprived early in life of every benefit of fortune, and set out to find the good which required no special dispensation but only the common lot and the common human endowment. He found that good to consist in the conviction of the necessity, made acceptable through the supremacy of the understanding. The like faith of the Stoics makes of no account the difference of fortune between Marcus the emperor and Epictetus the slave.

" For two reasons, then, it is right to be content with that which happens to thee; the one because it was done for thee and prescribed for thee, and in a manner had reference to thee, originally from the most ancient causes spun with thy destiny; and the other because even that which comes severally to every man is to the power which administers the universe a cause of felicity and perfection, nay even of its very continuance. For the integrity of the whole is mutilated, if thou cuttest off anything whatever from the conjunction and the continuity either of the parts or of the causes. And thou dost cut off, as far as it is in thy power, when thou art dissatisfied, and in a manner triest to put anything out of the way." [16]

[16] Marcus Aurelius Antoninus: *Thoughts.* Translation by Long, p. 141.

CHAPTER XI

§ 171. ABSOLUTE idealism is the most elaborately constructive of all the historical types of
General
Constructive
Character of
Absolute
Idealism.
philosophy. Though it may have over-
looked elementary truths, and have
sought to combine irreconcilable principles, it cannot be charged with lack of sophistication or subtlety. Its great virtue is its recognition
of problems—its exceeding circumspection; while
its great promise is due to its comprehensiveness—
its generous provision for all interests and points
of view. But its very breadth and complexity render this philosophy peculiarly liable to the equivo-
cal use of conceptions. This may be readily
understood from the nature of the central doctrine
of absolute idealism. According to this doctrine
it is proposed to define the universe as an *abso-*

[1] By *Absolute Idealism* is meant that system of philosophy
which defines the universe as the *absolute spirit*, which is
the human *moral, cognitive,* or *appreciative consciousness*
universalized; or as the *absolute, transcendental mind,* whose
state of *complete knowledge* is implied in all finite thinking.

lute spirit; or a being infinite, ultimate, eternal, and self-sufficient, like the being of Plato and Spinoza, but possessing at the same time the distinguishing properties of spirit. Such conceptions as self-consciousness, will, knowledge, and moral goodness are carried over from the realm of human endeavor and social relations to the unitary and all-inclusive reality. Now it has been objected that this procedure is either meaningless, in that it so applies the term spirit as to contradict its meaning; or prejudicial to spiritual interests, in that it neutralizes the properties of spirit through so extending their use. Thus one may contend that to affirm that the universe as a whole is spirit is meaningless, since moral goodness requires special conditions and relations that cannot be attributed to the universe as a whole; or one may contend that such doctrine is prejudicial to moral interests because by attributing spiritual perfection to the totality of being it discredits all moral loyalties and antagonisms. The difficulties that lie in the way of absolute idealism are due, then, to the complexity of its synthesis, to its complementary recognition of differences and resolution of them into unity. But this synthesis is due to the urgency of certain great problems which the first

or realistic expression of the absolutist motive left
undiscovered and unsolved.

§ 172. It is natural to approach so deliberate
and calculating a philosophy from the stand-point

The Great
Outstanding
Problems of
Absolutism.

of the problems which it proposes to
solve. One of these is the epistemological problem of the relation between
the state of knowledge and its object. Naturalism
and absolute realism side with common-sense in
its assumption that although the real object is essential to the valid state of knowledge, its being
known is not essential to the real object. Subjectivism, on the other hand, maintains that being
is essentially the content of a knowing state, or
an activity of the knower himself. Absolute idealism proposes to accept the general epistemological
principle of subjectivism; but to satisfy the realistic demand for a standard, compelling object, by
setting up an *absolute knower,* with whom all valid
knowledge must be in agreement. This epistemological statement of absolute idealism is its
most mature phase; and the culminating phase, in
which it shows unmistakable signs of passing over
into another doctrine. We must look for its pris-
tine inspiration in its solution of another fundamental problem: that of the relation between the

absolute and the empirical. Like absolute realism, this philosophy regards the universe as a unitary and internally necessary being, and undertakes to hold that being accountable for every item of experience. But we have found that absolute realism is beset with the difficulty of thus accounting for the fragmentariness and isolation of the individual. The contention that the universe must really be a rational or perfect unity is disputed by the evident multiplicity, irrelevance, and imperfection in the foreground of experience. The inference to perfection and the confession of imperfection seem equally unavoidable. Rational necessities and empirical facts are out of joint.

§ 173. Even Plato had been conscious of a certain responsibility for matters of fact. Inasmuch

The Greek Philosophers and the Problem of Evil. The Task of the New Absolutism.

as he attached the predicate of reality to the absolute perfection, he made that being the only source to which they could be referred. Perhaps, then, he suggests, they are due to the very bounteousness of God.

"He was good, and no goodness can ever have any jealousy of anything. And being free from jealousy, he desired that all things should be as like himself as possible."[2]

[2] Plato: *Timæus*. 29. Translation by Jowett.

Plotinus, in whom Platonism is leavened by the spirit of an age which is convinced of sin, and which is therefore more keenly aware of the positive existence of the imperfect, follows out this suggestion. Creation is " emanation "—the overflow of God's excess of goodness. But one does not readily understand how goodness, desiring all things to be like itself, should thereupon create evil—even to make it good. The Aristotelian philosophy, with its conception of the gradation of substances, would seem to be better equipped to meet the difficulty. A development requires stages; and every finite thing may thus be perfect in its way and perfect in its place, while in the absolute truth or God there is realized the meaning of the whole order. But if so, there is evidently something that escapes God, to wit, the meaningless and unfitness, the error and evil, of the stages in their successive isolation. Nor is it of any avail to insist (as did Plato, Aristotle, and Spinoza alike) that these are only privation, and therefore not to be counted in the sum of reality. For privation is itself an experience, with a great variety of implications, moral and psychological; and these cannot be attributed to God or deduced from him, in consideration of his absolute perfection.

The task of the new absolutism is now in clear view. The perfect must be amended to admit the imperfect. The absolute significance must be so construed as to provide for the evident facts; for the unmeaning things and changes of the natural order; for ignorance, sin, despair, and every human deficiency. The new philosophy is to solve this problem by defining a *spiritual absolute,* and by so construing the life or dynamics of spirit, as to demonstrate the necessity of the very imperfection and opposition which is so baffling to the realist.

§ 174. Absolute idealism, which is essentially a modern doctrine, does not begin with rhapsodies, but with a very sober analysis of familiar truths, conducted by the most sober of all philosophers, Immanuel Kant. This philosopher lived in Königsberg, Germany, at the close of the eighteenth century. He is related to absolute idealism much as Socrates is related to Platonism: he was not himself speculative, but employed a critical method which was transformed by his followers into a metaphysical construction. It is essential to the understanding both of Kant and of his more speculative successors, to observe that he begins with the recognition of certain non-philosophical truths—

The Beginning of Absolute Idealism in Kant's Analysis of Experience.

those of *natural science* and *the moral conscious-ness*. He accepts the order of nature formulated in the Newtonian dynamics, and the moral order acknowledged in the common human conviction of duty. And he is interested in discovering the ground upon which these common affirmations rest, the structure which virtually supports them as types of knowledge. But a general importance attaches to the analysis because these two types of knowledge (together with the æsthetic judg-ment, which is similarly analyzed) are regarded by Kant as coextensive with experience itself. The *very least experience* that can be reported upon at all is an experience of nature or duty, and as such will be informed with their char-acteristic principles. Let us consider the former type. The simplest instance of nature is the ex-perience of the single perceived object. In the first place, such an object will be perceived as in space and time. These Kant calls the *forms of intuition*. An object cannot even be presented or given without them. But, furthermore, it will be regarded as substance, that is, as having a sub-stratum that persists through changes of position or quality. It will also be regarded as causally dependent upon other objects like itself. Causality, substance, and like principles to the number of twelve, Kant calls the *categories of the understanding*. Both intuition and understanding are indispensable to the experience of any object whatsoever. They may be said to condition the object in general. Their principles condition the process of making something out of the manifold of sensation. But similarly, every moral experience recognizes what Kant calls *the categorical imperative*. The categorical imperative is the law of reasonableness or impartiality in conduct, requiring the individual to act on a maxim which he can "will to be law universal." No state of desire or situation calling for action means anything morally except in the light of this obligation. Thus certain principles of thought and action are said to be implicit in all experience. They are universal and necessary in the sense that they are discovered as the conditions not of any particular experience, but of experience in general. This implicit or virtual presence in experience in general, Kant calls their transcendental character, and the process of explicating them is his famous *Transcendental Deduction*.

§ 175. The restriction which Kant puts upon his method is quite essential to its meaning. I deduce the categories, for example, just in so far as I find them to be necessary to perception.

Without them my perception is blind, I make nothing of it; with them my experience becomes systematic and rational. But categories which I so deduce must be forever limited to the rôle for which they are defined. Categories without perceptions are " empty "; they have validity solely with reference to the experience which they set in order. Indeed, I cannot even complete that order. The orderly arrangement of parts of experience suggests, and suggests irresistibly, a perfect system. I can even define the ideas and ideals through which such a perfect system might be realized. But I cannot in the Kantian sense attach reality to it because it is not indispensable to experience. It must remain an ideal which regulates my thinking of such parts of it as fall within the range of my perception; or it may through my moral nature become the realm of my living and an object of faith. In short, Kant's is essentially a " critical philosophy," a logical and analytical study of the special terms and relations of human knowledge. He denies the validity of these terms and relations beyond this realm. His critiques are an inventory of the conditions, principles, and prospects of that cognition which, although not alone ideally conceivable, is alone possible.

§ 176. With the successors of Kant, as with the successors of Socrates, a criticism becomes a system of metaphysics. This transformation is effected in the post-Kantians by *a generalization of the human cognitive consciousness.* According to Kant's analysis it contains a manifold of sense which must be organized by categories in obedience to the ideal of a rational universe. The whole enterprise, with its problems given in perception, its instruments available in the activities of the understanding, and its ideals revealed in the reason, is an organic spiritual unity, manifesting itself in the self-consciousness of the thinker. Now in absolute idealism this very enterprise of knowledge, made universal and called the *absolute spirit* or *mind*, is taken to be the ultimate reality. And here at length would seem to be afforded the conception of a being to which the problematic and the rational, the data and the principles, the natural and the ideal, are alike indispensable. We are now to seek the real not in the ideal itself,

The Post-Kantian Metaphysics is a Generalization of the Cognitive and Moral Consciousness as Analyzed by Kant. The Absolute Spirit.

but in that spiritual unity in which appearance is the incentive to truth, and natural imperfection the spring to goodness. This may be translated into the language which Plato uses in the " Symposium," when Diotima is revealing to Socrates the meaning of love. The new reality will be not the loved one, but love itself.

" What then is Love?   Is he mortal?"
" No."
" What then?"
" As in the former instance, he is neither mortal nor immortal, but is a mean between them."
" What is he then, Diotima?"
" He is a great spirit, and like all that is spiritual he is intermediate between the divine and the mortal." [3]

Reality is no longer the God who mingles not with men, but that power which, as Diotima further says, " interprets and conveys to the gods the prayers and sacrifices of men, and to men the commands and rewards of the gods."

In speaking for such an idealism, Emerson says:

" Everything good is on the highway. The middle region of our being is the temperate zone. We may climb into the thin and cold realm of pure geometry and lifeless science, or sink into that of sensation. Between these extremes is the equator of life, of thought, of spirit, of poetry. . . .   The mid-world is best." [4]

[3] Plato: *Symposium*, 202.   Translation by Jowett.
[4] Emerson: *Essays, Second Series*, pp. 65-66.

The new reality is this highway of the spirit, the
very course and raceway of self-consciousness.   It
is traversed in the movement and self-correction
of thought, in the interest in ideals, or in the submission of the will to the control of the moral law.

§ 177. It is the last of these phases of self-consciousness that Fichte, who was Kant's immediate

Fichteanism,
or the Abso-
lute Spirit as
Moral
Activity.
successor, regards as of paramount importance.   As Platonism began with the
ideal of the good or the object of life,
so the new idealism begins with the conviction
of duty, or *the story of life*.   Being is the living
moral nature compelled to build itself a natural
order wherein it may obey the moral law, and to
divide itself into a community of moral selves
through which the moral virtues may be realized.
Nature and society flow from the conception of an
absolute moral activity, or ego.   Such an ego
could not be pure and isolated and yet be moral.
The evidence of this is the common moral consciousness.   My duty compels me to act upon the
not-self or environment, and to respect and coöperate with other selves.   Fichte's absolute is this
moral consciousness universalized and made eternal.   Moral value being its fundamental principle the universe must on that very account em-

brace both nature, or moral indifference, and humanity, or moral limitation.

§ 178. But the Romanticists, who followed close upon Fichte, were dissatisfied with so hard and exclusive a conception of spiritual being. Life, they said, is not all duty. Indeed, the true spiritual life is quite other, not harsh and constrained, but free and spontaneous—a wealth of feeling playing about a constantly shifting centre. Spirit is not consecutive and law-abiding, but capricious and wanton, seeking the beautiful in no orderly progression, but in a refined and versatile sensibility. If this be the nature of spirit, and if spirit be the nature of reality, then he is most wise who is most rich in sentiment. The Romanticists were the exponents of an absolute sentimentalism. And they did not prove it, but like good sentimentalists they felt it.

Romanticism, or the Absolute Spirit as Sentiment.

§ 179. Hegel, the master of the new idealism, set himself the task of construing spirit in terms as consecutive as those of Fichte, and as comprehensive as those of the Romanticists. Like Plato, he found in dialectic the supreme manifestation of the spiritual life. There is a certain flow of ideas which

Hegelianism, or the Absolute Spirit as Dialectic.

determines the meaning of experience, and is the truth of truths.   But the mark of the new prophet is this: the flow of ideas itself is *a process of self-correction due to a sense of error.*   Thus bare sensation is abstract and bare thought is abstract. The real, however, is not merely the concrete in which they are united, but the very process in the course of which through knowledge of abstraction thought arrives at the concrete.   The principle of negation is the very life of thought, and it is *the life of thought,* rather than the outcome of thought, which is reality.   The most general form of the dialectical process contains three moments: the moment of *thesis,* in which affirmation is made; the moment of *antithesis,* in which the opposite asserts itself; and the moment of *synthesis,* in which a reconciliation is effected in a new thesis.   Thus thought is the progressive overcoming of contradiction; not the state of freedom from contradiction, but the act of escaping it.   Such processes are more familiar in the moral life.   Morality consists, so even common-sense asserts, in the overcoming of evil.   Character is the resistance of temptation; goodness, a growth in grace through discipline.   Of such, for Hegel, is the very kingdom of heaven.   It is the task of the philosopher, a task to which Hegel applies himself most assiduously, to analyze the battle and the victory upon which spiritual being nourishes itself. And since the deeper processes are those of thought, the Hegelian philosophy centres in an ordering of notions, a demonstration of that necessary progression of thought which, in its whole dynamical logical history, constitutes the *absolute idea*.

§ 180. The Hegelian philosophy, with its emphasis upon difference, antagonism, and develop-

The Hegelian Philosophy of Nature and History. ment, is peculiarly qualified to be a philosophy of nature and history. Those principles of spiritual development which logic defines are conceived as incarnate in the evolution of the world. Nature, as the very antithesis to spirit, is now understood to be the foil of spirit. In nature spirit alienates itself in order to return enriched. The stages of nature are the preparation for the reviving of a spirituality that has been deliberately forfeited. The Romanticists, whether philosophers like Schelling or poets like Goethe and Wordsworth, were led by their feeling for the beauty of nature to attribute to it a much deeper and more direct spiritual significance. But Hegel and the Romanticists alike are truly expressed in Emerson's belief that the spiritual interpretation of nature is the "true science."

"The poet alone knows astronomy, chemistry, vegetation, and animation, for he does not stop at these facts, but employs them as signs. He knows why the plain or meadow of space was strown with these flowers we call suns and moons and stars; why the great deep is adorned with animals, with men, and gods; for in every word he speaks he rides on them as the horses of thought."[5]

The new awakening of spirit which is for Hegel the consummation of the natural evolution, begins with the individual or *subjective* spirit, and develops into the social or *objective* spirit, which is morality and history. History is a veritable dialectic of nations, in the course of which the consciousness of individual liberty is developed, and coördinated with the unity of the state. The highest stage of spirit incarnate is that of *absolute* spirit, embracing art, religion, and philosophy. In art the absolute idea obtains expression in sensuous existence, more perfectly in classical than in

[5] Emerson: *Op. cit.*, p. 25.
The possibility of conflict between this method of nature study and the empirical method of science is significantly attested by the circumstance that in the year 1801 Hegel published a paper in which he maintained, on the ground of certain numerical harmonies, that there could be no planet between Mars and Jupiter, while at almost exactly the same time Piazzi discovered Ceres, the first of the asteroids.

the symbolic art of the Orient, but most perfectly in the romantic art of the modern period. In religion the absolute idea is expressed in the imagination through worship. In Oriental pantheism, the individual is overwhelmed by his sense of the universal; in Greek religion, God is but a higher man; while in Christianity God and man are perfectly united in Christ. Finally, in philosophy the absolute idea reaches its highest possible expression in articulate thought.

§ 181. Such is absolute idealism approached from the stand-point of antecedent metaphysics.

Résumé. Failure of Absolute Idealism to Solve the Problem of Evil. It is the most elaborate and subtle provision for antagonistic differences within unity that the speculative mind of man has as yet been able to make. It is the last and most thorough attempt to resolve individual and universal, temporal and eternal, natural and ideal, good and evil, into an absolute unity in which the universal, eternal, ideal, and good shall dominate, and in which all terms shall be related with such necessity as obtains in the definitions and theorems of geometry. There is to be some absolute meaning which is rational to the uttermost and the necessary ground of all the incidents of existence. Thought could undertake no

more ambitious and exacting task. Nor is it evident after all that absolute idealism enjoys any
better success in this task than absolute realism.
The difference between them becomes much less
marked when we reflect that the former, like the
latter, must reserve the predicate of being for the
unity of the whole. Even though evil and contradiction belong to the essence of things, move in
the secret heart of a spiritual universe, the reality
is not these in their severalty, but that life within
which they fall, the story within which they
"earn a place." And if absolute idealism has
defined a new perfection, it has at the same time
defined a new imperfection. The perfection is
rich in contrast, and thus inclusive of both the
lights and shades of experience; but the perfection
belongs only to the composition of these elements
within a single view. It is not necessary to such
perfection that the evil should ever be viewed in
isolation. The idealist employs the analogy of the
drama or the picture whose very significance requires the balance of opposing forces; or the analogy of the symphony in which a higher musical
quality is realized through the resolution of discord
into harmony. But none of these unities requires
any element whatsoever that does not partake of its

beauty. It is quite irrelevant to the drama that
the hero should himself have his own view of
events with no understanding of their dramatic
value, as it is irrelevant to the picture that an unbalanced fragment of it should dwell apart, or
to the symphony that the discord should be heard
without the harmony.   One may multiply without
end the internal differences and antagonisms that
contribute to the internal meaning, and be as far
as ever from understanding the external detachment of experiences that are not rational or good
in themselves.   And it is precisely this kind of
fact that precipitates the whole problem.   We do
not judge of sin and error from experiences in
which they conduct to goodness and truth, but
from experiences in which they are stark and
unresolved.

In view of such considerations many idealists
have been willing to confess their inability to solve
this problem. To quote a recent expositor of
Hegel,

"We need not, after all, be surprised at the apparently
insoluble problem which confronts us. For the question
has developed into the old difficulty of the origin of evil,
which has always baffled both theologians and philosophers. An idealism which declares that the universe is
in reality perfect, can find, as most forms of popular

idealism do, an escape from the difficulties of the existence of evil, by declaring that the universe is as yet only growing towards its ideal perfection. But this refuge disappears with the reality of time, and we are left with an awkward difference between what philosophy tells us must be, and what our life tells us actually is."[6]

If the philosophy of eternal perfection persists in its fundamental doctrine in spite of this irreconcilable conflict with life, it is because it is believed that that doctrine *must* be true. Let us turn, then, to its more constructive and compelling argument.

§ 182. The proof of absolute idealism is supposed by the majority of its exponents to follow from the problem of epistemology, and more particularly from the manifest dependence of truth upon the knowing mind. In its initial phase absolute idealism is indistinguishable from subjectivism. Like that philosophy it finds that the object of knowledge is inseparable from the state of knowledge throughout the whole range of experience. Since the knower can never escape himself, it may be set down as an elementary fact that reality (at any rate whatever reality can be known or even talked about) owes its being to mind.

The Constructive Argument for Absolute Idealism is Based upon the Subjectivistic Theory of Knowledge.

[6] McTaggart: *Studies in Hegelian Dialectic*, p. 181.

Thus Green, the English neo-Hegelian, maintains that " an object which no consciousness presented to itself would not be an object at all," and wonders that this principle is not generally taken for granted and made the starting-point for philosophy.[7] However, unless the very term " object " is intended to imply presence to a subject, this principle is by no means self-evident, and must be traced to its sources.

We have already followed the fortunes of that empirical subjectivism which issues from the relativity of perception. At the very dawn of philosophy it was observed that what is seen, heard, or otherwise experienced through the senses, depends not only upon the use of sense-organs, but upon the special point of view occupied by each individual sentient being. It was therefore concluded that the perceptual world belonged to the human knower with his limitations and perspective, rather than to being itself. It was this epistemological principle upon which Berkeley founded his empirical idealism. Believing knowledge to consist essentially in perception, and believing perception to be subjective, he had to choose between the relegation of being to a region inac-

[7] Green: *Prolegomena to Ethics,* p. 15.

cessible to knowledge, and the definition of being
in terms of subjectivity.   To avoid scepticism he
accepted the latter alternative.   But among the
Greeks with whom this theory of perception origi-
nated, it drew its meaning in large part from the
distinction between perception and reason.   Thus
we read in Plato's " Sophist ":

"And you would allow that we participate in generation with the body, and by perception; but we participate
with the soul by thought in true essence, and essence
you would affirm to be always the same and immutable,
whereas generation varies." [8]

It is conceived that although in perception man
is condemned to a knowledge conditioned by the
affections and station of his body, he may nevertheless escape himself and lay hold on the
" true essence " of things, by virtue of thought.
In other words, knowledge, in contradistinction
to " opinion," is not made by the subject, but is
the soul's participation in the eternal natures
of things.   In the moment of insight the varying
course of the individual thinker coincides with the
unvarying truth; but in that moment the individual thinker is ennobled through being assimilated
to the truth, while the truth is no more, no less,
the truth than before.

[8] Plato: *The Sophist*, 248.   Translation by Jowett.

§ 183. In absolute idealism, the principle of subjectivism is extended to reason itself. This

The Principle of Subjectivism Extended to Reason. extension seems to have been originally due to moral and religious interests. From the moral stand-point the contemplation of the truth is a *state,* and the highest state of the individual life. The religious interest unifies the individual life and directs attention to its spiritual development. Among the Greeks of the middle period life was as yet viewed objectively as the fulfilment of capacities, and knowledge was regarded as perfection of function, the exercise of the highest of human prerogatives. But as moral and religious interests became more absorbing, the individual lived more and more in his own self-consciousness. Even before the Christian era the Greek philosophers themselves were preoccupied with the task of winning a state of inner serenity. Thus the Stoics and Epicureans came to look upon knowledge as a means to the attainment of an inner freedom from distress and bondage to the world. In other words, the very reason was regarded as an activity of the self, and its fruits were valued for their enhancement of the welfare of the self. And if this be true of the Stoics and the Epicureans, it is still more clearly true of the neo-Platonists of the Christian era, who mediate between the ancient and mediæval worlds.

§ 184. It is well known that the early period of Christianity was a period of the most vivid

Emphasis on Self-consciousness in Early Christian Philosophy.

self-consciousness. The individual believed that his natural and social environment was alien to his deeper spiritual interests. He therefore withdrew into himself. He believed himself to have but one duty, the salvation of his soul; and that duty required him to search his innermost springs of action in order to uproot any that might compromise him with the world and turn him from God. The drama of life was enacted within the circle of his own self-consciousness. Citizenship, bodily health, all forms of appreciation and knowledge, were identified in the parts they played here. In short the Christian consciousness, although renunciation was its deepest motive, was reflexive and centripetal to a degree hitherto unknown among the European peoples. And when with St. Augustine theoretical interests once more vigorously asserted themselves, this new emphasis was in the very foreground. St. Augustine wished to begin his system of thought with a first indubitable certainty, and selected neither being nor ideas, but *self*. St. Augustine's genius was primarily religious, and the " Confessions," in which he records the story of his hard winning of peace and right relations with God, is his most intimate book. How faithfully does he represent himself, and the blend of paganism and Christianity which was distinctive of his age, when in his systematic writings he draws upon religion for his knowledge of truth! In all my living, he argues, whether I sin or turn to God, whether I doubt or believe, whether I know or am ignorant, in all *I know that I am I.* Each and every state of my consciousness is a state of my self, and as such, sure evidence of my self's existence. If one were to follow St. Augustine's reflections further, one would find him reasoning from his own finite and evil self to an infinite and perfect Self, which centres like his in the conviction that I am I, but is endowed with all power and all worth. One would find him reflecting upon the possible union with God through the exaltation of the human self-consciousness. But this conception of God as the perfect self is so much a prophecy of things to come, that more than a dozen centuries elapsed before it was explicitly formulated by the post-Kantians. We must follow its more gradual development in the philosophies of Descartes and Kant.

§ 185. When at the close of the sixteenth century the Frenchman, René Descartes, sought to
Descartes's Argument for the Independence of the Thinking Self. construct philosophy anew and upon secure foundations, he too selected as the initial certainty of thought the thinker's knowledge of himself. This principle now received its classic formulation in the proposition, *Cogito ergo sum*—" I think, hence I am." The argument does not differ essentially from that of St. Augustine, but it now finds a place in a systematic and critical metaphysics. In that my thinking is certain of itself, says Descartes, in that I know myself before I know aught else, my self can never be dependent for its being upon anything else that I may come to know. A thinking self, with its knowledge and its volition, is quite capable of subsisting of itself. Such is, indeed, not the case with a finite self, for all finitude is significant of limitation, and in recognizing my limitations I postulate the infinite being or God. But the relation of my self to a physical world is quite without necessity. Human nature, with soul and body conjoined, is a combination of two substances, neither of which is a necessary consequence of the

other. As a result of this combination the soul is to some extent affected by the body, and the body is to some extent directed by the soul; but the body could conceivably be an automaton, as the soul could conceivably be, and will in another life become, a free spirit. The consequences of this dualism for epistemology are very grave. If knowledge be the activity of a self-subsistent thinking spirit, how can it reveal the nature of an external world? The natural order is now literally "external." It is true that the whole body of exact science, that mechanical system to which Descartes attached so much importance, falls within the range of the soul's own thinking. But what assurance is there that it refers to a province of its own—a physical world in space? Descartes can only suppose that "clear and distinct" ideas must be trusted as faithful representations. It is true the external world makes its presence known directly, when it breaks in upon the soul in sense-perception. But Descartes's rationalism and love of mathematics forbade his attaching importance to this criterion. Real nature, that exactly definable and predictable order of moving bodies defined in physics, is not known through sense-perception, but through thought. Its necessities are the necessities of reason. Descartes finds himself, then, in the perplexing position of seeking an internal criterion for an external world. The problem of knowledge so stated sets going the whole epistemological movement of the eighteenth century, from Locke through Berkeley and Hume to Kant. And the issue of this development is the absolute idealism of Kant's successors.

§ 186. Of the English philosophers who prepare the way for the epistemology of Kant, Hume

Empirical Reaction of the English Philosophers. is the most radical and momentous. It was he who roused Kant from his "dogmatic slumbers" to the task of the "Critical Philosophy." Hume is one of the two possible consequences of Descartes. One who attaches greater importance to the rational necessities of science than to its external reference, is not unwilling that nature should be swallowed up in mind. With Malebranche, Descartes's immediate successor in France, nature is thus provided for within the archetypal mind of God. With the English philosophers, on the other hand, externality is made the very mark of nature, and as a consequence sense-perception becomes the criterion of scientific truth. This empirical theory of knowledge, inaugurated and developed by Locke

and Berkeley, culminates in Hume's designation
of the *impression* as the distinguishing element of
nature, at once making up its content and certify-
ing to its externality. The processes of nature are
successions of impressions; and the laws of nature
are their uniformities, or the expectations of uniformity which their repetitions engender. Hume
does not hesitate to draw the logical conclusion.
If the final mark of truth is the presence to sense
of the individual element, then science can consist
only of items of information and probable generalizations concerning their sequences. The effect is
observed to follow upon the cause in fact, but there
is no understanding of its necessity; therefore no
absolute certainty attaches to the future effects of
any cause.

§ 187. But what has become of the dream of
the mathematical physicist? Is the whole system
To Save Exact of Newton, that brilliant triumph of the
Science Kant
Makes it mechanical method, unfounded and dog-
Dependent
on Mind. matic? It is the logical instability of
this body of knowledge, made manifest in the well
founded scepticism of Hume, that rouses Kant to
a reëxamination of the whole foundation of natural
science. The general outline of his analysis has
been developed above. It is of importance here

to understand its relations to the problem of Descartes. Contrary to the view of the English philosophers, natural science is, says Kant, the work of the mind. The certainty of the causal relation is due to the human inability to think otherwise. Hume is mistaken in supposing that mere sensation gives us any knowledge of nature. The very least experience of objects involves the employment of principles which are furnished by the mind. Without the employment of such principles, or in bare sensation, there is no intelligible meaning whatsoever. But once admit the employment of such principles and formulate them systematically, and the whole Newtonian order of nature is seen to follow from them. Furthermore, since these principles or categories are the conditions of human experience, are the very instruments of knowledge, they are valid wherever there is any experience or knowledge. There is but one way to make anything at all out of nature, and that is to conceive it as an order of necessary events in space and time. Newtonian science is part of such a general conception, and is therefore necessary if knowledge is to be possible at all, even the least. Thus Kant turns upon Hume, and shuts him up to the choice between the utter abnegation of all knowledge, including the knowledge of his own scepticism, and the acceptance of the whole body of exact science.

But with nature thus conditioned by the necessities of thought, what has become of its externality? That, Kant admits, has indeed vanished. Kant does not attempt, as did Descartes, to hold that the nature which mind constructs and controls, exists also outside of mind. The nature that is known is on that very account phenomenal, anthropocentric—created by its cognitive conditions. Descartes was right in maintaining that sense-perception certifies to the existence of a world outside the mind, but mistaken in calling it nature and identifying it with the realm of science. In short, Kant acknowledges the external world, and names it the *thing-in-itself;* but insists that because it is outside of mind it is outside of knowledge. Thus is the certainty of science saved at the cost of its metaphysical validity. It is necessarily true, but only of a conditioned or dependent world. And in saving science Kant has at the same time prejudiced metaphysics in general. For the human or naturalistic way of knowing is left in sole possession of the field, with the higher interest of reasons in the ultimate nature of being, degraded to the rank of practical faith.

§ 188. The transformation of this critical and agnostic doctrine into absolute idealism is inevi-

The Post-Kantians Transform Kant's Mind-in-general into an Absolute Mind.

table. The metaphysical interest was bound to avail itself of the speculative suggestiveness with which the Kantian philosophy abounds. The transformation turns upon Kant's assumption that whatever is constructed by the mind is on that account phenomenon or appearance. Kant has carried along the presumption that whatever is act or content of mind is on that account not *real* object or *thing-in-itself*. We have seen that this is generally accepted as true of the relativities of sense-perception. But is it true of thought? The post-Kantian idealist maintains that *that depends upon the thought.* The content of private individual thinking is in so far not real object; but it does not follow that this is true of such thinking as is universally valid. Now Kant has deduced his categories for thought in general. There are no empirical cases of thinking except the human thinkers; but the categories are not the property of any one human individual or any group of such individuals. They are the conditions of *experi-*

ence in general, and of every possibility of experience. The transition to absolute idealism is now readily made. *Thought in general* becomes the *absolute mind,* and experience in general its content. The thing-in-itself drops out as having no meaning. The objectivity to which it testified is provided for in the completeness and self-sufficiency which is attributed to the absolute experience. Indeed, an altogether new definition of subjective and objective replaces the old. The subjective is that which is only insufficiently thought, as in the case of relativity and error; the objective is that which is completely thought. Thus the natural order is indeed phenomenal; but only because the principles of science are not the highest principles of thought, and not because nature is the fruit of thought. Thus Hegel expresses his relation to Kant as follows:

" According to Kant, the things that we know about are *to us* appearances only, and we can never know their essential nature, which belongs to another world, which we cannot approach. . . . The true statement of the case is as follows. The things of which we have direct consciousness are mere phenomena, not for us only, but in their own nature; and the true and proper case of these things, finite as they are, is to have their existence founded not in themselves, but in the universal divine idea. This view of things, it is true, is as idealist as Kant's, but in contradistinction to the subjective idealism of the Critical Philosophy should be termed Absolute Idealism."[9]

§ 189. Absolute idealism is thus reached after a long and devious course of development. But the argument may be stated much more briefly. Plato, it will be remembered, found that experience tends ever to transcend itself. The thinker finds himself compelled to pursue the ideal of immutable and universal truth, and must identify the ultimate being with that ideal. Similarly Hegel says:

The Direct Argument. The Inference from the Finite Mind to the Infinite Mind.

"That upward spring of the mind signifies that the being which the world has is only a semblance, no real being, no absolute truth; it signifies that beyond and above that appearance, truth abides in God, so that true being is another name for God."[10]

The further argument of absolute idealism differs from that of Plato in that the dependence of truth upon the mind is accepted as a first principle. The ideal with which experience is informed is now *the state of perfect knowledge,* rather than the

[9] Hegel: *Encyclopädie*, § 45, lecture note. Quoted by McTaggart: *Op. cit.*, p. 69.

[10] Hegel: *Encyclopädie*, § 50. Quoted by McTaggart: *Op. cit.*, p. 70.

system of absolute truth. The content of the state of perfect knowledge will indeed be the system of absolute truth, but none the less *content,* precisely as finite knowledge is the content of a finite mind. In pursuing the truth, I who pursue, aim to realize in myself a certain highest state of knowledge. Were I to know all truth I should indeed have ceased to be the finite individual who began the quest, but the evolution would be continuous and the character of self-consciousness would never have been lost. I may say, in short, that God or being, is my perfect cognitive self.

The argument for absolute idealism is a constructive interpretation of the subjectivistic contention that knowledge can never escape the circle of its own activity and states. To meet the demand for a final and standard truth, a demand which realism meets with its doctrine of a being independent of any mind, this philosophy defines a *standard mind.* The impossibility of defining objects in terms of relativity to a finite self, conducts dialectically to the conception of the *absolute self.* The sequel to my error or exclusiveness, is truth or inclusiveness. The outcome of the dialectic is determined by the symmetry of the antithesis. Thus, corrected experience implies a last

correcting experience; partial cognition, complete
cognition; empirical subject, transcendental subject; finite mind, an absolute mind. The following statement is taken from a contemporary exponent of the philosophy:

"What you and I lack, when we lament our human
ignorance, is simply a certain desirable and logically
possible state of mind, or type of experience; to wit, a
state of mind in which we should wisely be able to say
that we had fulfilled in experience what we now have
merely in idea, namely, the knowledge, the immediate
and felt presence, of what we now call the Absolute
Reality. . . . There is an Absolute Experience for
which the conception of an absolute reality, *i. e.*, the
conception of a system of ideal truth, is fulfilled by the
very contents that get presented to this experience.
This Absolute Experience is related to our experience
as an organic whole to its own fragments. It is an experience which finds fulfilled all that the completest
thought can conceive as genuinely possible. Herein
lies its definition as an Absolute. For the Absolute
Experience, as for ours, there are data, contents, facts.
But these data, these contents, express, for the Absolute
Experience, its own meaning, its thought, its ideas.
Contents beyond these that it possesses, the Absolute
Experience knows to be, in genuine truth, impossible.
Hence its contents are indeed particular,—a selection
from the world of bare or merely conceptual possibilities,—but they form a self-determined whole, than
which nothing completer, more organic, more fulfilled,
more transparent, or more complete in meaning, is
concretely or genuinely possible. On the other hand,
these contents are not foreign to those of our finite

experience, but are inclusive of them in the unity of one life." [11]

§ 190. As has been already intimated, at the opening of this chapter, the inclusion of the whole **The Realistic** of reality within a single self is clearly **Tendency** a questionable proceeding. The need **in Absolute** **Idealism.** of avoiding the relativism of empirical idealism is evident. But if the very meaning of the self-consciousness be due to a certain selection and exclusion within the general field of experience, it is equally evident that the relativity of self-consciousness can never be overcome through appealing to a higher self. One must appeal *from* the self to the realm of things as they are. Indeed, although the exponents of this philosophy use the language of spiritualism, and accept the idealistic epistemology, their absolute being tends ever to escape the special characters of the self. And inasmuch as the absolute self is commonly set over against the finite or empirical self, as the standard and test of truth, it is the less distin-

[11] Royce: *Conception of God*, pp. 19, 43–44.
This argument is well summarized in Green's statement that " the existence of one connected world, which is the presupposition of knowledge, implies the action of one self-conditioning and self-determining mind." *Prolegomena to Ethics*, p. 181.

guishable from the realist's order of independent
beings.

§ 191. But however much absolute idealism
may tend to abandon its idealism for the sake of
its absolutism within the field of metaphysics, such is not the case within the
field of ethics and religion. The conception of the self here receives a new
emphasis. The same self-consciousness
which admits to the highest truth is the evidence
of man's practical dignity. In virtue of his immediate apprehension of the principles of self-
hood, and his direct participation in the life of
spirit, man may be said to possess the innermost
secret of the universe. In order to achieve goodness he must therefore recognize and express *himself*. The Kantian philosophy is here again the
starting-point. It was Kant who first gave adequate expression to the Christian idea of the moral
self-consciousness.

"Duty! Thou sublime and mighty name that dost
embrace nothing charming or insinuating, but requirest
submission, and yet seekest not to move the will by
threatening aught that would arouse natural aversion or
terror, but merely holdest forth a law which of itself
finds entrance into the mind, . . . a law before
which all inclinations are dumb, even though they

The margin note reads: The Conception of Self-consciousness Central in the Ethics of Absolute Idealism. Kant.

secretly counterwork it; what origin is there worthy of thee, and where is to be found the root of thy noble descent which proudly rejects all kindred with the inclinations . . . ? It can be nothing less than a power which elevates man above himself, . . . a power which connects him with an order of things that only the understanding can conceive, with a world which at the same time commands the whole sensible world, and with it the empirically determinable existence of man in time, as well as the sum total of all ends." [12]

With Kant there can be no morality except conduct be attended by the consciousness of this duty imposed by the higher nature upon the lower. It is this very recognition of a deeper self, of a personality that belongs to the sources and not to the consequences of nature, that constitutes man as a moral being, and only such action as is inspired with a reverence for it can be morally good. Kant does little more than to establish the uncompromising dignity of the moral will. In moral action man submits to a law that issues from himself in virtue of his rational nature. Here he yields nothing, as he owes nothing, to that appetency which binds him to the natural world. As a rational being he himself affirms the very principles which determine the organization of

[12] Kant: *Critical Examination of Practical Reason*. Translated by Abbott in *Kant's Theory of Ethics*, p. 180.

nature. This is his *freedom,* at once the ground and the implication of his duty. Man is free from nature to serve the higher law of his personality.

§ 192. There are two respects in which Kant's ethics has been regarded as inadequate by those

Kantian Ethics
Supplemented
through the
Conceptions
of Universal
and Objective
Spirit.

who draw from it their fundamental principles. It is said that Kant is too rigoristic, that he makes too stern a business of morality, in speaking so much of law and so little of love and spontaneity. There are good reasons for this. Kant seeks to isolate the moral consciousness, and dwell upon it in its purity, in order that he may demonstrate its incommensurability with the values of inclination and sensibility. Furthermore, Kant may speak of the principle of the absolute, and recognize the deeper eternal order as a law, but he may not, if he is to be consistent with his own critical principles, affirm the metaphysical being of such an order. With his idealistic followers it is possible to define the spiritual setting of the moral life, but with Kant it is only possible to define the antagonism of principles. Hence the greater optimism of the post-Kantians. They know that the higher law is the reality, and that he who obeys it thus unites himself with the absolute self. That which for Kant is only a resolute obedience to more valid principles, to rationally superior rules for action, is for idealism man's appropriation of his spiritual birthright. Since the law is the deeper nature, man may respect and obey it as valid, and at the same time act upon it gladly in the sure knowledge that it will enhance his eternal welfare. Indeed, the knowledge that the very universe is founded upon this law will make him less suspicious of nature and less exclusive in his adherence to any single law. He will be more confident of the essential goodness of all manifestations of a universe which he knows to be fundamentally spiritual.

But it has been urged, secondly, that the Kantian ethics is too formal, too little pertinent to the issues of life. Kant's moral law imposes only obedience to the law, or conduct conceived as suitable to a universal moral community. But what is the nature of such conduct in particular? It may be answered that to maintain the moral self-consciousness, to act dutifully and dutifully only, to be self-reliant and unswerving in the doing of what one ought to do, is to obtain a very specific character. But does this not leave the individual's conduct to his own interpretation of his duty?

It was just this element of individualism which
Hegel sought to eliminate through the application of his larger philosophical conception. If
that which expresses itself within the individual
consciousness as the moral law be indeed the law
of that self in which the universe is grounded, it
will appear as *objective spirit* in the evolution of
society. For Hegel, then, the most valid standard
of goodness is to be found in that customary morality which bespeaks the moral leadings of the
general humanity, and in those institutions, such as
the family and the state, which are the moral acts
of the absolute idea itself. Finally, in the realm
of *absolute spirit,* in art, in revealed religion, and
in philosophy, the individual may approach to the
self-consciousness which is the perfect truth and
goodness in and for itself.

§ 193. Where the law of life is the implication
in the finite self-consciousness of the eternal and

The Peculiar
Pantheism
and Mysticism
of Absolute
Idealism.

divine self-consciousness, there can be
no division between morality and religion, as there can be none between
thought and will. Whatever man seeks is in the
end God. As the perfect fulfilment of the thinking self, God is the truth; as the perfect fulfilment
of the willing self, God is the good. The finite

self-consciousness finds facts that are not understood, and so seeks to resolve itself into the perfect self wherein all that is given has meaning. On the other hand, the finite self-consciousness finds ideals that are not realized, and so seeks to resolve itself into that perfect self wherein all that is significant is given. All interests thus converge toward

"some state of conscious spirit in which the opposition of cognition and volition is overcome—in which we neither judge our ideas by the world, nor the world by our ideas, but are aware that inner and outer are in such close and necessary harmony that even the thought of possible discord has become impossible. In its unity not only cognition and volition, but feeling also, must be blended and united. In some way or another it must have overcome the rift in discursive knowledge, and the immediate must for it be no longer the alien. It must be as direct as art, as certain and universal as philosophy." [13]

The religious consciousness proper to absolute idealism is both pantheistic and mystical, but with distinction. Platonism is pantheistic in that nature is resolved into God. All that is not perfect is esteemed only for its promise of perfection. And Platonism is mystical in that the purification and universalization of the affections brings one

[13] Quoted from McTaggart: *Op. cit.*, pp. 231-232.

in the end to a perfection that exceeds all modes of thought and speech. With Spinoza, on the other hand, God may be said to be resolved into nature. Nature is made divine, but is none the less nature, for its divinity consists in its absolute necessity. Spinoza's pantheism passes over into mysticism because the absolute necessity exceeds in both unity and richness the laws known to the human understanding. In absolute idealism, finally, both God and nature are resolved into the self. For that which is divine in experience is self-consciousness, and this is at the same time the ground of nature. Thus in the highest knowledge the self is expanded and enriched without being left behind. The mystical experience proper to this philosophy is the consciousness of identity, together with the sense of universal immanence. The individual self may be directly sensible of the absolute self, for these are one spiritual life. Thus Emerson says:

"It is a secret which every intellectual man quickly learns, that beyond the energy of his possessed and conscious intellect he is capable of a new energy (as of an intellect doubled on itself), by abandonment to the nature of things; that beside his privacy of power as an individual man, there is a great public power upon which he can draw, by unlocking, at all risks, his human doors, and suffering the ethereal tides to roll and circulate through him; then he is caught up into the life of the Universe, his speech is thunder, his thought is law, and his words are universally intelligible as the plants and animals. The poet knows that he speaks adequately then only when he speaks somewhat wildly, or 'with the flower of the mind'; not with the intellect used as an organ, but with the intellect released from all service and suffered to take its direction from its celestial life."[14]

§ 194. But the distinguishing flavor and quality of this religion arises from its spiritual hospitality. It is not, like Platonism, a contemplation of the best; nor, like pluralistic idealisms, a moral knight-errantry. It is neither a religion of exclusion, nor a religion of reconstruction, but a profound willingness that things should be as they really are. For this reason its devotees have recognized in Spinoza their true forerunner. But idealism is not Spinozism, though it may contain this as one of its strains. For it is not the worship of necessity, Emerson's " beautiful necessity, which makes man brave in believing that he cannot shun a danger that is appointed, nor incur one that is not "; but the worship of *that which is* necessary.

The Religion of Exuberant Spirituality.

Not only must one understand that every effort, however despairing, is an element of sense in the universal significance;

[14] Emerson: *Op. cit.*, pp. 30-31.

"that the whole would not be what it is were not precisely this finite purpose left in its own uniqueness to speak precisely its own word—a word which no other purpose can speak in the language of the divine will"; [15]

but one must have a zest for such participation, and a heart for the divine will which it profits. Indeed, so much is this religion a love of life, that it may, as in the case of the Romanticists, be a love of caprice. Battle and death, pain and joy, error and truth—all that belongs to the story of this mortal world, are to be felt as the thrill of health, and relished as the essences of God. Religion is an exuberant spirituality, a fearless sensibility, a knowledge of both good and evil, and a will to serve the good, while exulting that the evil will not yield without a battle.

[15] Royce: *The World and the Individual, First Series*, p. 465.

CHAPTER XII

CONCLUSION

§ 195. ONE who consults a book of philosophy in the hope of finding there a definite body of

Liability of Philosophy to Revision, Due to its Systematic Character. truth, sanctioned by the consensus of experts, cannot fail to be disappointed. And it should now be plain that this is due not to the frailties of philosophers, but to the meaning of philosophy. Philosophy is not additive, but reconstructive. Natural science may advance step by step without ever losing ground; its empirical discoveries are in their severalty as true as they can ever be. Thus tho stars and the species of animals may be recorded successively, and each generation of astronomers and zoölogists may take up the work at the point reached by its forerunners. The formulation of results does, it is true, require constant correction and revision—but there is a central body of data which is little affected, and which accumulates from age to age. Now the finality of scientific truth is proportional to the modesty of its claims.

Items of truth persist, while the interpretation of them is subject to alteration with the general advance of knowledge; and, relatively speaking, science consists in items of truth, and philosophy in their interpretation. The liability to revision in science itself increases as that body of knowledge becomes more highly unified and systematic. Thus the present age, with its attempt to construct a single comprehensive system of mechanical science, is peculiarly an age when fundamental conceptions are subjected to a thorough reëxamination —when, for example, so ancient a conception as that of matter is threatened with displacement by that of energy. But philosophy is *essentially unitary and systematic*—and thus *superlatively liable to revision.*

§ 196. It is noteworthy that it is only in this age of a highly systematic natural science that

The One Science and the Many Philosophies.

different systems are projected, as in the case just noted of the rivalry between the strictly mechanical, or corpuscular, theory and the newer theory of energetics. It has heretofore been taken for granted that although there may be many philosophies, there is but one body of science. And it is still taken for granted that the experimental detail of the individual science is a common fund, to the progressive increase of which the individual scientist contributes the results of his special research; there being *rival* schools of mechanics, physics, or chemistry, only in so far as *fundamental conceptions* or *principles of orderly arrangement* are in question. But philosophy deals exclusively with the most fundamental conceptions and the most general principles of orderly arrangement. Hence it is significant of the very task of philosophy that there should be many tentative systems of philosophy, even that each philosopher should project and construct his own philosophy. Philosophy as the truth of synthesis and reconciliation, of comprehensiveness and coördination, must be a living unity. It is a thinking of entire experience, and can be sufficient only through being all-sufficient. The heart of every philosophy is a harmonizing insight, an intellectual prospect within which all human interests and studies compose themselves. Such knowledge cannot be delegated to isolated colaborers, but will be altogether missed if not loved and sought in its indivisible unity. There is no modest home-keeping philosophy; no safe and conservative philosophy, that can make sure of a part through renouncing the whole. There is no phi-

losophy without intellectual temerity, as there is no
religion without moral temerity. And the one is
the supreme interest of thought, as the other is the
supreme interest of life.

§ 197. Though the many philosophies be inevitable, it must not be concluded that there is
therefore no progress in philosophy.

Progress in
Philosophy.
The Sophistica-
tion or Eclec-
ticism of the
Present Age.

The solution from which every great
philosophy is precipitated is the mingled wisdom of some latest age, with
all of its inheritance. The " positive " knowledge
furnished by the sciences, the refinements and distinctions of the philosophers, the ideals of society
—these and the whole sum of civilization are its
ingredients. Where there is no single system of
philosophy significant enough to express the age,
as did the systems of Plato, Thomas Aquinas,
Descartes, Locke, Kant, Hegel, and the others who
belong to the roll of the great philosophers, there
exists a *general sophistication,* which is more elu-
sive but not less significant. The present age—at
any rate from its own stand-point—is not an age of
great philosophical systems. Such systems may
indeed be living in our midst unrecognized; but
historical perspective cannot safely be anticipated.
It is certain that no living voice is known to speak

for this generation as did Hegel, and even Spencer, for the last. There is, however, a significance in this very passing of Hegel and Spencer,—an enlightenment peculiar to an age which knows them, but has philosophically outlived them. There is a moral in the history of thought which just now no philosophy, whether naturalism or transcendentalism, realism or idealism, can fail to draw. The characterization of this contemporary eclecticism or sophistication, difficult and uncertain as it must needs be, affords the best summary and interpretation with which to conclude this brief survey of the fortunes of philosophy.

§ 198. Since the problem of metaphysics is the crucial problem of philosophy, the question of its

Metaphysics. The Antagonistic Doctrines of Naturalism and Absolutism. present status is fundamental in any characterization of the age. It will appear from the foregoing account of the course of metaphysical development that two fundamental tendencies have exhibited themselves from the beginning. The one of these is naturalistic and empirical, representing the claims of what common sense calls " matters of fact "; the other is transcendental and rational, representing the claims of the standards and ideals which are immanent in experience, and directly manifested in the great human interests of thought and action. These tendencies have on the whole been antagonistic; and the clear-cut and momentous systems of philosophy have been fundamentally determined by either the one or the other.

Thus materialism is due to the attempt to reduce all of experience to the elements and principles of connection which are employed by the physical sciences to set in order the actual motions, or changes of place, which the parts of experience undergo. Materialism maintains that the motions of bodies are indifferent to considerations of worth, and denies that they issue from a deeper cause of another order. The very ideas of such non-mechanical elements or principles are here provided with a mechanical origin. Similarly a phenomenalism, like that of Hume, takes immediate presence to sense as the norm of being and knowledge. Individual items, directly verified in the moment of their occurrence, are held to be at once the content of all real truth, and the source of those abstract ideas which the misguided rationalists mistake for real truth.

But the absolutist, on the other hand, contends that the thinker must *mean* something by the reality which he seeks. If he had it for the looking,

thought would not be, as it so evidently is, a purposive endeavor. And that which is meant by
reality can be nothing short of the fulfilment or
final realization of this endeavor of thought. To
find out what thought seeks, to anticipate the consummation of thought and posit it as real, is
therefore the first and fundamental procedure of
philosophy. The mechanism of nature, and all
matters of fact, must come to terms with this absolute reality, or be condemned as mere appearance. Thus Plato distinguishes the world of
" generation " in which we participate by perception, from the " true essence " in which we participate by thought; and Schelling speaks of the
modern experimental method as the " corruption "
of philosophy and physics, in that it fails to
construe nature in terms of spirit.

§ 199. Now it would never occur to a sophisticated philosopher of the present, to one who has

Concessions thought out to the end the whole tra-
from the Side
of Absolutism. dition of philosophy, and felt the grav-
Recognition
of Nature. ity of the great historical issues, to
The Neo-
Fichteans. suffer either of these motives to dominate him to the exclusion of the other. Absolutism has long since ceased to speak slightingly
of physical science, and of the world of perception.

It is conceded that motions must be known in the mechanical way, and matters of fact in the matter-of-fact way. Furthermore, the prestige which science enjoyed in the nineteenth century, and the prestige which the empirical and secular world of action has enjoyed to a degree that has steadily increased since the Renaissance, have convinced the absolutist of the intrinsic significance of these parts of experience. They are no longer reduced, but are permitted to flourish in their own right. From the very councils of absolute idealism there has issued a distinction which is fast becoming current, between the World of Appreciation, or the realm of moral and logical principles, and the World of Description, or the realm of empirical generalizations and mechanical causes.[1] It is indeed maintained that the former of these is metaphysically superior; but the latter is ranked without the disparagement of its own proper categories.

With the Fichteans this distinction corresponds to the distinction in the system of Fichte between the active moral ego, and the nature which it posits to act upon. But the *neo-Fichteans* are

[1] Cf. Josiah Royce: *The Spirit of Modern Philosophy*, Lecture XII; *The World and the Individual, Second Series*.

concerned to show that the nature so posited, or the World of Description, is the *realm of mechanical science,* and that the entire system of mathematical and physical truth is therefore morally necessary.[2]

§ 200. A more pronounced tendency in the same direction marks the work of the *neo-Kantians.* These philosophers repudiate the spiritualistic metaphysics of Schopenhauer, Fichte, and Hegel, believing the real significance of Kant to lie in his critical method, in his examination of the first principles of the different systems of knowledge, and especially in his analysis of the foundations of mathematics and physics.[3] In approaching mathematics and phys-

The Neo-Kantians.

[2] Cf. Hugo Münsterberg: *Psychology and Life.* The more important writings of this school are: *Die Philosophie im Boginn des zwanzigsten Jahrhunderts,* edited by Wilhelm Windelband, and contributed to by Windelband, H. Rickert, O. Liebmann, E. Troeltsch, B. Bauch, and others. This book contains an excellent bibliography. Also, Rickert: *Der Gegenstand der Erkenntnis; Die Grenzen der naturwissenschaftlichen Begriffsbildung,* and other works. Windelband: *Präludien; Geschichte und Naturwissenschaft.* Münsterberg: *Grundzüge der Psychologie.* Eucken: *Die Grundbegriffe der Gegenwart.*

[3] Cf. F. A. Lange: *History of Materialism,* Book II, Chap. I, on *Kant and Materialism;* also Alois Riehl: *Introduction to the Theory of Science and Metaphysics.* Translation by Fairbanks. The more important writings of this school are: Hermann Cohen: *Kant's Theorie der Erfahrung; Die*

ics from a general logical stand-point, these neo-Kantians become scarcely distinguishable in interest and temper from those scientists who approach logic from the mathematical and physical stand-point.

§ 201. The finite, moral individual, with his peculiar spiritual perspective, has long since been

Recognition of the Individual. Personal Idealism.

recognized as essential to the meaning of the universe rationally conceived. But in its first movement absolute idealism proposed to absorb him in the indivisible absolute self. It is now pointed out that Fichte, and even Hegel himself, means the absolute to be a plurality or society of persons.[4] It is commonly conceded that the will of the absolute must coincide with the wills of all finite creatures in their severalty, that God wills in and through men.[5] Corresponding to this individualistic tendency on the part of absolute idealism, there has been recently

Logik der reinen Erkenntniss, and other works. Paul Natorp: Sozialpädagogik; Einleitung in die Psychologie nach kritischer Methode, and other works. E. Cassirer: Leibniz' System in seinen wissenschaftlichen Grundlagen. Riehl: Der philosophische Kriticismus, und seine Bedeutung für die Positive Wissenschaft. Cf. also E. Husserl: Logische Untersuchungen.

[4] Cf. J. M. E. McTaggart: Studies in Hegelian Cosmology, Chap. III.

[5] Cf. Royce: The Conception of God, Supplementary Essay, pp. 135-322; The World and the Individual, First Series.

projected a *personal idealism,* or *humanism,* which springs freshly and directly from the same motive. This philosophy attributes ultimate importance to the human person with his freedom, his interests, his control over nature, and his hope of the advancement of the spiritual kingdom through co-operation with his fellows.[6]

§ 202. Naturalism exhibits a moderation and liberality that is not less striking than that of

Concessions from the Side of Naturalism. Recognition of Fundamental Principles.

absolutism. This abatement of its claims began in the last century with agnosticism. It was then conceded that there is an order other than that of natural science; but this order was held to be inaccessible to human knowledge. Such a theory is essentially unstable because it employs principles which define a non-natural order, but refuses to credit them or call them knowledge. The

---

[6] This movement began as a criticism of Hegelianism in behalf of the human personality. Cf. Andrew Seth: *Hegelianism and Personality; Man and the Cosmos; Two Lectures on Theism.* G. H. Howison: *The Limits of Evolution.* The important writings of the more independent movement are: William James: *The Will to Believe.* H. Sturt, editor: *Personal Idealism, Philosophical Essays by Eight Members of Oxford University.* F. C. S. Schiller: *Humanism.* Henri Bergson: *Essoi sur les données immédiates de la conscience; Matière et mémoire.* This movement is closely related to that of *Pragmatism.* See under § 203.

agnostic is in the paradoxical position of one who knows of an unknowable world. Present-day naturalism is more circumspect. It has interested itself in bringing to light that in the very procedure of science which, because it predetermines what nature shall be, cannot be included within nature. To this interest is due the rediscovery of the rational foundations of science. It was already known in the seventeenth century that exact science does not differ radically from mathematics, as mathematics does not differ radically from logic. Mathematics and mechanics are now being submitted to a critical examination which reveals the definitions and implications upon which they rest, and the general relation of these to the fundamental elements and necessities of thought.[7]

[7] Cf. Bertrand Russell: *Principles of Mathematics,* Vol. I. Among the more important writings of this movement are the following: Giuseppi. Peano: *Formulaire de Mathématique,* published by the *Rivista di matematica,* Tom. I–IV. Richard Dedekind: *Was sind und was sollen die Zahlen?* Georg Cantor: *Grundlagen einer allgemeinen Mannigfaltigkeitslehre.* Louis Couturat: *De l'Infini Mathématique,* and articles in *Revue de Metaphysique et de Morale.* A. N. Whitehead: *A Treatise on Universal Algebra.* Heinrich Hertz: *Die Prinzipien der Mechanik.* Henri Poincaré: *La Science et l'Hypothèse.* For the bearing of these investigations on philosophy, see Royce: *The Sciences of the Ideal,* in *Science,* Vol. XX, No. 510.

§ 203. This rationalistic tendency in natural-

Recognition
of the Will.
Pragmatism.

ism is balanced by a tendency which is more empirical, but equally subversive of the old ultra-naturalism. Goethe once wrote:

"I have observed that I hold that thought to be *true* which is *fruitful for me*. . . . When I know my relation to myself and to the outer world, I say that I possess the truth."

Similarly, it is now frequently observed that all knowledge is *humanly fruitful,* and it is proposed that this shall be regarded as the very criterion of truth. According to this principle science as a whole, even knowledge as a whole, is primarily a human utility. The nature which science defines is an artifact or construct. It is designed to express briefly and conveniently what man may practically expect from his environment. This tendency is known as *pragmatism.* It ranges from systematic doctrines, reminiscent of Fichte, which seek to define practical needs and deduce knowledge from them, to the more irresponsible utterances of those who liken science to " shorthand," [8] and mathematics to a game of chess. In any case pragmatism attributes to nature a certain dependence on will, and therefore implies, even when it

[8] The term used by Karl Pearson in his *Grammar of Science.*

does not avow, that will with its peculiar principles or values cannot be reduced to the terms of nature. In short, it would be more true to say that nature expresses will, than that will expresses nature.[9]

§ 204. Such, then, is the contemporary eclecticism as respects the central problem of meta- Summary, and physics. There are *naturalistic* and *in-dividualistic* tendencies in *absolutism;* *rationalistic* and *ethical* tendencies in *naturalism;* and finally the independent and spontaneous movements of *personal idealism* and *pragmatism.*

Summary, and Transition to Epistemology.

Since the rise of the Kantian and post-Kantian philosophy, metaphysics and epistemology have maintained relations so intimate that the present state of the former cannot be characterized without some reference to the present state of the latter. Indeed, the very issues upon which meta-

[9] The important English writings of the recent independent movement known as *pragmatism* are: C. S. Peirce: *Illustrations of the Logic of Science,* in *Popular Science Monthly,* Vol. XII. W. James: *The Pragmatic Method,* in *Journal of Philosophy, Psychology, and Scientific Methods,* Vol. I; *Humanism and Truth,* in *Mind,* Vol. XIII, N. S.; *The Essence of Humanism,* in *Jour. of Phil., Psych., and Sc. Meth.,* Vol. II (with bibliography); *The Will to Believe.* John Dewey: *Studies in Logical Theory.* W. Caldwell: *Pragmatism,* in *Mind,* Vol. XXV., N. S. See also literature on *personal idealism,* § 201. A similar tendency has appeared in France in Bergson, LeRoy, Milhaud, and in Germany in Simmel.

physicians divide are most commonly those provoked by the problem of knowledge. The counter-tendencies of naturalism and absolutism are always connected, and often coincide with, the epistemological opposition between empiricism, which proclaims perception, and rationalism, which proclaims reason, to be the proper organ of knowledge. The other great epistemological controversy does not bear so direct and simple a relation to the central metaphysical issues, and must be examined on its own account.

§ 205. The point of controversy is the dependence or independence of the object of knowledge

The Antagonistic Doctrines of Realism and Idealism. Realistic Tendency in Empirical Idealism.

on the state of knowledge; idealism maintaining that reality *is* the knower or his content of mind, realism, that being known is a circumstance which appertains to some reality, without being the indispensable condition of reality as such. Now the sophisticated thought of the present age exhibits a tendency on the part of these opposite doctrines to approach and converge. It has been already remarked that the empirical idealism of the Berkeleyan type could not avoid transcending itself. Hume, who omitted Berkeley's active spirits, no longer had any subjective seat or locus for the perceptions to which Berkeley had reduced the outer world. And perceptions which are not the states of any subject, retain only their intrinsic character and become a series of elements. When there is nothing beyond, which appears, and nothing within to which it appears, there ceases to be any sense in using such terms as appearance, phenomenon, or impression. The term sensation is at present employed in the same ill-considered manner. But empirical idealism has come gradually to insist upon the importance of the content of perception, rather than the relation of perception to a self as its state. The terms *element* and *experience,* which are replacing the subjectivistic terms, are frankly realistic.[10]

§ 206. There is a similar realistic trend in the development of absolute idealism. The pure Hegelian philosophy was notably objective. The principles of development in which it centres were conceived by Hegel himself to manifest themselves most clearly in the progressions of nature and history. Many of Hegel's followers have been led by moral and religious interests to emphasize con-

Realistic Tendency in Absolute Idealism. The Conception of Experience.

---

[10] Cf. Ernst Mach: *Analysis of Sensation.* Translation by Williams.

sciousness, and, upon epistemological grounds, to lay great stress upon the necessity of the union of the parts of experience within an enveloping self. But absolute idealism has much at heart the overcoming of relativism, and the absolute is defined in order to meet the demand for a being that shall not have the cognitive deficiencies of an object of finite thought. So it is quite possible for this philosophy, while maintaining its traditions on the whole, to abandon the term *self* to the finite subject, and regard its absolute as a system of rational and universal principles—self-sufficient because externally independent and internally necessary. Hence the renewed study of categories as logical, mathematical, or mechanical principles, and entirely apart from their being the acts of a thinking self.

Furthermore, it has been recognized that the general demand of idealism is met when reality is regarded as not outside of or other than knowledge, whatever be true of the question of dependence. Thus the conception of *experience* is equally convenient here, in that it signifies what is immediately present in knowledge, without affirming it to *consist in* being so presented.[11]

[11] Cf. F. H. Bradley: *Appearance and Reality*.

§ 207. And at this point idealism is met by a latter-day realism. The traditional modern real-

Idealistic Tendencies in Realism. The Immanence Philosophy.

ism springing from Descartes was dualistic. It was supposed that reality in itself was essentially extra-mental, and thus under the necessity of being either represented or misrepresented in thought. But the one of these alternatives is dogmatic, in that thought can never test the validity of its relation to that which is perpetually outside of it; while the other is agnostic, providing only for the knowledge of a world of appearance, an improper knowledge that is in fact not knowledge at all.

But realism is not necessarily dualistic, since it requires only that being shall not be dependent upon being known. Furthermore, since empiricism is congenial to naturalism, it is an easy step to say that nature is directly known in perception. This first takes the form of positivism, or the theory that only such nature as can be directly known can be really known. But this agnostic provision for an unknown world beyond, inevitably falls away and leaves *reality as that which is directly known, but not conditioned by knowledge.* Again the term *experience* is the most useful, and provides a common ground for *idealistic realism* with *realistic idealism*. A new epistemological movement makes this conception of experience its starting-point. What is known as the *immanence philosophy* defines reality as experience, and means by experience the subject matter of all knowledge —not defined as such, but regarded as capable of being such. Experience is conceived to be *both in and out* of selves, cognition being but one of the special systems into which experience may enter.[12]

§ 208. Does this eclecticism of the age open any philosophical prospect? Is it more than a general compromise—a confession of failure on the part of each and every radical and clear-cut doctrine of metaphysics and epistemology? There is no final answer to such a question short of an in-

The Interpretation of Tradition as the Basis for a New Construction.

---

[12] Cf. Carstanjen: *Richard Avenarius, and his General Theory of Knowledge, Empiriocriticism.* Translation by H. Bosanquet, in *Mind*, Vol. VI, N. S. Also James: *Does Consciousness Exist?* and *A World of Pure Experience*, in *Jour. of Phil., Psych., and Sc. Meth.*, Vol. I; *The Thing and its Relations, ibid.*, Vol. II.

The standard literature of this movement is unfortunately not available in English. Among the more important writings are: R. Avenarius: *Kritik der reinen Erfahrung; Der menschliche Weltbegriff*, and other works. Joseph Petzoldt: *Einführung in die Philosophie der reinen Erfahrung.* Ernst Mach: *Die Analyse der Empfindung und das Verhältniss des Physischen zum Psychischen, 2. Auff.* Wilhelm Schuppe: *Grund-*

dependent construction, and such procedure would exceed the scope of the present discussion. But there is an evident interpretation of tradition that suggests a possible basis for such construction.

§ 209. Suppose it to be granted that the categories of nature are quite self-sufficient. This

The Truth of the Physical System, but Failure of Attempt to Reduce All Experience to it.

would mean that there might conceivably be a strictly physical order, governed only by mechanical principles, and by the more general logical and mathematical principles. The body of physical science so extended as to include such general conceptions as identity, difference, number, quality, space, and time, is the account of such an order. This order need have no value, and need not be known. But reality as a whole is evidently not such a strictly physical order, for the definition of the physical order involves the rejection of many of the most familiar aspects of experience, such as its value and its being known in conscious selves. Materialism, in that it proposes to conceive the whole of reality as physical, must attempt to reduce the residuum to physical terms, and with no hope of success. Goodness and knowledge cannot be explained as mass and force, or shown to be mechanical necessities.

§ 210. Are we then to conclude that reality is not physical, and look for other terms to which we may reduce physical terms? There is no lack of such other terms. Indeed, we could as fairly have *begun* elsewhere. Thus some parts of experience compose the consciousness of the individual, and are said to be known by him. Experience so contained is connected by the special relation of being known together. But this relation is quite indifferent to physical, moral, and logical relations. Thus we may be conscious of things which are physically disconnected, morally repugnant, and logically contradictory, or in all of these respects utterly irrelevant. Subjectivism, in that it proposes to conceive the whole of reality as consciousness, must attempt to reduce physical, moral, and logical relations to that co-presence in consciousness from which they are so sharply distinguished in their very definition. The historical failure of this attempt was inevitable.

§ 211. But there is at least one further start-

Truth of Psychical Relations, but Impossibility of General Reduction to Them.

ing-point, the one adopted by the most subtle and elaborate of all reconstructive philosophies.

Truth of Logical and Ethical Principles. Validity of Ideal of Perfection, but Impossibility of Deducing the Whole of Experience from it. Logical necessities are as evidently real as bodies or selves. It is possible to define general types of inference, as well as compact and internally necessary systems such as those of mathematics. There is a perfectly distinguishable strain of pure rationality in the universe. Whether or not it be possible to conceive a pure rationality as self-subsistent, inasmuch as there are degrees it is at any rate possible to conceive of a maximum of rationality. But similarly there are degrees of moral goodness. It is possible to define with more or less exactness a morally perfect person, or an ideal moral community. Here again it may be impossible that pure and unalloyed goodness should constitute a universe of itself. But that a maximum of goodness, with all of the accessories which it might involve, should be thus self-subsistent, is quite conceivable. It is thus possible to define an absolute and perfect order, in which logical necessity, the interest of thought, or moral goodness, the interest of will, or both together, should be realized to the maximum. Absolutism conceives reality under the form of this ideal, and attempts to reconstruct experience accordingly. But is the prospect of success any better than in the cases of materialism and subjectivism? It is evident that the ideal of logical necessity is due to the fact that certain parts of knowledge approach it more closely than others. Thus mechanics contains more that is arbitrary than mathematics, and mathematics more than logic. Similarly, the theory of the evolution of the planetary system, in that it requires the assumption of particular distances and particular masses for the parts of the primeval nebula, is more arbitrary than rational dynamics. It is impossible, then, in view of the parts of knowledge which belong to the lower end of the scale of rationality, to regard reality as a whole as the maximum of rationality; for either a purely dynamical, a purely mathematical, or a purely logical, realm would be more rational. The similar disproof of the moral perfection of reality is so unmistakable as to require no elucidation. It is evident that even where natural necessities are not antagonistic to moral proprieties, they are at any rate indifferent to them.

§ 212. But thus far no reference has been made to error and to evil. These are the terms which

the ideals of rationality and goodness must repudiate if they are to retain their meaning. Never-
Error and Evil theless experience contains them and
Cannot be
Reduced to psychology describes them. We have
the Ideal. already followed the efforts which absolute idealism has made to show that logical perfection requires error, and that moral perfection
requires evil. Is it conceivable that such efforts
should be successful? Suppose a higher logic to
make the principle of contradiction the very bond
of rationality. What was formerly error is now
indispensable to truth. But what of the new
error—the unbalanced and mistaken thesis, the
unresolved antithesis, the scattered and disconnected terms of thought? These fall outside the
new truth as surely as the old error fell outside the
old truth. And the case of moral goodness is precisely parallel. The higher goodness may be so
defined as to require failure and sin. Thus it may
be maintained that there can be no true success
without struggle, and no true spiritual exaltation
except through repentance. But what of failure
unredeemed, sin unrepented, evil uncompensated
and unresolved? Nothing has been gained after
all but a new definition of goodness—and a new
definition of evil. And this is an ethical, not a

metaphysical question. The problem of evil, like the problem of error, is as far from solution as ever. Indeed, the very urgency of these problems is due to metaphysical absolutism. For this philosophy defines the universe as a perfect unity. Measured by the standard of such an ideal universe, the parts of finite experience take on a fragmentary and baffling character which they would not otherwise possess. The absolute perfection must by definition both determine and exclude the imperfect. Thus absolutism bankrupts the universe by holding it accountable for what it can never pay.

§ 213. If the attempt to construct experience in the special terms of some part of experience be

Collective Character of the Universe as a Whole.

abandoned, how is reality to be defined? It is evident that in that case there can be no definition of reality as such. It must be regarded as a collection of all elements, relations, principles, systems, that compose it. All truths will be true of it, and it will be the subject of all truths. Reality is at least physical, psychical, moral, and rational. That which is physical is not necessarily moral or psychical, but may be either or both of these. Thus it is a commonplace of experience that what has bulk and weight may or may not be good, and may or may not be known. Similarly, that which is psychical may or may not be physical, moral, or rational; and that which is moral or rational may or may not be physical and psychical. There is, then, an indeterminism in the universe, a mere coincidence of principles, in that it contains physical, psychical, moral, logical orders, without being in all respects either a physical, a psychical, a moral, or a logical necessity.[13] Reality or experience itself is neutral in the sense of being exclusively predetermined by no one of the several systems it contains. But the different systems of experience retain their specific and proper natures, without the compromise which is involved in all attempts to extend some one until it shall embrace them all. If such a universe seems inconceivably desultory and chaotic, one may always remind one's self by directly consulting experience that it is not only found immediately and unreflectively, but returned to and lived in after every theoretical excursion.

§ 214. But what implications for life would be

[13] It is not, of course, denied that there may be other orders, such as, e. g., an æsthetic order; or that there may be definite relations between these orders, such as, e. g., the psycho-physical relation.

contained in such a philosophy? Even if it be
theoretically clarifying, through being hospitable

Moral Impli-
cations of such
a Pluralistic
Philosophy.
Purity of the
Good.

to all differences and adequate to the
multifarious demands of experience, is
it not on that very account morally
dreary and stultifying? Is not its
refusal to establish the universe upon moral foundations destructive both of the validity of goodness,
and of the incentive to its attainment? Certainly
not—if the validity of goodness be determined by
criteria of worth, and if the incentive to goodness
be the possibility of making that which merely
exists, or is necessary, also good.

This philosophy does not, it is true, define the
good, but it makes ethics autonomous, thus distinguishing the good which it defines, and saving it
from compromise with matter-of-fact, and logical
or mechanical necessity. The criticism of life is
founded upon an independent basis, and affords
justification of a selective and exclusive moral
idealism. Just because it is not required that the
good shall be held accountable for whatever is real,
the ideal can be kept pure and intrinsically worthy.
The analogy of logic is most illuminating. If it
be insisted that whatever exists is logically necessary, logical necessity must be made to embrace

that from which it is distinguished by definition, such as contradiction, mere empirical existence, and error. The consequence is a logical chaos which has in truth forfeited the name of logic. Similarly a goodness defined to make possible the deduction from it of moral evil or moral indifference loses the very distinguishing properties of goodness. The consequence is an ethical neutrality which invalidates the moral will. A metaphysical neutrality, on the other hand, although denying that reality as such is predestined to morality—and thus affording no possibility of an ethical absolutism—becomes the true ground for an ethical purism.

§ 215. But, secondly, there can be no lack of incentive to goodness in a universe which, though

The Incentive to Goodness. not all-good, is in no respect incapable of becoming good. That which is mechanically or logically necessary, and that which is psychically present, *may be good*. And what can the realization of goodness mean if not that what is natural and necessary, actual and real, shall be also good. The world is not good, will not be good, merely through being what it is, but is or shall be made good through the accession of goodness. It is this belief that the real is not necessarily, but may be, good; that the ideal is not necessarily, but may be, realized; which has inspired every faith in action. Philosophically it is only a question of permitting such faith to be sincere, or condemning it as shallow. If the world be made good through good-will, then the faith of moral action is rational; but if the world be good because whatever is must be good, then moral action is a tread-mill, and its attendant and animating faith only self-deception. Moral endeavor is the elevation of physical and psychical existence to the level of goodness.

"Relate the inheritance to life, convert the tradition into a servant of character, draw upon the history for support in the struggles of the spirit, declare a war of extermination against the total evil of the world; and then raise new armies and organize into fighting force every belief available in the faith that has descended to you." [14]

Evil is here a practical, not a theoretical, problem. It is not to be solved by thinking it good, for to think it good is to deaden the very nerve of action; but by destroying it and replacing it with good.

§ 216. The justification of faith is in the prom-

[14] Quoted from George A. Gordon: *The New Epoch for Faith*, p. 27.

ise of reality. For what, after all, woul be the meaning of a faith which declares that all things, The Justifica- good, bad, and indifferent, are everlast-tion of Faith. ingly and necessarily what they are— even if it were concluded on philosophical grounds to call that ultimate necessity good. Faith has interests; faith is faith *in* goodness or beauty. Then what more just and potent cause of despair than the thought that the ideal must be held accountable for error, ugliness, and evil, or for the indifferent necessities of nature ? [15] Are ideals to be prized the less, or believed in the less, when there is no ground for their impeachment? How much more hopeful for what is worth the hoping, that nature should discern ideals and take some steps toward realizing them, than that ideals should have created nature—such as it is! How much better a report can we give of nature for its ideals, than of the ideals for their handiwork, if it be nature! Emerson writes:

"Suffice it for the joy of the universe that we have not arrived at a wall, but at interminable oceans. Our life seems not present so much as prospective; not for the affairs on which it is wasted, but as a hint of this vast-flowing vigor. Most of life seems to be mere ad-

[15] Cf. James: *The Will to Believe*, essay on *The Dilemma of Determinism, passim.*

vertisement of faculty; information is given us not to sell ourselves cheap; that we are very great. So, in particulars, our greatness is always in a tendency or direction, not in an action. It is for us to believe in the rule, not in the exception. The noble are thus known from the ignoble. So in accepting the leading of the sentiments, it is not what we believe concerning the immortality of the soul or the like, but *the universal impulse to believe*, that is the material circumstance and is the principal fact in the history of the globe." [16]

§ 217. If God be rid of the imputation of moral evil and indifference, he may be *intrinsically wor-*

The Worship and Service of God. *shipful,* because regarded under the form of the highest ideals. And if the great cause of goodness be in fact at stake, God may both command the adoration of men through his purity, and reënforce their virtuous living through representing to them that realization of goodness in the universe at large which both contains and exceeds their individual endeavor.

§ 218. Bishop Berkeley wrote in his "Commonplace Book":

" My speculations have the same effect as visiting foreign countries: in the end I return where I was before, but my heart at ease, and enjoying life with new satisfaction."

If it be essential to the meaning of philosophy that it should issue from life, it is equally essen-

[16] *Essays, Second Series,* p. 75.

tial that it should return to life. But this connection of philosophy with life does not mean its

The Philoso-
pher and the
Standards of
the Market-
place. reduction to the terms of life as conceived in the market-place. Philosophy
cannot emanate from life, and quicken
life, without elevating and ennobling it, and will
therefore always be incommensurable with life
narrowly conceived. Hence the philosopher must
always be as little understood by men of the street
as was Thales by the Thracian handmaiden. He
has an innocence and a wisdom peculiar to his
perspective.

" When he is reviled, he has nothing personal to say
in answer to the civilities of his adversaries, for he knows
no scandals of anyone, and they do not interest him;
and therefore he is laughed at for his sheepishness; and
when others are being praised and glorified, he cannot
help laughing very sincerely in the simplicity of his heart;
and this again makes him look like a fool. When he
hears a tyrant or king eulogized, he fancies that he is
listening to the praises of some keeper of cattle—a swine-
herd, or shepherd, or cowherd, who is being praised for
the quantity of milk which he squeezes from them; and
he remarks that the creature whom they tend, and out
of whom they squeeze the wealth, is of a less tractable
and more insidious nature. Then, again, he observes
that the great man is of necessity as ill-mannered and
uneducated as any shepherd, for he has no leisure, and
he is surrounded by a wall, which is his mountain-pen.
Hearing of enormous landed proprietors of ten thousand

acres and more, our philosopher deems this to be a trifle, because he has been accustomed to think of the whole earth; and when they sing the praises of family, and say that some one is a gentleman because he has had seven generations of wealthy ancestors, he thinks that their sentiments only betray the dulness and narrowness of vision of those who utter them, and who are not educated enough to look at the whole, nor to consider that every man has had thousands and thousands of progenitors, and among them have been rich and poor, kings and slaves, Hellenes and barbarians, many times over." [17]

It is not to be expected that the opinion of the "narrow, keen, little, legal mind" should appreciate the philosophy which has acquired the "music of speech," and hymns "the true life which is lived by immortals or men blessed of heaven." Complacency cannot understand reverence, nor secularism, religion.

§ 219. If we may believe the report of a contemporary philosopher, the present age is made insensible to the meaning of life through preoccupation with its very achievements:

The Secularism of the Present Age.

"The world of finite interests and objects has rounded itself, as it were, into a separate whole, within which the mind of man can fortify itself, and live *securus adversus deos*, in independence of the infinite. In the

[17] Plato: *Theætetus*, 174–175. Translation by Jowett.

sphere of *thought*, there has been forming itself an ever-increasing body of science, which, tracing out the relation of finite things to finite things, never finds it necessary to seek for a beginning or an end to its infinite series of phenomena, and which meets the claims of theology with the saying of the astronomer, 'I do not need that hypothesis.' In the sphere of *action*, again, the complexity of modern life presents a thousand isolated interests, crossing each other in ways too subtle to trace out—interests commercial, social, and political—in pursuing one or other of which the individual may find ample occupation for his existence, without ever feeling the need of any return upon himself, or seeing any reason to ask himself whether this endless striving has any meaning or object beyond itself." [18]

§ 220. There is no dignity in living except it be in the solemn presence of the universe; and only contemplation can summon such a presence. Moreover, the sessions must be not infrequent, for memory is short and visions fade. Truth does not require, however, to be followed out of the world. There is a speculative detachment from life which is less courageous, even if more noble, than worldliness. Such is Dante's exalted but mediæval intellectualism.

The Value of Contemplation for Life.

" And it may be said that (as true friendship between men consists in each wholly loving the other) the true philosopher loves every part of wisdom, and wisdom

[18] E. Caird: *Literature and Philosophy*, Vol. I, pp. 218–219.

every part of the philosopher, inasmuch as she draws all to herself, and allows no one of his thoughts to wander to other things."

Even though, as Aristotle thought, pure contemplation be alone proper to the gods in their perfection and blessedness, for the sublunary world this is less worthy than that balance and unity of faculty which distinguished the humanity of the Greek.

" Then," writes Thucydides, "we are lovers of the beautiful, yet simple in our tastes, and we cultivate the mind without loss of manliness. Wealth we employ, not for talk and ostentation, but when there is a real use for it. To avoid poverty with us is no disgrace; the true disgrace is in doing nothing to avoid it. An Athenian citizen does not neglect the State because he takes care of his own household; and even those of us who are engaged in business have a very fair idea of politics. We alone regard a man who takes no interest in public affairs not as a harmless, but as a useless character; and if few of us are originators, we are all sound judges, of a policy. The great impediment to action is, in our opinion, not discussion, but the want of that knowledge which is gained by discussion preparatory to action. For we have a peculiar power of thinking before we act, and of acting too, whereas other men are courageous from ignorance, but hesitate upon reflection." [19]

Thus life may be broadened and deepened without being made thin and ineffectual. As the civil

[19] Translation by Jowett. Quoted by Laurie in his *Pre-Christian Education*, p. 213.

community is related to the individual's private interests, so the community of the universe is related to the civil community. There is a citizenship in this larger community which requires a wider and more generous interest, rooted in a deeper and more quiet reflection. The world, however, is not to be left behind, but served with a new sense of proportion, with the peculiar fortitude and reverence which are the proper fruits of philosophy.

"This is that which will indeed dignify and exalt knowledge, if contemplation and action may be more nearly and straitly conjoined and united together than they have been; a conjunction like unto that of the two highest planets: Saturn, the planet of rest and contemplation, and Jupiter, the planet of civil society and action."[20]

[20] Bacon: *Advancement of Learning*, Book I.

BIBLIOGRAPHY

The references contained in this bibliography have been selected on the score of availability in English for the general reader and beginning student of philosophy. But I have sought wherever possible to include passages from the great philosophers and men of letters. These are placed first in the list, followed by references to contemporary writers and secondary sources.

CHAPTER I, THE PRACTICAL MAN AND THE PHILOSOPHER.

PLATO: *Republic*, especially Book VII. Translations by Jowett and Vaughan. *Theaetetus*, 172 ff. Translation by Jowett.
ARISTOTLE: *Ethics*, Book X. Translation by Welldon.
MARCUS AURELIUS: *Thoughts*. Translation by Long.
EPICTETUS: *Discourses*. Translation by Long.
BACON: *The Advancement of Learning*.
EMERSON: *Representative Men—Plato; or the Philosopher. Conduct of Life—Culture. Essays, Second Series —Experience.*

ROYCE, JOSIAH: *Spirit of Modern Philosophy*. Introduction.
HIBBEN, J. G.: *Problems of Philosophy*. Introduction.

CHAPTER II, POETRY AND PHILOSOPHY.

PLATO: *Republic*, Books II and III. Translation by Jowett. (Criticism of the poets as demoralizing.)
WORDSWORTH: *Observations Prefixed to the Second Edition of the Lyrical Ballads*.
SHELLEY: *Defence of Poetry*.

EVERETT, C. C.: *Poetry, Comedy, and Duty.* (Discussion of the philosophy of poetry.) *Essays, Theological and Literary.* (On the poetry of Emerson, Goethe, Tennyson, Browning.)

CAIRD, EDWARD: *Literature and Philosophy.* (Wordsworth, Dante, Goethe, etc.)

ROYCE, JOSIAH: *Studies of Good and Evil.* Essay on *Tennyson and Pessimism.*

SANTAYANA, GEORGE: *Poetry and Religion.* (Philosophy of poetry; Greek poetry, Shakespeare, etc.)

SNEATH, E. H.: *Philosophy in Poetry: A Study of Sir John Davies's Poem, "Nosce Teipsum."*

CHAPTERS III AND IV, RELIGION.

PLATO: *Republic*, Book III. Translations by Jowett and Vaughan. (Criticism of religion from the standpoint of morality and politics.)

ST. AUGUSTINE: *Confessions.* Translation by Pusey. (Document of religious experience.)

THOMAS Á KEMPIS: *Imitation of Christ.* Translation by Stanhope. (Mediæval programme of personal religion.)

SPINOZA: *Theological-Political Treatise.* Translation by Elwes. (One of the first great pleas for religious liberty and one of the first attempts to define the *essential* in religion.

KANT: *Critique of Pure Reason—The Canon of Pure Reason.* Translation by Max Müller. *Critique of Practical Reason.* Translation by Abbott in *Theory of Ethics.* (Defines religion as the province of faith, distinguishes it from knowledge, and relates it to morality.)

SCHLEIERMACHER: *On Religion. Speeches to its Cultured Despisers.* Translation by Oman. (Ponderous, dogmatic in its philosophy, but profound and sympathetic in its understanding of religion.)

ARNOLD: *Literature and Dogma.* (On the essence of religion as exemplified in Judaism and Christianity.)

SABATIER, A.: *Outlines of a Philosophy of Religion based on Psychology and History.* Translation by Seed. *Religions of Authority and the Religion of the Spirit.* Translation by Houghton. (These books emphasize the essential importance of the believer's attitude to God.)

JAMES, WILLIAM: *The Varieties of Religious Experience.* (A rich storehouse of religion, sympathetically interpreted.)

EVERETT, C. C.: *The Psychological Elements of Religious Faith.* (A study in the definition and *meaning* of religion.)

CAIRD, EDWARD: *Evolution of Religion.* (Indoctrinated with the author's idealistic philosophy.)

FIELDING, H.: *The Hearts of Men.* (A plea for the universal religion. Special feeling for Indian religions.)

HARNACK, A.: *What is Christianity?* Translation by Saunders. (Attempt to define the *essence* of Christianity.)

PALMER, G. H.: *The Field of Ethics,* Chapters V and VI. (On the relation of ethics and religion.)

BROWN, W. A.: *The Essence of Christianity.* (Special study of the definition of religion.)

JASTROW, M.: *The Study of Religion.* (Method of history and psychology of religion.)

SMITH, W. ROBERTSON: *The Religion of the Semites.* (Excellent study of tribal religions.)

CLARKE, W. N.: *What Shall We Think of Christianity?* (An interpretation of Christianity.)

LEUBA, J. H.: *Introduction to a Psychological Study of Religion.* In *The Monist,* Vol. XI, p. 195.

STARBUCK, E. D.: *The Psychology of Religion.*

CHAPTER V, THE PHILOSOPHICAL CRITICISM OF SCIENCE.*

PLATO: *Republic*, Book VII, 526 ff.   Translations by Jowett and Vaughan.   *Phaedo*, 96 ff.   Translation by Jowett.

BERKELEY: *Alciphron*, the Fourth Dialogue.   *Siris*, especially 234–264.   (On the failure of the scientist to grasp the deeper truth respecting causes and substances.)

DESCARTES: *Discourse on Method*.   Translation by Veitch.

SPINOZA: *On the Improvement of the Understanding*.   Translation by Elwes.

KANT: *Critique of Pure Reason—Transcendental Æsthetic* and *Transcendental Analytic*.   Translation by Max Müller.   (Studies of the Method of Science.)

WARD, JAMES: *Naturalism and Agnosticism*.   (Full but clear account of recent development of natural science, and criticism of its use as philosophy.)

MACH, ERNST: *Science of Mechanics*.   (Historical and methodological.)

JAMES, WILLIAM: *Principles of Psychology*, Vol. II, Chap. xxviii.   (Emphasizes the practical interest underlying science.)

ROYCE, JOSIAH: *The World and the Individual, Second Series, Man and Nature*.   (Interpretation of the province of natural science from the standpoint of absolute idealism.)

PEARSON, KARL: *The Grammar of Science*.   (The limits of science from the scientific stand-point.)

CLIFFORD, W. K.: *Lectures and Essays: On the Aims and Instruments of Scientific Thought; The Philosophy of the Pure Sciences; On the Ethics of Belief*.

* For further contemporary writings on this topic, see foot-notes under §§ 199, 200, 203.

HUXLEY, T. H.: *Method and Results.* (The positivistic position.)

MUENSTERBERG, HUGO: *Psychology and Life.* (Epistemological limitations of natural science applied to psychology, from idealistic stand-point.)

FULLERTON, G. E.: *A System of Metaphysics*, Part II.

TAYLOR, A. E.: *Elements of Metaphysics*, Book III.

CHAPTERS VI AND VII, THE SPECIAL PROBLEMS OF PHILOSOPHY.

PLATO: *Dialogues*, especially *Protagoras* and *Theaetetus*. Translation by Jowett. (The actual genesis of special problems.)

KUELPE, OSWALD: *Introduction to Philosophy.* Translation by Pillsbury and Titchener. (Full and accurate account of the traditional terms and doctrines of philosophy.)

HIBBEN, J. G.: *Problems of Philosophy.* (Brief and elementary.)

SIDGWICK, HENRY: *Philosophy, its Scope and Relations.*

PAULSEN, FRIEDRICH: *Introduction to Philosophy.* Translation by Thilly.

BALDWIN, J. M.: *Dictionary of Philosophy.* (Full, and convenient for reference.)

FERRIER, J. F.: *Lectures on Greek Philosophy.* (Interpretation of the beginning and early development of philosophy.)

BURNET, J.: *Early Greek Philosophy.* Translation of the sources.

FAIRBANKS, A.: *The First Philosophers of Greece.*

GOMPERZ, TH.: *Greek Thinkers*, Vol. I. Translation by Magnus. (On the first development of philosophical problems.)

PALMER, G. H.: *The Field of Ethics.* (On the relations of the ethical problem.)

PUFFER, ETHEL: *The Psychology of Beauty.* (On the relations of the æsthetical problem.)

CHAPTER VIII, NATURALISM.*

LUCRETIUS: *On the Nature of Things.* Translation by Munro. (Early materialism.)

HOBBES: *Metaphysical System.* Edited by Calkins. *Leviathan*, Part I. (Modern materialism.)

BUECHNER, LOUIS: *Force and Matter.* Translation by Collingwood. (Nineteenth century materialism.)

JANET, PAUL: *Materialism of the Present Day.* Translation by Masson.

LANGE, F. A.: *History of Materialism.* Translation by Thomas.

HAECKEL, ERNST: *The Riddle of the Universe.* Translation by McCabe. ("Monism of Energy.")

CLIFFORD, W. K.: *Lectures and Essays: The Ethics of Belief; Cosmic Emotion; Body and Mind.* (Positivism.)

HUXLEY, T. H.: *Evolution and Ethics; Prologomena.* (Distinguishes between the moral and natural.) *Science and Hebrew Tradition; Science and Christian Tradition.* (Controversies of the naturalist with Gladstone and Duke of Argyle.)

SPENCER, HERBERT: *First Principles.* (The systematic evolutionary philosophy.) *Principles of Ethics.* (Ethics of naturalism.) *The Nature and Reality of Religion.* (Controversy with Frederick Harrison.)

BALFOUR, A. J.: *Foundations of Belief*, Part I. (On the religious, moral, and æsthetic consequences of naturalism.)

PATER, WALTER: *Marius the Epicurean.* (Refined hedonism.)

ROMANES, G. J.: *Thoughts on Religion.* (Approached from stand-point of science.)

---

* For histories of philosophy, see supplementary bibliography at end.

BENTHAM, J.: *Introduction to the Principles of Morals and Legislation.* (Utilitarian.)

STEPHEN, L.: *Science of Ethics.* (Evolutionary and social.)

CHAPTER IX, SUBJECTIVISM.

PLATO: *Theaetetus.* Translation by Jowett. (Exposition and criticism of Protagoras.)

BERKELEY: *Three Dialogues between Hylas and Philonous; Principles of Human Knowledge.*

HUME: *An Enquiry Concerning Human Understanding.*

SCHOPENHAUER: *The World as Will and Idea.* Translation by Haldane and Kemp.

MILL, J. S.: *An Examination of Sir William Hamilton's Philosophy,* X–XIII.

CLIFFORD, W. K.: *Lectures and Essays: On the Nature of Things in Themselves.* (Panpsychism.)

DEUSSEN, PAUL: *Elements of Metaphysics.* Translation by Duff. (Following Schopenhauer and Oriental philosophy.)

PAULSEN, FR.: *Introduction to Philosophy.* (Panpsychism.)

STRONG, C. A.: *Why the Mind Has a Body.* (Panpsychism.)

JAMES, WILLIAM: *Reflex Action and Theism,* in *The Will to Believe.* (Morality and religion of individualism.)

CHAPTER X, ABSOLUTE REALISM.

PARMENIDES: *Fragments.* Arrangement and translation by Burnet or Fairbanks.

PLATO: *Republic,* Books VI and VII. Translations by Jowett and Vaughan. *Symposium, Phœdrus, Phœdo, Philebus.* Translation by Jowett.

ARISTOTLE *: *Psychology.* Translations by Hammond and Wallace. *Ethics.* Translation by Welldon.

* The Metaphysics of Aristotle, Fichte, and Hegel must be found by the English reader mainly in the secondary sources.

SPINOZA: *Ethics*, especially Parts I and V. Translations by
    Elwes and Willis.
LEIBNIZ: *Monadology*, and Selections. Translation by Latta.
    Discourse on Metaphysics. Translation by Mont-
    gomery.
MARCUS AURELIUS: *Thoughts*. Translation by Long.
EPICTETUS: *Discourses*. Translation by Long.

————

CAIRD, EDWARD: *The Evolution of Theology in the Greek Phi-
                losophers*. (The central conceptions of
                Plato and Aristotle.)
JOACHIM: *A Study of the Ethics of Spinoza.*

CHAPTER XI, ABSOLUTE IDEALISM.

DESCARTES: *Meditations*. Translation by Veitch.
KANT: *Critique of Pure Reason*. Translation by Max Müller.
    Critique of Practical Reason. Translation by Ab-
    bott, in *Kant's Theory of Ethics*.
FICHTE*: *Science of Ethics*. Translation by Kroeger. *Popu-
    lar Works: The Nature of the Scholar; The Voca-
    tion of Man; The Doctrine of Religion*. Transla-
    tion by Smith.
SCHILLER: *Æsthetic Letters, Essays, and Philosophical Letters.*
    Translation by Weiss. (Romanticism.)
HEGEL*: *Ethics*. Translation by Sterrett. *Logic*. Transla-
    tion, with Introduction, by Wallace. *Philosophy
    of Mind*. Translation, with Introduction, by
    Wallace. *Philosophy of Religion*. Translation
    by Spiers and Sanderson. *Philosophy of Right*.
    Translation by Dyde.
GREEN, T. H.: *Prolegomena to Ethics.*
EMERSON: *The Conduct of Life—Fate. Essays, First Series—
    The Over-Soul; Circles. Essays, Second Series—
    The Poet; Experience; Nature*. (The apprecia-
    tion of life consistent with absolute idealism.)
WORDSWORTH: *Poems, passim.*
COLERIDGE: *Aids to Reflection. The Friend.*

ROYCE, J.: *Spirit of Modern Philosophy*. (Sympathetic exposition of Kant, Fichte, Romanticism, and Hegel.) *The Conception of God*. (The epistemological argument.) *The World and the Individual, First Series*. (Systematic development of absolute idealism; its moral and religious aspects.)

CAIRD, EDWARD: *The Critical Philosophy of Kant*. (Exposition and interpretation from stand-point of later idealism.)

EVERETT, C. C.: *Fichte's Science of Knowledge*.

MCTAGGART, J. M. E.: *Studies in Hegelian Dialectic*. *Studies in Hegelian Cosmology*.

SUPPLEMENTARY BIBLIOGRAPHY ON THE HISTORY OF PHILOSOPHY.

I.—GENERAL.

ROGERS: *Student's History of Philosophy*. (Elementary and clear; copious quotations.)

WEBER: *History of Philosophy*. Translation by Thilly. (Comprehensive and compact.)

WINDELBAND: *A History of Philosophy*. Translation by Tufts. (Emphasis upon the *problems* and their development.)

ERDMANN: *History of Philosophy*. Translation edited by Hough; in three volumes. (Detailed and accurate exposition.)

UEBERWEG: *A History of Philosophy*. Translation by Morris and Porter, in two volumes. (Very complete; excellent account of the literature.)

II.—SPECIAL PERIODS.

FERRIER: *Lectures on Greek Philosophy*. (Excellent introduction.)

MARSHALL: *Short History of Greek Philosophy*. (Brief and clear.)

WINDELBAND: *History of Ancient Philosophy.* Translation by Cushman. (Very accurate and scholarly; also brief.)

ZELLER: *Pre-Socratic Philosophy.* Translation by Alleyne. *Socrates and the Socratic Schools.* Translation by Reichel. (Full and accurate.)

GOMPERZ: *Greek Thinkers.* Translated by Magnus, in four volumes. (Very full; especially on Plato. Goes no further than Plato.)

BURNET: *Early Greek Philosophy.* (Translations of fragments, with commentary.)

FAIRBANKS: *The First Philosophers of Greece.* (Translations of fragments, with commentary.)

TURNER: *History of Philosophy.* (Excellent account of Scholastic philosophy.)

ROYCE: *The Spirit of Modern Philosophy.* (Very illuminating introductory exposition of modern idealism.)

FALCKENBERG: *History of Modern Philosophy.*

HOEFFDING: *History of Modern Philosophy.* Translation by Meyer, in two volumes. (Full and good.)

INDEX